The Wilderness Westwards

The Wilderness Westwards
American Trappers & the Oregon
Expeditions of the Early 19th Century

Journal of a Trapper—or—
Nine Years in the Rocky Mountains 1834-1843

Osborne Russell

Journal of Captain Nathaniel J. Wyeth's
Expeditions to the Oregon Country

Nathaniel J. Wyeth

The Wilderness Westwards
American Trappers & the Oregon Expeditions of the Early 19th Century
Journal of a Trapper—or—Nine Years in the Rocky Mountains 1834-1843
by Osborne Russell
Journal of Captain Nathaniel J. Wyeth's Expeditions to the Oregon Country
by Nathaniel J. Wyeth

FIRST EDITION

First published under the titles
Journal of a Trapper—or—Nine Years in the Rocky Mountains 1834-1843
and
The Correspondence and Journals of Captain Nathaniel J. Wyeth 1831-6 (Extract)

Leonaur is an imprint
of Oakpast Ltd

Copyright in this form © 2014 Oakpast Ltd

ISBN: 978-1-78282-347-6 (hardcover)
ISBN: 978-1-78282-348-3 (softcover)

http://www.leonaur.com

Publisher's Notes
The views expressed in this book are not necessarily those of the publisher.

Contents

Journal of a Trapper—or—Nine Years in the Rocky Mountains 1834-1843   7

Journal of Captain Nathaniel J. Wyeth's Expeditions to the Oregon Country   181

Journal of a Trapper—or—
Nine Years in the Rocky Mountains 1834-1843

Contents

Publisher's Note	11
Preface	21
Expedition Left Independence, Missouri, April 28, 1834	23
Meeting With Captain B. S. Bonneville and Party	27
Hunting Party Suffers From Hunger	31
Attacked by Indians, One Man Wounded	36
Lost	41
In the Yellowstone Country	49
Encounter with Blackfeet Indians	53
Finally Reaches Fort Hall	58
Joins Bridger's Company as a Trapper	62
Rendezvous at Green River	65
Yellowstone National Park	68
"Howell's Encampment"	71
Brilliant Display of "Northern Lights"	77
The Arrival of Wagon Train and Supplies	83
Back Again to the Hunting Grounds	86
Thieving Indians Steal Most of the Horses	90

Stampeded Buffalo	94
Threatened and Robbed by the Crow Indians	97
Fort William	103
Leave for Powder River with Supplies	107
Spring Hunt	109
Battle With the Blackfeet	113
Fall Hunt	117
Spring Hunt	121
Another Viewpoint	125
Wounded by Arrows of Blackfeet	130
Supply Train Reaches Fort Hall on June 14, 1840	138
Christmas Dinner à l'Indian	141
Solitary Hunting Bouts in the Early Spring of 1841	145
A Visit to the Eutaw Indian Village	149
Old Partners Reunite	152
Closing Incidents of an Interesting Experience	155
Appendix	159

Publisher's Note

This journal ends so abruptly, with no hint of the personal fortunes of this most interesting author (who, by the way, was a great uncle of the writer of these explanatory notes), that we have gathered such information as we were able from surviving relatives, and append it hereto.

Osborne Russell was born in Maine June 12, 1814. He had very little schooling, and like most of the boys raised on the Kennebec River, dreamed of going to sea. Forbidden by his father to indulge this desire, at the age of sixteen he ran away from home and shipped on a sailing vessel. They had a hard skipper and the crew deserted the vessel when she touched New York. Here he joined the Northwest Fur Trapping & Trading Company, operating principally in Wisconsin and Minnesota. Two or three years in the employ of this company brings the author to the initial chapter of his *Journal*, April, 1834. The *Journal* records his fortunes up till June 6, 1843.

From information gathered it appears that Mr. Russell took a prominent part in political affairs, and was a member of the Executive Committee of the Provisional Government of Oregon. The family recollection has it that he was the defeated candidate for Governor of Oregon at the first election under Territorial organisation, his defeat being due, in part at least, to his outspoken disapproval of the government's policy in western affairs—notably, refusing military protection to the settlers from the Indians, and at the same time attempting to recruit soldiers from that domain for the war in Mexico.

Hon. John Hailey, pioneer of Oregon and Idaho, who had charge of the Idaho Historical Society exhibit in the Capitol building, has a copy of *Recollections and Opinions of an Old Pioneer*, written by Peter H. Burnett, the first governor of the State of California. Judge Burnett was prominent in the political history of Oregon 1843-8, and we find the following mention of Osborne Russell in his very interesting book, written about the year of 1860.

I have already mentioned the name of Judge O. Russell as one of the Rocky Mountain men. He is a native of the State of Maine, and came to the mountains when a young man, in pursuit of health. All his comrades agreed that he never lost his virtuous habits, but always remained true to his principles. He was never married. He was at one time one of the Executive committee [1] of our Provisional Government in Oregon, and most faithfully did he perform his duty. He is a man of education and of refined feelings. After the discovery of gold he came to the mines, and has been engaged in mining in El Dorado County, California, ever since, (1914). When in Oregon he was occasionally a guest at my house, and would for hours together entertain us with descriptions of mountain life and scenery. His descriptive powers were fine, and he would talk till a late hour at night. My whole family were deeply attentive and my children yet remember the Judge with great pleasure. He was always a most welcome guest at my house. He did not tell so many extraordinary stories as the average Rocky Mountain trapper and hunter, but those he did tell were true.

Then followed a description of the encounter with a grizzly, practically as recorded in this book.

In 1848 Mr. Russell left Oregon for Sacramento, California, and the gold fields. The following letters, which are in good state of preservation, explains conditions better than we could describe them and we give them *verbatim*:

Oregon, Polk County, April 4th, 1848,

Dear Sister:

I received the letters from Martha and yourself dated January 31st, '47, on the 18th day of September, last; your own experience will dictate to you the inexpressible delight which I felt on the receipt of them, better than my pen can describe it. A person by the name of Hanford brought these letters from the States to Oregon but I have never been able to see him, or learn

---

1. We are informed by Hon. John Hailey that under the Provisional Government of Oregon, the three members of the Executive Committee had practically the same powers and functions as the governor would have, or in other words, instead of electing a governor, they elected three men to act in that capacity.—Original Ed.

anything from your friend Haket. This is the first opportunity I have had of answering your letter; a party is now about to start across the mountains to the States, to which I entrust the care of a letter to yourself and one to Martha Ann.

I cannot answer my brother's letters until I receive them. It would afford me the greatest satisfaction to comply with your earnest request "to come home" and visit with you all, but it is a pleasure which reason dictates that I must forego at present, as my presence in Oregon is indispensably necessary, until the United States extend their jurisdiction over us, in order to acquire title to my lands and property. Nevertheless, I sincerely hope the time is not far distant, when my ardent desires to see my native land will be fulfilled.

It affords me consolation to know that you have a partner suited to your wishes. May your days glide smoothly in uninterrupted happiness and may you continue to dwell in the affections of your husband and favour of your God, and may Lemuel by a faithful discharge of the duties he owes to his family, to society, to his country and his God, continue to merit those affections. We have had one of the most pleasant winters I ever experienced. The grass has been remarkably fine all winter, and the finest quality of beef now killed from the natural pastures. Garden vegetables such as beets, onions, turnips, potatoes, and in fact nearly all roots, do the best in this country, to stand in the ground all winter, especially where the soil is inclined to be sandy, as we never have frost sufficient to injure them. The wheat promises an extraordinary crop this year; it is thought it will average twenty-five bushels to the acre throughout the country.

It was generally put in the ground in autumn or the early part of winter, although winter wheat can be sown here in any month of the year. You who have never seen what is called a prairie country, can form but a faint idea of the beauty of its scenery. A diversity of oak-covered hills, cleared of underbrush as if by the hand of art, and plains covered with the most luxuriant verdure, intersected with small streams from the mountains, whose serpentine courses divide them into convenient farms, which are supplied with wood and timber from the narrow groves along their banks, or the oak groves on the intervening hills, constitute the face of this valley as viewed from my residence eastward, until the sight is lost in the smoky atmosphere thirty miles distant, or rests on the towering peaks of Mount Washington and Jefferson, with their snow-crowned heads,

That oft-times pierce the onward fleeting mists,
Whose feet are washed by gentle summer showers,
Whilst Phoebus' rays play on their sparkling crests.

But, my dear sister, beautiful as this country is, that is, this portion of it (for I now speak only of the Willamette valley) my better reason would not prompt me to wish you were here at present, although the contemplation of the scenery around me often dictates the wish that not only you, but all the family were here. We have to undergo, the best of us, in this country, privations of which you are little acquainted, and which must always be expected in the settlement of a new country.

We are now engaged in an expensive Indian war which we have been unavoidably drawn into, but the theatre of action is 200 miles from this valley. The particulars of this war I have briefly described in Martha's letter.

My health is very good in comparison to what it has formerly been.

Give my best respects to your husband, and tell him that although we are not personally acquainted, yet a letter from him would be received as a favour. Give my love to your children and my respects to all inquiring friends.

Write every opportunity.

And now, that the God of heaven may bless you and yours, and his spirit guide you in the path of duty, direct through and protect you from the snares and temptations which the flesh is subject to in this world, and bring you to everlasting happiness, is the sincere prayer of your affectionate brother,

Osborne Russell.

Oregon, Polk County, April 3, 1848.

Dear Sister:

I received your letter, dated January 31st, '47, on the 18th of September last, and the one dated 16th March on the 1st of October; and if your last letter speaks the language of your heart (which I do not doubt) you can imagine in some degree my feelings upon receipt of letters from the dearest female relations I have on earth. And when your eyes rest upon the date of this letter, do not impute it to a want of regard or negligence, that an answer to your letters has so long been delayed. In Oregon we are all mere creatures of chance so far at least as regards communication with the civilized world; and indeed, I sometimes fear the "masterly inactivity" of the government of the United States towards affording protection to the people of Oregon will drive them to a desperate extreme.

Congress has treated us with a shameful neglect which we do not deserve.

Notwithstanding our feeble resources, we are now involved in an expensive Indian war, the cause of which I shall briefly relate.

On the 29th of November last, the Cayuse Indians, who live 300 miles up the Columbia, massacred fourteen white persons, most of whom were missionaries residing among them, among whom were Dr. Marcus Whitman and his estimable lady, who had founded the mission among the Cayuses in 1837 under the auspices of the American Board of Boston. The only cause they could assign for the commission of such an atrocious deed was a report secretly spread among them, that Dr. Whitman and the whites wished to kill them and take their lands, and for that purpose, the last immigration from the States had introduced the measles among them. It is true the last immigration did fetch the measles into all the inhabited parts of Oregon, the effects of which have proven severe on the Indians from their mode of treating the disease. There were several families of whites amounting to upwards of seventy persons residing among the Cayuses at the mission. The men were nearly all killed and the women subjected to indignities too horrid to be described, for about twelve days, when their freedom was purchased by the Hudson's Bay Company.

The name of Peter S. Ogden will long be remembered with gratitude, not only by those he so timely released from such a dreadful captivity, but by every American in Oregon who has a heart susceptible of feeling.

Our Legislature being in session at the time the distressing news arrived at Oregon City, measures were immediately adopted for raising and equipping 500 men for the purpose of punishing the Cayuses as their crime deserved.

Whilst seated at the table writing this letter I have received intelligence from the regiment, which started on the campaign in January last. They have had several skirmishes with the Indians and killed sixty of them. The whites have lost four killed and fifteen wounded. The colonel has been killed in camp by an accidental shot from a rifle. The lieutenant colonel has been wounded in the knee. A treaty has been concluded with the neighbouring tribes, and the Cayuses have been informed that a treaty of peace will be made with them on no other consideration than delivering up the murderers and paying of the war expenses. And worse than all, the regiment is much in want of ammunition. I said worse than all, but I recall the expression; our worst treatment comes from our mother country who, instead of affording us the protection we have so long prayed for, she has sent a ship to us modestly requesting 500 men to assist in the war with Mexico!

Alas! has it come to this? A colony of American citizens living on American soil, continually imploring protection in the most humiliating manner for nine years, and then meet with such a response as this! It is but too true. Citizens and subjects of foreign governments deride us with the neglect of our government, and what can we say in its defence? With shame and confusion we are subjected to the humiliating confession of the truth. We are informed that Congress at their last session passed an act to establish a mail by sea from the United States to Oregon, but the information of such an act being passed is all the benefit we have as yet derived from it.

But our political circumstance is too gloomy a subject for me to dwell longer upon, even if time and space would permit. And now, my dear sister, since the rehearsal of a few out of the many of our political misfortunes have put me somewhat in an ill humour, I hope to be forgiven if you should feel a little of its effects.

Are you aware that your letter dated January 31st, the first I ever received from you, and which now lays open before me, is not even embellished with your signature, and your name nowhere to be seen on the sheet? Now, I think such a nice, clean, and above all, such an affectionate letter, should not have been ashamed to bear the signature of its fair author, and the only excuse I can frame for the omission was the indisposition of which you complained when you wrote.

I return you an affectionate brother's thanks for the souvenir I received enclosed in your second letter, which although of small nominal value, I assure you is highly esteemed, and would be doubly so had the letters comprising the motto been wrought with your own fair hair.

You seemed to be pleased that I was not married, but I assure you that should I get married in this country, or should death (who is no respecter of persons) overtake me, my last will will testify my regard for you. Your affectionate letters have added much to my anxiety to visit Maine. I have not at present the least inclination to marry in this country. But I must first secure the title to my lands before I can visit the United States.

My health since I wrote last has been better than formerly.

The past winter has been the finest I ever saw; the finest quality of beef is now being killed from the natural pastures. Oregon promises a more abundant crop of wheat this year than was ever before known in this country.

I have sent my journal of mine residence in the Rocky Mountains to New York for publication, and have instructed my agent at that place to forward you a copy of it when published.

Give my best wishes to Daniel, Lemuel and families, and tell them that I cannot anticipate the contents of their letters enough to answer them before I receive them. Since the year 1834 I have received five letters from my relatives, *viz.*, one from Daniel, one from Samuel, one from Eleanor, and two from yourself.

You thought I had better go to Maine and get a load of Kennebec girls and fetch out to Oregon. Such a cargo would doubtless find a ready market in Oregon, if the policy of insurance upon it were not purchased too dear, and I think no man in his right senses would ship such a cargo without having it insured, not only against the insults of Neptune, but the wantonness of Cupid.

Give my best compliments to Uncle Sam and Ursula, and tell the old gentleman I have known jokes accidentally turned into hard earnest. And tell those who are solicitous about gaining mother's consent on my behalf that it is not impossible that I may appear among them some day like Irving's Dutchman after twenty years' sleep.

Give my respects to old Mr. Boswell and family and all others who feel enough interested to inquire for me.

It is a great consolation to me to think that you live happy and contented. Notwithstanding my philosophy has never taught me how happy three clams can live in a junk bottle, it teaches me that true happiness is contentment, and *vice versa*.

Give mother the love of an affectionate son and William that of a brother. Tell mother I should be extremely glad to grant her request to "come home," but it is impossible for me to do so at present without a sacrifice which, I dare say, she would not wish me to make; but do not despair of seeing me at no far distant period. I should have been in Hallowell before this, had the United States extended their jurisdiction and gave security to my property.

Another subject occurs to my memory which I had almost forgotten. Before I left Maine, grandfather sent to the family a recipe for making pills; if that recipe is in being I wish to obtain a copy of it, and shall consider it a great favour if you will forward it by the first opportunity.

You half expressed a wish to be with me to enjoy with me the evening hours. Could I harbour a wish that you should leave mother, the next one of all others would be that you were with me. Write every opportunity. If the mail goes into operation this year by way of Panama, we shall have a better opportunity for communication. I write to Eleanor tomorrow in answer to her letter. My time is brief and the sheet full; I will therefore close this epistle by imploring the blessing of that Being in whom we live, move and have our being, now and forever. *Adieu* from your brother,

Osborne Russell.

California (Gold Mines) Nov. 10, 1849.

Dear Sister:—You will not probably be astonished when you see my locality at the date of this letter, as I think Maine, and even Hallowell, must by this time have had a touch of the gold fever.

I left Oregon last September for this country by land, and arrived here on the 25th of the same, and on the 20th of October was attacked with the bilious fever, which lasted until winter. I remained in the mines during the winter and until now, and shall also spend this winter in the mines.

Owing to my ill health last winter I engaged in merchandising; in March commenced collecting gold with my own hands and continued working until the first of October, when I commenced business under the firm of Russell & Gilliam—provision store and boarding house—my partner, an old neighbour from Oregon, having his family here. We are doing a thriving business for this country. About 30,000 people have come across land to this country this season. The old miners, I think average from $12 to $16 per day, estimating gold at $6 per ounce.

Cities and towns are rising up among the hills and mountains in the gold region as if by the effect of magic.

The place where we are located is called Gallowstown. It is situated fifty-five miles east of the city of Sacramento, on the south side, within four miles of the American River. It takes the name from the fact of our having hung three men for murder last winter. Your brother sat as one of the judges *pro tempore* on the trial . Since that dreadful execution, this has been one of the most quiet communities I ever lived in.

Some people here are getting gold by the pound per day, and others not making more than their board, and I am informed it is the same throughout the mines, which are nearly 400 miles in length—confined entirely to the hills, mountain streams and ravines. The most I have ever dug in a day was $100, but have frequently obtained $40 to $60 per day.

The gold here in this place is coarse, from one-half dollar to six ounces in a piece, yet some is so fine that it can hardly be seen with the naked eye. But let this suffice for the gold diggings and let something else take its place.

I received a letter from Martha, dated September 24th, 1848, in which she informed me that she was to be married in December, and that is the only cause why she does not get an answer from me. Not that I have the least wish to prevent her from uniting with the man of her choice, but I must hear of her being certainly married, and to whom, before I shall know how to direct a letter to her, as this life is filled with uncertainties.

A gentleman from Thomaston, Maine, with whom I became acquainted this spring, stepping into the store today, told me he should start for Maine on the 12th and should pass through Lewiston, as he had some relatives living there. I also having a dear relative living there, determined at once to send her a letter, although she has not yet answered my last.

I am in good health, good spirits, and full of business at present, and it is now near eleven o'clock at night and I must yet write a few lines to Daniel before I sleep. When I shall see Maine I cannot tell, but expect to see it before long and fetch with me some of the California gold. But people value not gold here as they would in the United States. The sight of so much of it makes it familiar to them and depreciates its value. Silver coin seems like iron.

Give my best respects to Mr. Read and an uncle's love to your children, with compliments to all inquiring friends.

Send your letters to Sacramento City, California, by the first opportunity, and believe me to be your most affectionate brother,

Osborne Russell.

To his sister Eleanor.

The letter had no envelope, but was folded and sealed with wax, as was customary at that date, and addressed on the back as follows:

Mrs, Eleanor Read,
Lewiston, Maine,
By the politeness of Mr. Kinney.

Mrs. Read was our grandmother. "Martha," to whom he refers, was his younger sister, and Daniel was his cousin.

To continue. It seems that Osborne Russell prospered in his mining and merchandising, and that he and a partner later acquired two vessels which plied between Sacramento and Portland. During one of his trips to the mines, the partner absconded, after collecting all he could of the firm's money, taking a loaded boat to Oregon and also disposing of that. Mr. Russell spent the balance of his days trying to repay their creditors, finally being attacked by what was termed "miner's rheumatism," which paralysed him from the waist down, and he spent the last year of his eventful life in the county hospital at Placerville, El Dorado County. We have been unable to get the date of his death, but have been informed that he was satisfied to die, and at peace with the world and his Maker.

A limited edition of this *Journal* was published by us in 1914 and distributed to relatives, friends and historical societies. There has later been such an insistent demand for copies of this work that we have printed another edition, adding the "Appendix" which was omitted by us in the former book.

L. A. York.

Boise, Idaho, July 25, 1921.

Preface

Reader, if you are in search of the travels of a classical and scientific tourist, please to lay this volume down, and pass on, for this simply informs you what a trapper has seen and experienced. But if you wish to peruse a hunter's rambles among the wild regions of the Rocky Mountains, please to read this, and forgive the author's foibles and imperfections, considering as you pass along that he has been chiefly educated in Nature's school under that rigid tutor, Experience, and you will also bear in mind the author does not hold himself responsible for the correctness of statements made otherwise than from observation.

The Author.

"I envy no man who knows more than myself and pity them that know less." —Sir T. Brown

CHAPTER 1

Expedition Left Independence, Missouri, April 28, 1834

At the town of Independence, Mo., on the 4th of April, 1834, 1 joined an expedition fitted out for the Rocky Mountains and mouth of the Columbia River, by a company formed in Boston under the name and style of the Columbia River Fishing and Trading Company. The same firm had fitted out a brig of two hundred tons burden, freighted with the necessary assortment of merchandise for the salmon and fur trade, with orders to sail to the mouth of the Columbia River, whilst the land party, under the direction of Mr. Nathaniel J. Wyeth, should proceed across the Rocky Mountains and unite with the brig's company in establishing a post on the Columbia near the Pacific.

Our party consisted of forty men engaged in the service, accompanied by Messrs. Nutall and Townsend, botanists and ornithologists, with two attendants; likewise Revs. Jason and Daniel Lee, Methodist missionaries, with four attendants, on their way to establish a mission in Oregon, which brought our numbers (including six independent trappers) to fifty-eight men. From the 23rd to the 27th of April we were engaged in arranging our packs and moving to a place about four miles from Independence. On the morning of the 28th we were all equipped and mounted hunter-like. About forty men leading two loaded horses each were marched out in double file with joyous hearts, enlivened by anticipated prospects, led by Mr. Wyeth, a persevering adventurer and lover of enterprise, whilst the remainder of the party, with twenty head of extra horses and as many cattle to supply emergencies brought up the rear under the direction of Captain Joseph Thing, eminent navigator and fearless son of Neptune, who had been employed by the company in Boston to accompany the party and measure the route across the Rocky Mountains by astronomical observation.

We travelled slowly through the beautiful, verdant and widely extended prairie until about two o'clock p. m. and encamped at a small grove of timber near a spring. On the 29th we took up our march and travelled across a large and beautifully undulating prairie, intersected by small streams skirted with timber intermingled with shrubbery, until the 3rd day of May, when we arrived at the Kaw or Kansas River, near the residence of the United States agent for those Indians.

The Kaw or Kansas Indians are the most filthy, indolent and degraded set of human beings I ever saw. They live in small, oval huts four or five feet high, formed of willow branches and covered with, deer, elk or buffalo skins.

On the 4th of May we crossed the river and on the 5th resumed our march into the interior, travelling over beautiful rolling prairies and encamping on small streams at night until the 10th, when we arrived at the River Platte. We followed up this river to the forks, then forded the south fork and travelled up the north until the 1st day of June, when we arrived at Laramie's Fork of the Platte, where is the first perceptible commencement of the Rocky Mountains. We crossed this fork and travelled up the main river until night and encamped. The next day we left the river and travelled across Black Hills nearly parallel with the general course of the Platte until the 9th of June, when we came to the river again and crossed it at a place called the Red Buttes (high mountains of red rock from which the river issues). The next day we left the river on our left and travelled a northwest direction, and stopped at night on a small spring branch, nearly destitute of wood or shrubbery. The next day we arrived at a stream running into the Platte, called Sweetwater.

This we ascended to a rocky, mountainous country until the 15th of June, then left it and crossed the divide between the waters of the Atlantic and Pacific oceans, and encamped on Sandy Creek, a branch running into Green River, which flows into the Colourado of the West. The next day we moved down Sandy west northwest direction and arrived at Green River on the 18th of June. Here we found some white hunters, who informed us that the grand rendezvous of the whites and Indians would be on a small western branch of the river about twenty miles distant, in a southwest direction. Next day, June 20th, we arrived at the destined place. Here we met with two companies of trappers and traders. One was a branch of the American

Fur Company, under the direction of Messrs. Dripps and Fontanell; the other was called the Rocky Mountain Fur Company. The names of the partners were Thomas Fitzpatrick, Milton Sublett and James Bridger. The two companies consisted of about 600 men, including men engaged in the service, white, half-breed and Indian fur trappers. This stream was called Ham's Fork of Green River. The face of the adjacent country was very mountainous and broken, except the small alluvial bottoms along the streams.

It abounded with buffalo, antelope, elk and bear and some few deer along the river. Here Mr. Wyeth disposed of a part of his loads to the Rocky Mountain Fur Company, and on the 2nd of July we renewed our march towards the Columbia River. After leaving Ham's Fork we took across a high range of hills in a northwest direction and fell on a stream called Bear River, which emptied into the Big Salt Lake. This was a beautiful country. The river, which was about twenty yards wide, ran through large, fertile bottoms bordered by rolling ridges which gradually ascended on each side of the river to the high ranges of dark and lofty mountains upon whose tops the snow remained nearly the year round. We travelled down this river northwest about fifteen miles and encamped opposite a lake of fresh water about sixty miles in circumference, which outlet into the river on the west side.

Along the west border of this lake the country was generally smooth, ascending gradually into the interior and terminating in a high range of mountains which nearly surrounded the lake, approaching close to the shore on the east. The next day, the 7th, we travelled down the river and on the 9th we encamped at a place called the Sheep Rock, so called from a point of the mountain terminating at the river bank in a perpendicular high rock. The river curved around the foot of this rock and formed a half circle, which brought its course to the southwest, from whence it ran in the same direction to the Salt Lake, about eighty miles distant. The sheep occupied this prominent elevation (which overlooked the surrounding country to a great extent) at all seasons of the year.

On the right hand or east side of the river about two miles above the rock were five or six mineral springs, some of which had precisely the taste of soda water when taken up and drank immediately; others had a sour, sulphurous taste; none of them had any outlet, but boiled and bubbled in small holes a few inches from the surface of the ground. This place which looked so lonely, visited only by the rambling trapper or solitary savage, will doubtless at no distant; day, be a resort for thousands of the gay and fashionable world, as; well as invalids and spectators. The country immediately adjacent seemed to have all undergone volcanic action at some remote period, the evidences of which, however, still remained in the deep and frightful chasms which might be found in the rocks throughout this portion of the country and which could only have been formed by some terrible convulsion of nature. The ground about these springs was very strongly impregnated with *salsoda*. There were also large beds of clay in the vicinity, of a snowy whiteness, used by the Indians for cleansing their clothes and skins, it not being inferior to any soap for cleansing woollens or skins, dressed after the Indian fashion.

CHAPTER 2

Meeting With Captain B. S. Bonneville and Party

On July 11th we left Bear River and crossed low ridges of broken country for about fifteen miles in a northeast direction, and fell on to a stream which ran into the Snake River, called Blackfoot. Here we met with Captain B. S. Bonneville and a party of ten or twelve men. He was on his way to the Columbia and was employed killing and drying buffalo meat for the journey. The next day we travelled in a westerly direction over a rough, mountainous country about twenty-five miles, and the day following, after travelling about twenty miles in the same direction, we emerged from the mountains into the great valley of the Snake River. On the 16th we crossed the valley and reached the river in about twenty-five miles travel west. Here Mr. Wyeth concluded to stop, build a fort and deposit the remainder of his merchandise, leaving a few men to protect them, and trade with the Snake and Bannock Indians.

On the 18th we commenced the fort, which was a stockade eighty feet square, built of cottonwood trees set on end, sunk two and one-half feet in the ground and standing about fifteen feet above, with two bastions eight feet square at the opposite angles. On the 4th of August the fort was completed and on the 5th the "Stars and Stripes" were unfurled to the breeze at sunrise in the centre of a savage and uncivilized country, over an American trading post.

The next day Mr. Wyeth departed for the mouth of the Columbia River with all the party excepting twelve men (myself included) who were stationed at the fort. I now began to experience the difficulties attending a mountaineer, we being all raw hands, excepting the man who had charge of the fort, and a *mulatto*, the two latter having but very little experience in hunting game with the rifle, and although the country abounded with game, still it wanted experience to kill it.

On the 12th of August myself and three others (the *mulatto* included) started from the fort to hunt buffalo. We proceeded up the stream running into Snake River near the fort called Ross Fork in an easterly direction about twenty-five miles, crossed a low mountain in the same direction about five miles and fell on to a stream called the Portneuf. Here we found several large bands of buffalo. We went to a small stream and encamped. I now prepared myself for the first time in my life to kill meat for my supper, with a rifle. I had an elegant one, but had little experience in using it.

However, I approached the band of buffaloes, crawling on my hands and knees within about eighty yards of them, then raised my body erect, took aim and shot at a bull. At the crack of the gun the buffaloes all ran off excepting the bull which I had wounded. I then reloaded and shot as fast as I could until I had driven twenty-five bullets at, in and about him, which was all that I had in my bullet pouch, while the bull still stood, apparently riveted to the spot. I watched him anxiously for half an hour in hopes of seeing him fall, but to no purpose. I was obliged to give it up as a bad job and retreat to our encampment without meat; but the *mulatto* had better luck—he had killed a fat cow while shooting fifteen bullets at the band. The next day we succeeded in killing another cow and two bulls. We butchered them, took the meat and returned to the fort.

Experience with a Grizzly Bear

On the 20th of August we started again to hunt meat. We left the fort and travelled about six miles, when we discovered a grizzly bear digging and eating roots in a piece of marshy ground near a large bunch of willows. The *mulatto* approached within 100 yards and shot him through the left shoulder. He gave a hideous growl and sprang into the thicket. The *mulatto* then said: "Let him go; he is a dangerous varmint," but not being acquainted with the nature of these animals I determined on making another trial, and persuaded the *mulatto* to assist me. We walked around the bunch of willows where the bear lay, keeping close together, with our rifles ready cocked and presented towards the bushes, until near the place where he had entered, when we heard a sullen growl about ten feet from us, which was instantly followed by a spring of the bear toward us, his enormous jaws extended and eyes flashing fire.

Oh Heavens! was ever anything so hideous? We could not retain sufficient presence of mind to shoot at him but took to our heels, separating as we ran, the bear taking after me. Finding I could outrun him, he left and turned to the other, who wheeled about and discharged his rifle, covering the bear with smoke and fire, the ball, however, missing him. He turned and bounded toward me. I could go no further without jumping into a large quagmire which hemmed me in on three sides. I was obliged to turn about and face him. He came within about ten paces of me, then suddenly stopped and raised his ponderous body erect, his mouth wide open, gazing at me with a beastly laugh.

At this moment I pulled trigger, as I knew not what else to do and hardly knew that I did this, but it accidentally happened that my rifle was pointed towards the bear when I pulled and the ball piercing his heart, he gave one bound from me, uttered a deathly howl and fell dead, but I trembled as if I had an ague fit for half an hour after. We butchered him, as he was very fat, packed the meat and skin on our horses and returned to the fort with the trophies of our bravery, but I secretly determined in my own mind never to molest another wounded grizzly bear in a marsh or thicket.

On the 26th of September, our stock of provisions beginning to get short, four men started again to hunt buffalo. As I had been out several times in succession, I concluded to stay in the fort awhile and let others try it. This was the most lonely and dreary place I think I ever saw—not a human to be seen excepting the men about the fort. The country was very smoky and the weather sultry and hot. On the first day of October our hunters arrived with news which caused some little excitement among us. They had discovered a village of Indians on Blackfoot Creek, about twenty-five miles from the fort in a north-easterly direction, consisting of about sixty lodges. They had ridden, greenhorn-like, into the village without any ceremony or knowledge of the friendly or hostile disposition of the Indians, neither could they inform us to what nation they belonged. It happened, however, that they were Snake, friendly to the whites, and treated our men in a hospitable manner.

After remaining all night with them three of the Indians accompanied our hunters to the fort. From these we gathered (through the *mulatto* who could speak a little of their language) much desired information. The next day myself and the *mulatto* started to the village, where we arrived about sun half an hour high. We were conducted to the chief's lodge, where we dismounted and were cheerfully saluted by the chief, who was called by the whites "Iron Wristbands" and by the Indians "*Pah-dasher-wah-un-dah*" or "The Hiding Bear." Our horses were taken to grass and we followed him into his lodge, when he soon ordered supper to be prepared for us. He seemed very much pleased when we told him the whites had built a trading post on Snake River. He said the village would go to the fort in three or four days to trade.

We left them next morning loaded with as much fat, dried buffalo meat as our horses could carry, which had been given as a gratuity. We were accompanied on our return to the fort by six of the men. On the 10th the village arrived and pitched their lodges within about 200 yards of the fort. I now commenced learning the Snake language and progressed so far in a short time that I was able to understand most of their words employed in the matters of trade.

October 20th a village of Bannocks consisting of 250 lodges, arrived at the fort. From these we traded a considerable quantity of furs, a large supply of dried meat, deer, elk and sheep skins. In the meantime we were employed building small log houses and making other necessary preparations for the approaching winter.

CHAPTER 3

Hunting Party Suffers From Hunger

November 5th some white hunters arrived at the fort who had been defeated by the Blackfoot Indians on Ham's Fork of Green River. One of them had his arm broken by a fusee ball, but by the salutary relief which he obtained from the fort he was soon enabled to return to his associates. On the 16th two more white men arrived and reported that Captain Bonneville had returned from the lower country and was passing within thirty miles of the fort on his way to Green River. On the 20th four white men arrived and reported that a party of the Rocky Mountain Fur Company, consisting of sixty men under the direction of one of the partners (Mr. Bridger), were at the forks of Snake River, about sixty miles above the fort, where they intended to pass the winter. We were also informed that the two fur companies had formed a coalition. December 15th the ground was still bare, but frozen, and the weather very cold.

On the 24th Captain Thing arrived from the mouth of the Columbia with ten men, fetching supplies for the fort. Times now began to have a different appearance. The whites and Indians were very numerous in the valley. All came to pass the winter on the Snake River. On the 20th of January twelve of Mr. Bridger's men left his camp and came to the fort to get employment. They immediately made an engagement with Captain Thing to form a party for hunting and trapping. On the 15th of March the party was fitted out, consisting often trappers and seven camp keepers (myself being one of the latter), under the direction of Mr. Joseph Gale, a native of the City of Washington. March 25th we left the fort and travelled about six miles northeast and encamped on a stream running into the river about twelve miles below the fort, called Portneuf.

The next day we followed up this stream in an easterly direction about fifteen miles. Here we found the snow very deep. From this we took a south course in the direction of Bear River. Our animals being so poor and the travelling being so bad, we had to make short marches, and reached Bear River on the 1st day of April. The place where we struck the river was called Cache Valley, so called from its having been formerly a place of deposit for the fur traders. The country on the north and west side of the river was somewhat broken and uneven and covered with wild sage. The snow had disappeared only upon the south sides of the hills. On the south and east sides of the river lay the valley, but it appeared very white and the river nearly overflowing its banks, insomuch that it was very difficult crossing, and should we have been able to have crossed, the snow would have prevented us gaining the foot of the mountain on the east side of the valley. This place being entirely destitute of game, we had to live chiefly upon roots for ten days.

On the 11th of April we swam the river with our horses and baggage and pushed our way through the snow across the valley to the foot of the mountain. Here we found the ground bare and dry, but we had to stay another night without supper. About four o'clock the next day the meat of two fat grizzly bears was brought into camp. Our camp kettles had not been greased for some time, as we were continually boiling thistle roots in them during the day, but now four of them containing about three gallons each were soon filled with fat bear meat, cut in very small pieces, and hung over a fire, which all hands were employed in keeping up with the utmost impatience.

An old, experienced hand who stood six feet six and was never in a hurry about anything, was selected by a unanimous vote to say when the stew (as we called it) was done, but I thought, with my comrades, that it took a longer time to cook than any meal I ever saw prepared, and after repeated appeals to his long and hungry stewardship by all hands, he at length consented that it might be seasoned with salt and pepper and dished out to cool. But it had not much time for cooling before we commenced operations, and all pronounced it the best meal they had ever eaten, as a matter of course where men had been starving.

The next morning I took a walk up a smooth spur of the mountain to look at the country. This valley commenced about thirty miles below the Soda Springs, the river running west of south entering the valley through a deep cut in the high hills. After winding its way through the north and west borders of the valley, it turned due west and ran through the deep canyon of perpendicular rocks on its way to the Salt Lake. The valley laid in a sort of semi-circle or rather an oblong on the south and east of about twenty miles in length by five miles in diameter and nearly surrounded by high and rugged mountains from which flowed large numbers of small streams, crossing the valley and emptying into the river. There were large quantities of beaver and otter living in these streams, but the snow melting raised the water so high that our trappers made but slow progress in catching them.

We stopped in this valley until the 20th of April, then moved to the southeast extremity and made an attempt to cross the mountain. The next day we travelled up a stream called Rush Creek in an easterly direction, through a deep gorge in the mountain for about twelve miles, which then widened about a mile into a smooth and rolling country. Here we staid the following day. We then took a northeast course over the divide and travelled about twelve miles through snow two or three feet deep and in many places drifts; to the depth of six or eight feet deep. At night we encamped on a small dry spot of ground on the south side of a steep mountain, where there was little or no vegetation excepting wild sage.

Sometime after we had stopped it was disclosed that one man was missing—a young English shoemaker from Bristol. We found he had been seen last dismounted and stopping to drink at a small branch at some distance before we entered the snow. On the following morning I was ordered to go back in search of him. I started on the snow, which was frozen hard enough to bear me and my horse. I went to the place where he was last seen and found his trail, which I followed on to a high mountain, when I lost it among the rocks. I then built a large fire, shot my gun several times, and after hunting till near sunset without hopes of finding him, I gave it up and went to the edge of the snow and stopped for the night. The next morning I started at daylight in a gallop on the snow, traversing mountain and valley smoothed up with snow so hard frozen that a galloping horse scarcely left a foot print.

About noon I arrived on a high ridge which overlooked the Snake Lake and the valley southwest of it, which had apparently been clear of snow for some length of rime. At the southern extremity of the lake lay the camp, about two miles distant northeast of me. I descended the mountain and entered the camp. On the 27th of April we travelled down the west side of the lake to the outlet of the Bear River. Here we found about 300 lodges of Snake Indians. We encamped at the village and staid three days. In the meantime our trappers were engaged hunting beaver in the river and small streams. We then crossed the river and ascended a branch called Thomas' Fork, in a northerly direction about ten miles. The next day we started across the mountain in a northerly direction and after travelling about five miles we discovered a grizzly bear about 200 yards ahead of us. One of our hunters approached and shot him dead on the spot. We all rode up and dismounted to butcher him. He was an enormous animal, a hideous brute, a savage looking beast. On removing his skin we found the fat on his back measured six inches deep. He had probably not left his winter quarters more than two hours, as we saw his tracks on the snow where he had just left the thick forest of pines on the side of the mountain.

We put the meat on our pack animals and travelled up the mountain about five miles and encamped. The next morning we started about two hours before day and crossed the mountain on the snow, which was frozen hard enough to bear our animals, and at ten o'clock a. m. we found ourselves travelling down a beautiful green vale which led us to the valley of the Salt River, where we encamped about two o'clock p. m. This river derived its name from the numerous salt springs found on its branches. It ran through the middle of a smooth valley about forty miles long and ten wide, emptying its waters into Lewis' Fork of Snake River, its course being almost due north. This was a beautiful valley, covered with green grass and herbage, surrounded by towering mountains covered with snow, spotted with groves of tall spruce pines, which, from their vast elevation, resembled small twigs half immersed in the snow, whilst thousands of buffaloes carelessly feeding in the green vales contributed to the wild and romantic splendour of the surrounding scenery.

On the 10th of May we moved down the river about twelve miles to a stream running into it on the west side called Scott's Fork. Here were some fine salt springs, the salt forming on the pebbles by evaporation to the depth of five or six inches in a short time after the snow had disappeared. May 11th, after gathering a supply of salt, we travelled down the river about fifteen miles and encamped near the mouth of a stream on the west side called Gardner's Fork. Here we met with Mr. Bridger and his party, who informed us that the country around and below was much infested with Blackfeet. They had had several skirmishes with them in which they had lost a number of horses and traps and one young man had been wounded in the shoulder by a ball from a fusee. Upon the receipt of this information our leader concluded to shape his course toward the fort.

On the 14th of May we ascended Gardner's Fork about fifteen miles through a deep gorge in the high, craggy mountain. May 15th, travelled up this stream west about ten miles, when the country opened into a valley ten miles long and two wide. Here we left Gardner's Fork, which turns almost due north into the high mountains, with the bend of it just cutting the north end of this valley. We travelled south about three miles and encamped on Blackfoot, which runs into Snake River, after a course of about 100 miles. Here the snow was very deep over nearly the whole plain, which was surrounded by high mountains. On the 16th we travelled down Blackfoot, which runs southwest across the valley, then turns west and runs into a deep cut in the mountain, upwards of a thousand feet above the bed of the stream, the entrance of which seems barely wide enough to admit its waters. We travelled through this canyon for about ten miles, when it opened into a large plain extending to the Sheep Rock on Bear River, which appeared to be about forty miles distant to the southwest.

There Blackfoot makes a sweeping curve to the southwest, then gradually turning to the north enters a narrow gorge of basaltic rock, through which it rushes with impetuosity for about fifteen miles, then emerges into the great plain of the Snake River. 17th—We travelled down this stream about fifteen miles and stopped to kill and dry buffalo meat sufficient to load our loose horses. On the 22nd we moved down ten miles, where we found thousands of buffalo bulls and killed a great number of them, the cows being very poor at this season of the year. May 30th we travelled down to the plains and on the following day arrived at the fort after travelling about thirty miles in a southwest direction. On arriving at the fort we learned Captain Thing had started in April with twelve men for the purpose of establishing a trading post on a branch of Salmon River, but had been defeated by the Blackfeet, with the total loss of his outfit excepting his men and horses.

CHAPTER 4

Attacked by Indians, One Man Wounded

On the 10th of June a small party belonging to the Hudson Bay Company arrived from Fort Vancouver on the Columbia River, under the direction of Mr. F. Ermatinger, accompanied by Captain Wm. Stewart, an English half-pay officer who had passed the winter at Vancouver and was on a tour of pleasure in the Rocky Mountains. On the 12th they left Fort Hall and started for the grand rendezvous on Green River. We now began to make preparations for what the trappers termed the "Fall Hunt," and all being ready on the 15th, we started. Our party (under our former leader) consisted of twenty-four men, fourteen trappers and ten camp keepers. It was the intention of our leader to proceed to the Yellowstone Lake and hunt the country which lay in the vicinity of our route; from thence proceed to the headwaters of the Missouri and Snake Rivers on our return back to Fort Hall, where it was intended we should arrive about the middle of October next. We travelled up to the mouth of Blackfoot Creek, about ten miles.

16th—Up Blackfoot about fifteen miles.

17th—Followed up this stream about ten miles farther, then left it to our right and took a northeast course through the dry plains covered with dry sage and sand hills, about fifteen miles, to the foot of the mountain and encamped at a small spring which sinks in the plain soon after leaving the mountain. Here we killed a couple of fine bulls and took some of the best meat.

18th—We crossed a low mountain in an easterly direction, about twelve miles, and encamped on a stream called Gray's Creek, which empties into Snake River about forty miles above Fort Hall.

19th—Travelled east over a rough, broken mountainous country about twelve miles and encamped on a branch of the same stream. This country afforded no timber excepting the quaking asp, which grows in small, scrubby groves in the nooks and ravines among the hills.

20th—We left the waters of Gray's Creek and crossed a low place in the mountain in an easterly direction, fell on to a small stream running into Lewis' Fork—distance ten miles.

21st—Travelled east, following this stream to the mouth, about fifteen miles, which was about thirty miles below the mouth of Salt River. Here we were obliged to cross Lewis' Fork, which is about 300 yards wide and might be forded at a low stage of water, but at that time was almost overflowing its banks and running at the rate of about six miles per hour. We commenced making a boat by sewing two raw bull hides together, which we stretched over a frame formed of green willow branches, and then dried it gradually over a slow fire during the night, aid—Our boat being completed, we commenced crossing our equipage, and while five of us were employed at this a young man by the name of Abram Patterson attempted to cross on horseback.

In spite of all the advice and entreaty of those present, his wild and rash temper got the better of his reason and after a desperate struggle to reach the opposite bank he abandoned his horse,! made a few springs, and sank to rise no more. He was a native of Pennsylvania, about twenty-three years of age. We succeeded in crossing our baggage and encamped on the east side for the night. Lewis' Fork at this place was timbered with large cottonwood trees along the banks on both sides. On the east lay a valley about twenty-eight miles long and three or four wide in an oblong shape, half enclosed by a range of towering mountains which approached the river at each extremity of the valley.

23rd—We crossed the north point of the valley and ascended a small stream about fifteen miles northeast where we encamped among the mountains, thickly covered with tall pines intermingled with fallen timber.

24th—Crossed the mountain, twelve miles easterly course, and descended into the southwest extremity of a valley called Pierre's Hole, where we staid the next day. This valley lies north and south in an oblong form, about thirty miles long and ten wide, surrounded except on the north by wild and rugged mountains; the east range resembles mountains piled on mountains and capped with three spiral peaks which pierce the clouds.

These peaks bear the French name of Tetons or Teats. The Snake Indians called them "The Hoary Headed Fathers." This was a beautiful valley, consisting of a smooth plain intersected by small streams and thickly clothed with grass and herbage and abounding with buffalo, elk, deer, antelope, etc.

On the 27th we travelled to the north end of the valley and encamped on one of the numerous branches which unite at the northern extremity and forms a stream called Pierre's Fork, which discharges its waters into Henry's Fork of Snake River. The stream on which we encamped flows directly from the central Teton and is narrowly skirted with cottonwood trees, closely intermingled with underbrush on both sides. We were encamped on the south side in a place partially clear of brush, under the shade of the large cottonwoods.

On the 28th about nine o'clock a. m. we were aroused by an alarm of "Indians." We ran to our horses. All was confusion, each trying to catch his horses. We succeeded in driving them into camp, where we caught all but six, which escaped into the prairies. In the meantime the Indians appeared before our camp to the number of sixty, of which fifteen or twenty were mounted on horseback and the remainder on foot, all being entirely naked, armed with fusees, bows, arrows, etc. They immediately caught the horses which had escaped from us and commenced riding to and fro within gunshot of our camp with all the speed their horses were capable of producing, without shooting a single gun, for about twenty minutes, brandishing their war weapons and yelling at the top of their voices.

Some had scalps suspended on small poles which they waved in the air, others had pieces of scarlet cloth with one end fastened round their heads while the other trailed after them. After securing my horses I took my gun, examined the priming, set the breech on the ground and hand on the muzzle, with my arms folded, gazed at the novelty of this scene for some minutes, quite unconscious of danger, until the whistling of balls about my ears gave me to understand that these were something more than mere pictures of imagination and gave me assurance that these living creatures were a little more dangerous than those I had been accustomed to see portrayed upon canvas.

The first gun was fired by one of our party, which was taken as the signal for attack on both sides, but the well directed fire from our rifles soon compelled them to retire from the front and take to the brush behind us, where they had the advantage until seven or eight of our men glided into the brush and concealing themselves until their left wing approached within about thirty feet of them before they shot a gun, they then raised and attacked them in the flank. The Indians did not stop to return the fire, but retreated through the brush as fast as possible, dragging their wounded along with them and leaving their dead on the spot. In the meantime myself and the remainder of our party were closely engaged with the centre and right.

I took advantage of a large tree which stood near the edge of the brush between the Indians and our horses. They approached until the smoke of our guns met. I kept a large German horse pistol loaded by me in case they should make a charge when my gun was empty. When I first stationed myself at the tree I placed a hat on some twigs which grew at the foot of it and would put it in motion by kicking the twigs with my foot in order that they might shoot at the hat and give me a better chance at their heads, but I soon found this was no joke for the poor horses behind me were killed and wounded by the balls intended for me. The Indians stood the fight for about two hours, then retreated through the brush with a dismal lamentation. We then began to look about to find what damage they had done to us.

One of our comrades was found under the side of an old root, wounded by balls in three places in the right and one in the left leg below the knee, no bones having been broken. Another had received a slight wound in the groin. We lost three horses killed on the spot and several more were wounded, but not so bad as to be unable to travel. Towards night some of our men followed down the stream about a mile and found the place where they had stopped and laid their wounded comrades on the ground in a circle. The blood was still standing congealed in nine places where they had apparently been dressing the wounds.

29th—Staid at the same place, fearing no further attempt by the same party of Indians. 30th—Travelled up the main branch about ten miles.

July 1st—Travelled to the southeast extremity of the valley and encamped for the night. Our wounded comrade suffered very much in riding, although everything was done which lay in our power to ease his sufferings. A pallet was made upon the best gaited horse belonging to the party for him to ride on and one man appointed to lead the animal.

On the 2nd we crossed the Teton Mountains in an easterly direction, about fifteen miles. The ascent was very steep and rugged, covered with tall pines, but the descent was somewhat smoother.

Chapter 5

Lost

Here we again fell on to Lewis' Fork, which runs in a southerly direction through a valley about eighty miles long, there turning to the mountains through a narrow cut in the mountain to the mouth of Salt River, about thirty miles. This valley was called "Jackson Hole." It is generally from five to fifteen miles wide. The southern part where the river enters the mountains is hilly and uneven, but the northern portion is wide, smooth and comparatively even, the whole being covered with wild sage and surrounded by high and rugged mountains upon whose summit the snow remains during the hottest months in summer. The alluvial bottoms along the river and streams intersecting it through the valley produced a luxuriant growth of vegetation, among which wild flax and a species of onion were abundant. The great altitude of this place, however, connected with the cold descending from the mountains at night, I think would be a serious obstruction to the growth of most kinds of cultivated grains. This valley, like all other parts of the country, abounded with game.

Here we again attempted to cross Lewis Fork with a bull skin boat. July 4th, our boat being completed, we loaded it with the baggage And crossed to the other side, but on returning ran it into some brush, when it instantly filled and sank, but without further accident than the loss of the boat. We had already forded half the distance across the river upon horseback and were now upon an island in the middle, having previously driven our horses to the other shore. We now commenced making a raft of logs that had drifted on the island. On this, when completed, we put the remainder of our equipment about two o'clock p. m. and ten of us started with it for the other side, but no sooner reached the rapid current than our raft, which was constructed of large timber, became unmanageable and all efforts to reach either side were vain, and, fearing lest we should run on to the dreadful rapids to which we were fast approaching, we abandoned the raft and committed ourselves to the mercy of the current.

We being all tolerably good swimmers excepting myself, I would fain have called for help, but at this critical period every one had to shift for himself. Fortunately I scrambled to the shore among the best swimmers. We were now on the side from whence we started without a single article of bedding except an old cloth tent, whilst the rain poured incessantly. Fortunately we had built a large fire previous to our departure on the raft, which was still burning.

I now began to reflect on the miserable condition of myself and those around me—without clothing, provisions or firearms and all drenched to the skin with rain.

I thought of those who were perhaps at that moment celebrating the anniversary of our independence in my native land or seated around tables loaded with the richest dainties that a rich, independent and enlightened country could afford, or perhaps collected in the gay salon relating the heroic deeds of our ancestors or joining in the nimble dance, forgetful of cares and toils, whilst here presented a group of human beings crouched around a fire which the rain was fast diminishing, meditating on their deplorable condition, not knowing at what moment we might be aroused by the shrill war cry of the hostile savages with which the country was infested, whilst not an article for defence, excepting our butcher knives, remained in our possession.

The night at length came on and we lay down to await the events of the morrow. Daylight appeared and we started down along the shore in hopes of finding something that might get loose from the raft and drift upon the beach. We had not gone a mile when we discovered the raft lodged on a gravel bar which projected from the island, where it had been driven by the current. We hastened through the water waist deep to the spot, where to our great surprise and satisfaction we found everything safe upon the raft in the same manner we had left it. We also discovered that the river, with some difficulty, could be forded on horseback at this place. Accordingly, we had our horses driven across to us, packed them up and mounted, and crossed without further accident, and the day being fair, we spent the remainder of it and the following day drying our equipage.

7th—Left the river and followed up a stream called the Grosbent Fork in an easterly direction about eight miles. This stream was very high and rapid. In fording it we lost two rifles.

8th—We followed the stream through the mountains east, passing through narrow defiles, over rocky precipices and deep gulches for fifteen miles.

9th—Travelled up the stream about ten miles east, then turned up a left hand fork about eight miles northeast and encamped among the high, rough mountains, thickly covered with pine timber. There was not a man in the party who had ever been at this place or at the Yellowstone Lake where we intended to go, but our leader received information from some person at the fort and had written the direction on a piece of paper which he carried with him. They directed us to go from the place where we now were due north, but he said the direction must be wrong, as he could discover no passage through the mountains to the north of us.

10th—We took a narrow defile which led us in an easterly direction about twelve miles, on to a stream running southeast. This we followed down about six miles, when the defile opened into a beautiful valley about fifteen miles in circumference, through which the stream ran in the direction above stated and entered the mountains on the east side. Here a dispute arose about the part of the country we were in. Our leader maintained that this was a branch of the Yellowstone River, but some of the trappers had been in this valley before and knew it to be a branch of Wind River. They pointed out their old encampment and the beaver lodges where they had been trapping two years previous. But our man at the helm was inflexible; he commanded the party and had a right to call these streams by what names he pleased, and as a matter of course this was called the Yellowstone. Three of the party, however, called it Wind River and left us, but not before one of them had given our *charge d'affaires* a sound drubbing about some small matters of little importance to anyone but themselves.

11th—We left the stream and crossed the valley in a north-easterly direction, ascended a high point of mountain thickly covered with pines, then descended over cliffs and crags, crossing deep gulches, among the dark forests of pines and logs until about noon, when we came into a smooth, grassy spot about a mile in circumference, watered by a small rivulet which fell from the rocks above, passed through the valley and fell into a chasm on the southeast side among the pines. On the north and west were towering rocks, several thousand feet high, which seemed to overhang this little vale. Thousands of mountain sheep were scattered up and down feeding on the short grass which grew among the cliffs and crevices, some so high that it required a telescope to see them. Our wounded companion suffered severely by this day's travel and our director concluded to remain at this place the next day. He now began to think that these were not the waters of the Yellowstone, as all the branches ran southeast. He finally gave it up and openly declared he could form no distinct idea what part of the country we were in.

12th—Myself and another had orders to mount two of the best mules and ascend the mountain to see if we could find any pass to the northwest of us. We left the camp and travelled in a northerly direction about two miles, then turning to our left around a high point of perpendicular rock entered a narrow glen which led northwest up the mountain. Through this we directed our course, ascending over the loose fragments of rock which had fallen from the dark threatening precipices that seemed suspended in the air above us on either side, for about five miles, when the ascent became so steep that we were obliged to dismount and lead our mules. After climbing about a mile further we came to large banks of snow eight or ten feet deep and so hard that we were compelled to cut steps with our butcher knives to place our feet in, whilst our mules followed in the same track.

These places were from fifty to two hundred yards across and so steep that we had to use both hands and feet dog-like in climbing over them. We succeeded in reaching what we at first supposed to be the summit, when another peak appeared in view, completely shrouded with snow, dotted here and there with a few dwarfish, weather-beaten cedars. We now seated ourselves for a few minutes to rest our wearied limbs and gaze on surrounding objects near us. On either hand were large bands of mountain sheep carelessly feeding upon the short grass and herbage which grew among the crags and cliffs, whilst crowds of little lambs were nimbly skipping and playing upon the banks of snow. After resting ourselves a short time, we resumed our march over the snow, leaving the mules behind. We reached the highest summit in about a mile of travel.

On the top of this elevation was a flat place of about a quarter of a mile in circumference. On the west and north of us was presented one vast pile of huge mountains crowned with snow, but none appeared so high as the one on which we stood. On the south and east nothing could be seen in the distance but the dense, blue atmosphere. We did not prolong our stay in this place, for the north wind blew keen and cold as the month of January in a northern climate. We hurried down to where we had left the mules in order to descend to a more temperate climate before the night came on.

Our next object was to find a place to descend with our mules, it being impossible to; retrace our steps without the greatest danger. After hunting around some time, we at length found a place on the northeast side where we concluded to try it. We drove our mules on to the snow, which being hard and slippery, their feet tripped and after sliding about 300 feet they arrived in a smooth green spot at the foot of the declivity. We then let ourselves down by cutting steps with our butcher knives and the breeches of our guns. After travelling down out of the snow, we encamped on a smooth, green spot and turned our mules loose to feed. At sunset we built a large, fire, ate supper and laid down to sleep. The next morning at daybreak I arose and kindled a large fire, and seeing the mules grazing at a short distance, I filled my tobacco pipe and sat down to smoke.

Presently I cast my eyes down the mountain and discovered two Indians approaching within 200 yards of us. I immediately aroused my companion, who was still sleeping. We grasped our guns and presented them upon the intruders upon our solitude. They quickly accosted us in the Snake tongue, saying they were Shoshonies and friends to the whites. I invited them to approach and sit down, then gave them some meat and tobacco. They seemed astonished to find us here with mules, saying they knew of but one place where they thought mules or horses could ascend the mountain, and that was in a north-easterly direction. The small stream which was formed by the melting of the snow above us, after running past where we sat rushed down a fearful chasm and was lost in spray. After our visitors had eaten and smoked, we began to question them concerning their families and the country around them. They said their families were some distance below in a northerly direction and that there was a large lake beyond all the snowy peaks in sight to the northwest.

They also pointed out the place where we could descend the mountain and told us that this stream ran down through the mountain and united with a larger stream, which, after running a long distance north, turned toward the rising of the sun, into a large plain, where there were plenty of buffalo and Crow Indians. After getting this desired information, we left these sons of the wilderness to hunt their sheep and we went to hunt our camp as we could. We travelled over a high point of rocks composed of granite and coarse sandstone. In many places we saw large quantities of petrifaction, nearly whole trees broken in pieces from one to three feet long completely petrified. We also saw immense pieces of rock on the top of the mountain composed of coarse sand, pebbles and sea shells of various sizes and kinds. After crossing the summit we fell into a defile which led a winding course down the mountain. Near the foot of this defile we found a stone jar which would contain three gallons, neatly cut from a piece of granite, well shaped and smooth. After travelling all day over broken rocks, fallen timber and rough country, we arrived at the camp about dark.

On the 14th we raised camp and travelled north northeast over rough, craggy spurs about fifteen miles and encamped in a narrow glen between two enormous peaks of rocks. As we were passing along over a spur of the mountain we came to a place from which the earth had slid at some previous period and left the steep inclined ledge bare and difficult to cross. Our horses were obliged to place their feet in the small holes and fissures in the rock to keep themselves from sliding off. An unfortunate pack horse, however, missed his footing and slid down the declivity near the brink of a deep and frightful canyon through which the cataract nearby dashed some hundred feet below. Fortunately his foot caught in some roots which projected from a crevice in the rock and arrested his terrible course until we could attach ropes to him and drag him from his perilous situation.

15th—We followed the windings of the glen east as far as we could ride, and then all dismounted and walked except the wounded man, who rode until the mountain became so steep his horse could carry him no longer. We then assisted him from his horse and carried or pushed him to the top of the divide over the snow. In the meantime it commenced snowing very hard. After gaining the summit we unloaded our animals and rushed them on to the snow on the other side, which being hard, they went helter-skelter down to a warmer climate and were arrested by a smooth, grassy spot.

We then lowered the wounded man down by cords and put our saddles and baggage together on the snow, jumped on the top and started down, slowly at first, but the velocity soon increased until we brought up tumbling heels over head in a grassy bench in a more moderate climate. Now we were down, but whether we could get out was a question yet to be solved. Tremendous, towering mountains of rocks surrounded us excepting on the southeast, where a small stream ran from the snow into a dismal chasm below. But for my part I was well contented, for an eye could scarcely be cast in any direction around, above or below, without seeing the fat sheep gazing at us with anxious curiosity or lazily feeding among the rocks and scrubby pines. The bench where we encamped contained about 500 acres nearly level.

16th—We staid at this place, as our wounded comrade had suffered severely the day before. Some went down the stream to hunt a passage, while others went to hunt sheep. Being in camp about ten o'clock I heard the faint report of a rifle overhead. I looked up and saw a sheep tumble down the rocks, which stopped close to where I stood, but the man who shot it had to travel three or four miles before he could descend with safety to the camp. The sheep were all very fat, so that this could be called no other than high living, both as regarded altitude and rich provisions.

17th—Travelled down the stream through difficult and dangerous passage about ten miles, where we struck another branch on the left. This we ascended due north about eight miles and encamped on another green spot near the snow at the head of the glen.

18th—We ascended the mountain at the head of this branch and crossed the divide and descended another branch, which ran in a northerly direction about eight miles, and encamped in an enormous gorge

19th—Travelled about fifteen miles down stream and encamped on the edge of a plain.

20th—Travelled down to the two forks of this stream, about five miles, and stopped for the night. Here some of the trappers knew the country. This stream was called Stinking River, a branch of the Big Horn, which, after running about forty miles through the big plain, enters the above river about fifteen miles above the lower Big Horn mountain. It takes its name from several hot springs about five miles below the forks, producing a sulphurous stench which is often carried by the wind to the distance of five or six miles. Here were also large quarries of gypsum almost transparent, of the finest quality, and also appearances of lead, with large, rich beds of iron and bituminous coal. We stopped at this place and rested our animals until the 23rd. By this time our wounded comrade had recovered so far as to be able to hobble about on crutches.

24th—We took up the right hand fork in a north-westerly direction about fifteen miles, through a rugged defile in the mountain.

25th—Travelled about eighteen miles in the same direction, still following the stream, which ran very rapid down through the dense piles of mountains, which are formed of granite, slate and stone, covered with pines where there was sufficient soil to support them.

26th—Followed the stream almost due north about eight miles and encamped, where we staid the next day.

CHAPTER 6

In the Yellowstone Country

On the 28th we crossed the mountain in a westerly direction through the thick pines and fallen timber, about twelve miles, and encamped in a small prairie about a mile in circumference. Through this valley ran a small stream in a northerly direction, which all agreed in believing to be a branch of the Yellowstone.

29th—We descended the stream about fifteen miles through the dense forest and at length came to a beautiful valley about eight miles long and three or four wide, surrounded by dark and lofty mountains. The stream, after running through the centre in a north-westerly direction, rushed down a tremendous canyon of basaltic rock apparently just wide enough to admit its waters. The banks of the stream in the valley were low and skirted in many places with beautiful cottonwood groves.

Here we found a few Snake Indians comprising six men, seven women and eight or ten children, who were the only inhabitants of the lonely and secluded spot. They were all neatly clothed in dressed deer and sheep skins of the best quality and seemed to be perfectly contented and happy. They were rather surprised at our approach and retreated to the heights, where they might have a view of us without apprehending any danger, but having persuaded them of our pacific intentions we succeeded in getting them to encamp with us. Their personal property consisted of one old butcher knife nearly worn to the back, two old, shattered fusees which had long since become useless for want of ammunition, a small stone pot and about thirty dogs on which they carried their skins, clothing, provisions, etc., on their hunting excursions.

They were well armed with bows and arrows pointed with obsidian. The bows were beautifully wrought from sheep, buffalo and elk horns, secured with deer and elk sinews, and ornamented with porcupine quills, and generally about three feet long. We obtained a large number of deer, elk and sheep skins from them of the finest quality, and three large, neatly dressed panther skins, in return for awls and axes, kettles, tobacco, ammunition, etc. They would throw the skins at our feet and say, "Give us whatever you please for them and we are satisfied; we can get plenty of skins, but we do not often see the *Tibuboes*" (or "People of the Sun"). They said there had been a great many beavers on the branches of this stream, but they had killed nearly all of them, and, being ignorant of the value of fur had singed it off with fire in order to drip the meat more conveniently.

They had seen some whites some years previous who had passed through the valley and left a horse behind, but he had died during the first winter. They are never at a loss for fire, which they produce by the friction of two pieces of wood which are rubbed together with a quick and steady motion. One of them drew a map of the country around us on a white elk skin with a piece of charcoal, after which he explained the direction of the different passes, streams, etc. From these we discovered that it was about one day's travel in a south-westerly direction to the outlet or northern extremity of the Yellowstone Lake, but the route, from his description being difficult, and beaver comparatively scarce, our leader gave up the idea of going to it this season, as our horses were much jaded and their feet badly worn. Our geographer also told us that this stream united with the Yellowstone after leaving this valley half a day's travel in a westerly direction. The river then ran a long distance through a tremendous cut in the mountain in the same direction and emerged into a large plain, the extent of which was beyond his geographical knowledge or conception.

30th—We stopped at this place and for my own part I almost wished I could spend the remainder of my days in a place like this, where happiness and contentment seemed to reign in wild, romantic splendour, surrounded by majestic battlements which seemed to support the heavens and shut out all hostile intruders.

Another Man Lost

31st—We left the valley and descended the stream by a narrow, difficult path, winding among the huge fragments of basaltic rock for about twelve miles, when the trail came to an end and the towering rocks seemed to overhang the river on either side, forbidding further progress of man or beast, and obliged us to halt for the night. About dark some of our trappers came to camp and reported one of their comrades to be lost or met with some serious accident. The next day we concluded to stop at this place for the lost man and four men went in search of him, and returned at night without any tidings of him whatever. It was then agreed that either his gun had bursted and killed him or his horse had fallen over some tremendous precipice. He was a man about fifty-five years of age and of thirty years' experience as a hunter. Our leader concluded that further search was useless in this rocky, pathless and pine covered country.

August 2nd we forded the Yellowstone with some difficulty to the south side. The river at this place was about 200 yards wide and nearly swimming to the horses. A short distance below it rushes down a chasm with a dreadful roar echoing among the mountains. After crossing we took up a steep and narrow defile in a southerly direction and on gaining the summit in about three miles we found the country to open south and west of us into rolling prairie hills. We descended the mountain and encamped on a small stream running west.

3rd—Travelled about twenty-five miles due west, the route broken and uneven in the latter part of the day, and in some places thickly covered with pines. Encamped at night in a valley called "Gardner's Hole." This valley was about forty miles in circumference, surrounded, except on the north and west, by low, puny mountains. On the west was a high, narrow range of mountains running north and south, dividing the waters of the Yellowstone from those of the Gallatin Fork of the Missouri. We stopped in this valley until the 20th, the trappers being continually employed in hunting and trapping beaver.

On the 21st we crossed the mountains through a defile in a westerly direction and fell on to a small branch of the Gallatin. Here we encamped on a small clear spot and killed the fattest elk I ever saw. It was a large bull. The fat on his rump measured seven inches thick. He had fourteen spikes on the left horn and twelve on the right.

22nd—After we had started in the morning, five of our party (four trappers and one camp tender) secretly, dropped behind with their packs and riding horses and took a different direction, forming a party of their own, but they could not be much blamed for leaving, as our fractious leader was continually wrangling with the trappers by endeavouring to exercise his authority tyrannically. We followed down this branch to the Gallatin, about ten miles west, encamped and staid the next day.

24th—Down the Gallatin north northwest, the river running between two high ranges of mountains, skirted along the bank by a narrow valley.

25th—Left the defile and took up the Gallatin in an easterly direction, crossed the mountain and fell on to a stream running into the Yellowstone, and finding no beaver, returned to the Gallatin the next day the route we had come.

28th—Up the Gallatin to the place where we had struck it on the 22nd.

29th—Took up the stream a southerly course about ten miles, then left it to the left hand and proceeded about four miles south through a low pass and fell on to a branch of the Madison Fork of the Missouri running south. This we followed down about six miles further and encamped, where we staid next day. This pass was formed by the minor ranges of hills or spurs on the two high ranges of mountains on either side of us, which approach toward each other and terminate in a low defile completely covered with pines except along the stream, where small prairies may be found thickly clothed with grass, forming beautiful encampments.

CHAPTER 7

Encounter with Blackfeet Indians

31st—Travelled southwest down the stream about ten miles, when we came to the "Burnt Hole," a prairie valley about eighty miles in circumference, surrounded by low spurs of pine-covered mountains which are the sources of great numbers of streams which by uniting in this valley form the Madison Fork.

Sept. 1st—Travelled down the stream about twelve miles northwest and encamped during a heavy snowstorm. This stream, after leaving the valley, enters a gorge in the mountains in a north-westerly direction.

2nd—We stopped in the entrance of this gorge until the 8th. Travelled down about fifteen miles, where the country opened into a large plain, through which the stream turned in a sweeping curve due north.

9th—Crossed the valley in a westerly direction, travelled up a small branch and encamped about three miles from the river in a place with high bluffs on each side of us. We had been encamped about an hour when fourteen white trappers came to us in full gallop. They were of Mr. Bridger's party, who was encamped at Henry's Lake, about twenty miles in a southerly direction, and expected to arrive at the Madison the next day. His party consisted of sixty white men and about twenty Flathead Indians. These trappers remained with us during the night, telling mountain "yarns" and the news from the States. Early next morning eight of them started down the stream to set traps on the main fork, but returned in about an hour closely pursued by about eighty Blackfeet.

We immediately secured our horses in a yard previously made for

53

the purpose, and prepared for battle. In the meantime the Indians had gained the bluffs and commenced shooting into the camp from both sides. The bluff on the east side was very steep and rocky, covered with tall pines, the foot approaching within forty yards of us. On the west the bluffs were covered with thick groves of quaking asps. From these heights they poured in fusee balls without mercy or even damage, except killing our animals which were exposed to their fire. In the meantime we concealed ourselves in the thicket around the camp to await a nearer approach, but they were too much afraid of our rifles to come near enough for us to use ammunition. We lay almost silently about three hours, when finding they could not arouse us to action by their long shots, they commenced setting fire to the dry grass and rubbish with which we were surrounded.

The wind blowing brisk from the south, in a few moments the fire was converted into one circle of flame and smoke which united over our heads. This was the most horrible position I was ever placed in. Death seemed almost inevitable, but we did not despair, and all hands began immediately to remove the rubbish around the encampment and setting fire to it to act against the flames that were hovering over our heads. This plan proved successful beyond our expectations. Scarce half an hour had elapsed when the fire had passed around us and driven our enemies from their position. At length we saw an Indian whom we supposed to be the chief standing on a high point of rock and giving the signal for retiring, which was done by taking hold of the opposite corners of his robe, lifting it up and striking it three times on the ground.

The cracking of guns then ceased and the party moved off in silence. They had killed two horses and one of the mules on the spot and five more were badly wounded. It was about four o'clock in the afternoon when the firing ceased. We then saddled and packed our remaining animals and started for Mr. Bridger's camp, which we found on the Madison at the place where we had left it. Our party was now so disabled from the previous desertion of men and loss of animals that our leader concluded to travel with Mr. Bridger until we should arrive at the forks of the Snake River, where the latter intended to pass the winter.

On the 11th myself with five others returned to the battleground to get some traps which had been set for beaver on the stream above our encampment, whilst the main camp was to travel down the river about five miles and stop the remainder of the day to await our return.

We went for the traps and returned to the camp about three o'clock p. m.

12th—At sunrise an alarm of "Blackfeet!" echoed through the camp. In a moment all were under arms and inquiring "Where are they?" when 'twas replied, "On the hills to the west." I cast a glance along the high range of hills which projected toward the river from the mountain and discovered them standing in a line on a ridge. In their centre stood a small pole and from it waved an American flag, displaying a wish to make peace. About thirty of us walked up within about 300 yards of their line, when they made a signal for us to halt and send two men to meet the same number of theirs and treat for peace. Two of the whites who could speak the Blackfoot language were appointed to negotiate, while the respective lines sat upon the ground to await the event. After talking and smoking for half an hour the negotiators separated and returned to their respective parties. Ours reported them to be a party of Pagans, a small tribe of the Blackfeet, who desired to make peace with the whites and for that purpose had procured the flag from an American trading post on the Missouri. There were forty-five members, well armed and equipped.

We gave them a general invitation to our camp, which they accepted with a great deal of reluctance, when they were informed of the battle on the 10th, but arriving at the camp and receiving friendly treatment, their fears in a manner subsided. After smoking several rounds of the big pipe, the chief began to relate his adventures. He said he had been in several battles with the whites and some of the party were at the battle in "Pierre's Hole" on the 28th of June, last, in which there were four Indians killed on the spot and eight died of their wounds on the way to the village, but he denied having any knowledge of the late battle, but said there were several parties of the Blood Indians lurking about the mountains around us. They stopped with us until nearly night and all left except one, who concluded to remain.

13th—We left the Madison Fork with Mr. Bridger's camp and ascended a small branch in a westerly direction through the mountains about twenty miles, and encamped on the divide. After we had encamped a Frenchman started down the mountain to set his traps for beaver, contrary to the advice and persuasion of his comrades. He had gone but a few miles when he was fired upon by a party of Blackfeet, killed and scalped.

On the 14th we travelled down the mountain about fifteen miles northwest, and encamped on a stream called "Stinking Creek," which runs into the Jefferson Fork of the Missouri. After we had encamped some trappers ascended the stream, but were driven back by the Blackfeet. Others went below and shared the same fate from another party, but escaped to the camp unhurt.

15th—Moved down this stream about twelve miles north. This part of the country was comprised of high, bald hills on either side of the stream, which terminated in rough, pine-covered mountains.

16th—We travelled down the stream northwest about eight miles. The valley opened wider as we descended, and large numbers of buffalo were scattered over the plains and among the hills.

17th—Down about ten miles northwest, the mountains on the west side descending to a sloping spur, from thence to a plain.

18th—We did not raise camp, and about noon some Flathead Indians arrived and told us their village was on a branch of the Jefferson called "Beaverhead Creek," about thirty miles in a westerly direction. The next day we went to their village, which consisted of 180 lodges of Flatheads and Pend d'Oreilles (or Hanging Ears). Here we found a trading party belonging to the Hudson Bay Company. They were under the direction of Mr. Francis Ermatinger, who was endeavouring to trade every beaver skin as fast as they were taken from the water by the Indians. 20th—The whole cavalcade moved *en masse* up the stream about twelve miles southwest and encamped with another village of the same tribe consisting of 130 lodges.

From this place was a large plain, slightly undulating, extending nearly to the junction of the three forks of the Missouri. The Flatheads were a brave, friendly, generous and hospitable tribe, strictly honest, with a mixture of pride which exalts them far above the rude appellation of savages, when contrasted with the tribes around them. They boast of never injuring the whites and consider it a disgrace to their tribe if they are not treated like brothers whilst in company with them. Sorcery, fornication and adultery are severely punished. Their chiefs are obeyed with a reverence due to their station and rank.

23rd—We left the village in company with Mr. Bridger and his party and travelled southeast across the plain about six miles to the foot of the hills and encamped at a spring.

24th—Travelled about eighteen miles southeast over high, rolling hills, beautifully clothed with bunch grass.

25th—Travelled in the same direction twelve miles and encamped in a smooth valley about eighty miles in circumference, surrounded on the north and east by a high range of mountains. At the northeast extremity was a marshy lake about twelve miles in circumference. From this flowed the head stream of the Jefferson Fork of the Missouri, which curved to the southwest through the valley and entered the low mountains on the west through a narrow cut, still continuing the curve encircling a large portion of country previous to its arrival at the junction.

26th—Crossed the valley about sixteen miles and encamped on the east side. This valley, as a mountaineer would say, was full of buffalo when we entered it and large numbers of them were killed by our hunters. We repeatedly saw signs of Blackfeet about us to waylay the trappers.

27th—We stopped at this place and encamped on Camas Creek on the northwest extremity of the great plain of the Snake River. Here the leader of our party desired me to go to Fort Hall and get some horses to assist them to the fort, as we were dependent on Mr. Bridger for animals to move camp.

CHAPTER 8

Finally Reaches Fort Hall

30th—After getting the necessary information from our leader, I started, contrary to the advice and remonstrances of Mr. Bridger and his men, rather than be impeached of cowardice by our autocratic director. I travelled according to his directions south until dark amid thousands of buffaloes. The route was very rocky and my horse's feet (he not being shod) were worn nearly to the quick, which caused him to limp very much. After travelling about thirty miles I lay down and slept sound during the night. The next morning I arose and proceeded on my journey down the stream. About nine o'clock I came to where it formed a lake, where it sank in the dry and sandy plain. From this I took a south-easterly course, as directed, towards a high butte which stood in the almost barren plain.

By passing to the east of this butte, I was informed that it was about twenty-five miles to Snake River. In this direction I travelled until about two hours after dark. My horse had been previously wounded by a ball in the loins, and though nearly recovered before I started, yet travelling over the rocks and gravel with tender feet and his wound together had nearly exhausted him. I turned him loose among the rocks and wild sage and laid myself down to meditate on the follies of myself and others.

In about two hours I fell asleep to dream of cool springs, rich feasts and cool shade. In the morning I arose and looked around me. My horse was near by me picking the scanty blades of sunburned grass which grew among the sage. On surveying the place I found I could go no further in a south or east direction, as there lay before me a range of broken, basaltic rock which appeared to extend for five or six miles on either hand and five or six miles wide, thrown together promiscuously in such a manner that it was impossible for a horse to cross them. The butte stood to the southwest about ten miles, which I was informed was about half the distance from Camas Lake to Snake River.

I now found that either from ignorance or some other motive less pure, our leader had given me directions entirely false, and came to the conclusion to put no further confidence in what he had told me, but return to the lake I had left, as it was the nearest water I knew of. This point being settled, I saddled my horse and started on foot, leading him by the bridle, and travelled all day in the direction of the lake over the hot sand and gravel. After daylight disappeared I took a star for my guide, but it led me south of the lake, where I came on to several large bands of buffalo, which would start on my near approach and run in all directions. It was near midnight when I laid down to rest. I had plenty of provisions, but could not eat. Water! Water was the object of my wishes. Travelling for two days in the hot burning sun without water is by no means a pleasant way of passing the time. I soon fell asleep and dreamed again of bathing in the cool rivulets issuing from the snow topped mountains. About an hour before day I was awakened by the howling of wolves, they having formed a complete circle within thirty paces of me and my horse. At the flashing of my pistol, however, they soon dispersed.

At daylight I discovered some willows about three miles distant to the west, where large numbers of buffalo had assembled, apparently for water. In two hours I had dispersed the brutes and lay by the water side. After drinking and bathing for half an hour, I travelled up the stream about a mile and lay down among some willows to sleep in the shade, whilst my horse was carelessly grazing among the bushes. The next day being the 4th, I lay all day and watched the buffalo, which were feeding in immense bands all about me.

5th—I arose in the morning at sunrise and looking to the southwest I discovered the dust arising in a defile which led through the mountain about five miles distant. The buffaloes were carelessly feeding all over the plain as far as the eye could reach. I watched the motion of the dust for a few minutes, when I saw a body of men on horseback pouring out of the defile among the buffalo. In a few minutes the dust rose to the heavens. The whole mass of buffalo became agitated, producing a sound resembling distant thunder. At length an Indian pursued a cow close to me. Running alongside of her he let slip an arrow and she fell. I immediately recognised him to be a Bannock with whom I was acquainted.

On discovering me he came to me and saluted me in Snake, which I answered in the same tongue. He told me the village would come and encamp where I was. In the meantime he pulled off some of his clothing and hung it on a stick as a signal for the place where his squaw should set his lodge. He then said he had killed three fat cows but would kill one more and stop. So saying he wheeled his foaming charger and the next moment disappeared in the cloud of dust. In about half an hour the old chief came up with the village and invited me to stop with him, which I accepted.

While the squaws were putting up and stretching their lodges, I walked out with the chief on to a small hillock to view the field of slaughter, the cloud of dust having passed away, and the prairie was covered with the slain. Upward of one thousand cows were killed without burning one single grain of gunpowder. The village consisted of 332 lodges and averaged six persons, young and old, to each lodge. They were just returning from the salmon fishing to feast on fat buffalo. After the lodges were pitched I returned to the village. This chief was called "*Aikenlo-ruckkup*" (or "The Tongue Cut With a Flint"). He was the brother of the celebrated Horn Chief, who was killed in a battle with the Blackfeet some years before, and it was related by the Bannocks, without the least scruple, that he was killed by a piece of antelope horn, the only manner in which he could have been taken, as he was protected by a supernatural power from all other harm. My worthy host spared no pains to make my situation as comfortable as his circumstances would permit.

The next morning I took a walk through the village and found there were fifteen lodges of Snakes with whom I had formed an acquaintance the year before. On my first entering the village I was informed that two white trappers belonging to Mr. Wyeth's party had been lately killed by the Bannocks in the lower country and that the two Indians who had killed or caused them to be killed were then in the village. The old chief had pointed them out to me as we walked through the village and asked me what the white men would do about it. I told him they would hang them if they caught them at the fort. He said it was good; that they deserved death, for said he, "I believe they have murdered the two white men to get their property, and lost it all in gambling, for," continued he, "ill gained wealth often flies away and does the owners no good. But," said he, "you need not be under any apprehension of danger whilst you stop with the village." The squaws were employed cutting and drying meat for two days, at the end of which time the ground on which the village stood seemed covered with meat scaffolds bending beneath their rich loads of fat buffalo meat.

13th—My horse being somewhat recruited, I left the village with a good supply of boiled buffalo tongue prepared by my landlady, and the necessary directions and precautions from the old chief. I travelled due east about twenty-five miles, which brought me to the forks of Snake River. When approaching to the waters I discovered fresh human footprints. I immediately turned my horse and rode out from the river about a quarter of a mile, intending to travel parallel with the river in order to avoid any straggling party of Blackfeet, which might be secreted in the timber growing along the bank. I had not gone far when I discovered three Indians on horseback running a bull toward me. I jumped my horse into a ravine and out of sight and crawled up among the high sage to watch their movements.

As they approached nearer to me I saw they were Snakes and showed myself to them. They left the bull and galloped up to me. After the usual salutation, I followed them to their village, which was on the east bank of the river. The village consisted of fifteen lodges under the direction of a chief called "Comb Daughter" by the Snakes and by the whites "Lame Chief." He welcomed me to his lodge in the utmost good humour and jocular manner I had ever experienced among the Indians, and I was sufficiently acquainted with the Snake language to repay his jokes in his own coin without hesitation. I passed the time very agreeably for six days among these simple but well-fed and good-humoured savages.

On the 19th, learning that Bridger was approaching the forks and the party of hunters to which I had belonged had passed down the river toward the fort, I mounted my horse, started down the river and arrived at the fort next day about noon, the distance being about sixty miles south southwest.

When I arrived the party had given up all hopes of ever seeing me again and had already fancied my lifeless body lying on the plains, after having been scalped by the savages.

CHAPTER 9

Joins Bridger's Company as a Trapper

The time for which myself and all of Mr. Wyeth's men were engaged had recently expired, so that now I was independent of the world and no longer to be termed a "greenhorn." At least I determined not to be so green as to bind myself to an arbitrary Rocky Mountain Chieftain to be kicked over hill and dale at his pleasure.

November 15th Captain Thing arrived from the Columbia with supplies for the fort. In the meantime the men about the fort were doing nothing and I was lending them a hand until Mr. Wyeth should arrive and give us our discharge.

December 20th Mr. Wyeth arrived, when I bid *adieu* to the Columbia River Fishing and Trading Company and started, in company with fifteen of my old messmates, to pass the winter at a place called "Mutton Hill," on Portneuf, about forty miles south-east from Fort Hall. Mr. Wyeth had brought a new recruit of sailors and Sandwich islanders to supply our places at the fort. We lived on fat mutton until the snow drove us from the mountains in February. Our party then dispersing, I joined Mr. Bridger's company, who were passing the winter on Blackfoot Creek, about fifteen miles from the fort, where we staid until the latter part of March. Mr. Bridger's men lived very poor and it was their own fault, for the valley was covered with fat cows when they arrived in November, but instead of approaching and killing their meat for the winter they began to kill by running on horseback, which had driven the buffalo all over the mountain to the head of the Missouri, and the snow falling deep, they could not return during the winter.

They killed plenty of bulls, but they were so poor that their meat was perfectly blue, yet this was their only article of food, as bread and vegetables were out of the question in the Rocky Mountains, except a few kinds of roots of spontaneous growth, which the Indians dig and prepare for food. It would doubtless be amusing to a disinterested spectator to witness the process of cooking poor bull meat as practiced by this camp during the winter of 1835-6.

On going through the camp at any time in the day heaps of ashes might be seen with the fire burning on the summit and an independent looking individual, who is termed a camp kicker, sitting with a "two-year-old club" in his hand watching the pile with as much seeming impatience as Philoctele did the burning of Hercules. At length, poking over the ashes with his club, it bounds five or six feet from the ground like a huge ball of gum elastic. This operation, frequently repeated, divests the ashes adhering to it and prepares it for carving. He then drops his club and draws his butcher knife calling to his comrades, "Come Major, Judge, Squire, Dollar, Pike, Cotton and Gabe, won't you take a lunch of Simon?" each of whom acts according to the dictates of his appetite in accepting or refusing the invitation.

I have often witnessed these philosophical and independent dignitaries collected round a bull's ham just torn from a pile of embers, good-humouredly observing as they hacked the huge slices from the lean mass that this was tough eating but that it was tougher where there was none, and consoling themselves with a promise to make the fat cows suffer before the year rolled around. The camp remained on Blackfoot until the latter part of March, when the winter broke up and we commenced travelling and hunting beaver.

We left winter quarters on the 28th and travelled along the foot of the mountain in a northerly direction to Lewis Fork and ascended it southeast to the mouth of Muddy Creek, where we arrived on the 7th of April. Here Mr. Bridger ordered a party of twelve trappers to branch off to the right and hunt the head waters of Gray and Blackfoot Creeks. I was included in the number and felt anxious to try my skill in trapping.

10th—We set off, leaving the main camp, to proceed leisurely to Saltrim valley and from thence to the mouth of Thomas Fork of Bear River, where we were instructed to meet them. We ascended Muddy Creek and crossed the mountain on to Gray's Creek. Here we found the snow disappearing very fast and the streams so much swollen that we made but slow progress in taking beaver. We travelled the numerous branches of this stream to and fro, setting traps where the water would permit, until the 25th of April, when we left the waters of Gray's Creek and travelled about forty miles in a southwest direction from where we had struck it, crossed a low mountain about eight miles and fell on to Blackfoot. This we ascended two days and hunted until the 5th of May, when three of our party were waylaid and fired upon by a party of Blackfeet whilst ascending the stream through a canyon. One of them was slightly wounded in the side by a fusee ball, but all escaped to the camp and reported the Indians to be about twenty-five in number. On the 7th of May we left Blackfoot and crossed the mountain southwest through deep snow and thick pines and at night fell into the valley on Bear River and encamped about twenty-five miles above the soda springs.

8th—Travelled up Bear River to Thomas Fork, where we found the main camp, likewise Mr. A. Dripps and his party, consisting of about sixty whites and nearly as many half breeds, who were encamped with 400 lodges of Snakes and Bannocks and 100 lodges of Nez Perces and Flatheads.

9th—We all camped together in the beautiful plain on Bear River above the mouth of Smith's Fork.

11th—The whole company of Indians and whites left Bear River and travelled to Ham's Fork, excepting Mr, Dripps and a small party, who went round to Black's Fork of Green River to get some furs and other articles deposited there in the ground. After reaching Ham's Fork the Indians concluded to separate in different directions, as we were in too large a body and had too many horses to thrive long together. They were instructed to be on the mouth of Horse Creek on Green River about the 1st of July, as we expected supplies from the United States about that time. We laid about on the branches of Green River until the 28th of June, when we arrived at the destined place of rendezvous. On the 1st of July Mr. Wyeth arrived from the mouth of the Columbia on his way to the United States, with a small party of men.

CHAPTER 10

Rendezvous at Green River

On the 3rd the outfit arrived from St. Louis, consisting of forty men having twenty horse carts drawn by mules and loaded with the supplies for the ensuing year. They were accompanied by Doctor Marcus Whitman and lady, Mr. H. H. Spaulding and lady, and Mr. W. H. Gray, Presbyterian missionaries, on their way to the Columbia to establish a mission among the Indians in that quarter. The two ladies were gazed on with wonder and astonishment by the rude savages, they being the first white women ever seen by these Indians and the first that had ever penetrated into these wild and rocky regions.

We remained at the rendezvous until the 16th of July and then began to branch off into parties for the fall hunt in different directions.

Mr. Bridger's party, as usual, was destined for the Blackfoot country. It contained most of the American trappers and amounted I to sixty men. I started with a party of fifteen trappers and two camp keepers, ordered by Mr. Bridger to proceed to the Yellowstone Lake and there await his arrival with the rest of the party. July 24th we set off and travelled up Green River twenty-five miles in a northerly direction.

25th—Up Green River fifteen miles in the same direction, then left it to our right and took up a small branch, keeping a northeast course still. The course of the river where we left it turns abruptly to the east and heads in a high, craggy mountain, covered with snow, about thirty miles distant. This mountain is a spur of the Wind River range and is commonly called the Sweetwater mountain, as that stream heads in its southern termination. After leaving the river we travelled about four miles to the head of the branch and encamped in a smooth, grassy plain on the divide between Green and Snake Rivers, which head within 200 paces of each other at this place.

26th—Travelled north about fifteen miles, descending a small stream through a rough, mountainous country covered with pine trees and underbrush, and encamped on Grosvent Fork.

27th—We descended the Grosvent Fork to "Jackson's Hole" about twenty miles, general course west.

28th—We followed Lewis Fork through the valley, crossing several large streams coming in from the east. We then left the valley and followed the river about five miles through a piece of rough, piney country, and came to Jackson's Lake, which is formed by the river. We encamped at the outlet at a small prairie about a mile in circumference. This lake is about twenty-five miles long and three miles wide, lying north and south, bordered on the east by pine swamps and marshes extending from one to two miles from the lake, to the spurs of the mountain. On the southwest stands the three Tetons, whose dark, frightful forms rising abruptly from the lake, towering above the clouds, cast a gloomy shade upon the waters beneath, whilst the water rushes in torrents down the awful precipices from the snow by which they are crowned. The high range of mountains on the west, after leaving the Tetons, slope gradually to the north and spread into low piney mountains.

This place, like all other marshes and swamps among the mountains, is infested with innumerable swarms of horseflies and mosquitoes, to the great annoyance of man and beast during the day, but the cold air descending from the mountain at night compels them to seek shelter among the leaves and grasses at an early hour. Game is plentiful and the river and lake abound with fish. After hunting the streams and marshes about this lake, we left it on the 7th of August and travelled down Lewis Fork about four miles to the second stream running into it on the east side below the lake. This we ascended about twelve miles east and encamped among the pines close to where it emerged from a deep canyon in the mountain.

8th—We took across a high spur thickly covered with pines, intermingled with brush and fallen timber, in a northeast direction for about twelve miles, where we fell into a small valley on a left hand branch of the stream we had left.

9th—We took up this branch due north about ten miles, when, it turning short to the right, we left it and ascended a narrow glen, keeping a north course, sometimes travelling through thick pines and then crossing small green spots through which little streams were running from the remaining banks of snow lying among the pines in the shade of the mountains, for about six miles, when we came to a smooth prairie about two miles long and half a mile wide, lying east and west, surrounded by pines. On the south side, about midway of the prairie, stood a high snowy peak from whence issued a stream of water which, after entering the plain, divided equally, one-half running west and the other east, thus bidding *adieu* to each other, one bound for the Pacific and the other for the Atlantic ocean. Here a trout of twelve inches in length may cross the mountains in safety. Poets have sung of the "meeting of the waters" and fish climbing cataracts, but the "*parting of the waters and fish crossing mountains*," I believe, remains unsung as yet by all except the solitary trapper who sits under the shade of a spreading pine whistling blank verse and beating time to the tune with a whip on his trap sack whilst musing on the parting advice of those waters.

10th—We took down the east branch and followed it about eight miles to the Yellowstone River, which is about eighty yards wide and at the shallowest place nearly swimming to our horses. To this place it comes from a deep gorge in the mountains, enters a valley lying north and south about fifteen miles long and three miles wide, through which it winds its way slowly to the north through swamps and marshes and calmly reposes in the bosom of the Yellowstone Lake. The south extremity of this valley was smoother and thickly clothed with high meadow grass, surrounded by high, craggy mountains, topped with snow. We stopped at this place trapping until the 3rd of August, when we travelled down the lake to the inlet or southern extremity.

Chapter 9

Yellowstone National Park

16th—Mr. Bridger came up with the remainder of the party.

18th—The whole camp moved down the east shore of the lake through thick pines and fallen timber about eighteen miles and encamped in a small prairie.

19th—Continued down the shore to the outlet about twenty miles, and encamped in a beautiful plain which extended along the northern extremity of the lake. This valley was interspersed with scattering groves of tall pines, forming shady retreats for the numerous elk and deer during the heat of the day. The lake is about 100 miles in circumference, bordered on the east by high ranges of mountains whose spurs terminate at the shore and on the west by a low bed of piney mountains. Its greatest width is about fifteen miles, lying in an oblong form south to north, or rather in the shape of a crescent. Near where we encamped were several hot springs which boiled perpetually. Near these was an opening in the ground about eight inches in diameter from which hot steam issued continually with a noise similar to that made by the steam issuing from the safety valve of an engine, and could be heard five or six miles distant.

I should think the steam issued with sufficient force to work an engine of thirty horsepower. We encamped about three o'clock p.m. and after resting our horses about an hour, seven of us were ordered to go out and hunt some streams running into the Yellowstone some distance below the lake. We started from the camp in an easterly direction, crossed the plain and entered the pines, and after travelling about an hour through dense forests we fell into a broken tract of country which seemed to be all on fire at some distance below the surface. It being very difficult to get around this place, we concluded to follow an elk trail across it for about half a mile. The treading of our horses sounded like travelling on a plank platform covering an immense cavity in the earth, whilst the hot water and steam were spouting and hissing around us in all directions.

As we were walking and leading our horses across this place, the horse that was before me broke through the crust with one hind foot and the blue steam rushed forth from the hole. The whole place was covered with a crust of lime stone of a dazzling whiteness, formed by the overflowing of the boiling water. Shortly after leaving this resemblance of the infernal regions, we killed a fat elk and camped at sunset in a smooth, grassy spot between two high, shaggy ridges, watered by a small stream which came tumbling down the gorge behind us. As we had passed the infernal regions we thought, as a matter of course, this must be a commencement of the Elysian Fields, and accordingly commenced preparing a feast. A large fire was soon blazing, encircled with sides of elk ribs and meat: cut in slices, supported on sticks, down which the grease ran in torrents.

The repast being over, the jovial tale goes round the circle, the peals of loud laughter break upon the stillness of the night which, after being mimicked in the echo from rock to rock dies away in the solitary gloom. Every tale reminds an auditor of something similar to it but under different circumstances, which, being told, the "laughing part" gives rise to increasing merriment and furnishes more subjects for good jokes and witty sayings such as a Swift never dreamed of. Thus the evening passed, with eating, drinking and stories, enlivened with witty humour until near midnight, all being wrapped in their blankets lying round the fire, gradually falling to sleep one by one, until the last tale is encored by the snoring of the drowsy audience. The speaker takes the hint, breaks off the subject and wrapping his blanket more closely about him, soon joins the snoring party.

The light of the fire being superseded by that of the moon just rising from behind the eastern mountain, a sullen gloom is cast over the remaining fragments of the feast and all is silent except the occasional howling of the solitary wolf on the neighbouring mountain, whose senses are attracted by the flavour of roasted meat, but fearing to approach nearer, he sits upon a rock and bewails his calamities in piteous moans which are re-echoed among the mountains.

Aug. 20th—Took over a high, rugged mountain about twelve miles northeast and fell into the secluded valley which I have described in my last year's journal. There we found some of those indifferent and happy natives of whom I gave a description. We traded some beaver and dressed skins from them and hunted the streams running into the valley for several days. There is something in the wild, romantic scenery of this valley which I cannot, nor will I attempt, to describe, but the impressions made upon my mind while gazing from a high eminence on the surrounding landscape one evening as the sun was gently gliding behind the western mountains and casting its gigantic shadow across the vale were such as time can never efface from my memory, but as I am neither poet, painter nor romance writer I must content myself to be what I am—a humble journalist—and leave this beautiful vale in obscurity until visited by some more skilful admirer of the beauties of nature, who may chance to stroll this way at some future period.

25th—Left the valley and travelled down to the Yellowstone and crossed it at the ford.

26th—Crossed the mountain in a southwest direction and fell on to Gardner's Fork. Here myself and another set some traps and stopped for the night whilst the remainder of the party went in different directions to hunt setting.

27th—We crossed the mountain southwest to "Gardner's Hole," where we found the main camp.

28th—Camp left "Gardner's Hole" and travelled north to the Yellowstone about twenty miles.

29th—The whole party followed the river out of the mountain into the great Yellowstone plain, distance about twelve miles. The trappers then scattered out in small parties of from two to five in number, leaving Mr. Bridger with twenty-five camp keepers to travel slowly down the river. Myself and another travelled down the river about forty miles northeast to a branch called "Twenty-five Yard River," This we ascended about twenty-five miles in a northerly direction, where we remained trapping several days. The country lying on this stream is mostly comprised of high rolling ridges, thickly clothed with grass and herbage and crowded with immense bands of buffalo, intermingled with bands of antelope.

CHAPTER 12

"Howell's Encampment"

Sept. 1st—We returned to the camp, which we found at the mouth of this stream, where we found also ten Delaware Indians who had joined the camp in order to hunt beaver with greater security.

2nd—Travelled down the Yellowstone River about twenty miles. This is a beautiful country, the large plains widely extending on either side of the river, intersected with streams and occasional low spurs of mountains, whilst thousands of buffaloes may be seen in almost every direction, and deer, elk and grizzly bear are abundant. The latter are more numerous than in any other part of the mountains, owing to the vast quantities of cherries, plums and other wild fruits which this section of the country affords. In going to visit my traps, a distance of three or four miles, early in the morning, I have frequently seen seven or eight standing about the clumps of cherry bushes on their hind legs, gathering cherries with surprising dexterity, not even deigning to turn their grizzly heads to gape at the passing trapper, but merely casting a sidelong glance at him without altering their position.

3rd—Left the camp on the Yellowstone and started across a low and somewhat broken tract of country in a south-easterly direction to a stream called the Rosebud, accompanied by another trapper.

5th—The camp came to us on the Rosebud and the next day passed on in the same direction, whilst myself and comrade stopped behind to trap.

7th—We overtook the camp on a stream called Rocky Fork, a branch of Clark's Fork of the Yellowstone. When we arrived at camp we were told the sad news of the death of a French trapper named Bodah, who had been waylaid and killed by a party of Blackfeet while setting his traps, and one of the Delawares had been shot through the hip by the rifle of one of his comrades going off accidentally, and several war parties of Blackfeet had been seen scouting about the country. We had been in camp but a few minutes when two trappers rode up whom we called "Major Meek" and "Dave Crow." The former, a tall Virginian who had been in the mountains some twelve years, was riding a white Indian pony. On dismounting some blood was discovered which had apparently been running down his horse's neck and dried on the hair.

He was immediately asked where he had been and what was the news. "News!" exclaimed he, "I have been, me and Dave, over on to Prior's Fork to set our traps and found old Benj. Johnson's boys over there, just walking up and down them 'ar streams with their hands on their hips gathering plums. They gave me a tilt, and turned me a somerset or two, shot my horse, 'Too Shebit,' in the neck and sent us heels over head in a pile together, but we raised a-runnin'. Gabe, do you know where Prior leaves the cut bluffs, goin' up it?"

"Yes," replied Bridger. "Well, after you get out of the hills on the right hand fork there is scrubby box elders about three miles along the creek up to where a little right hand spring branch puts in with lots and slivers of plum trees about the mouth of it and some old beaver dams at the mouth of the main creek. Well, sir, we went up there and set yesterday morning. I set two traps right below the mouth of that little branch and in them old dams, and Dave set his down the creek apiece. So after we had got our traps set we cruised around and eat plums a while. The best plums I ever saw are there. The trees are loaded and breaking down to the ground with the finest kind, as large as pheasant eggs and sweet as sugar. They'll almost melt in yo' mouth; no wonder them rascally savages like that place so well. Well, sir, after we had eat what plums we wanted, me and Dave took down the creek and staid all night on a little branch in the hills, and this morning started to our traps.

"We came up to Dave's traps and in the first there was a four-year-old 'spade,' the next was false licked, went to the next and it had cut a foot and none of the rest disturbed. We then went up to mine to the mouth of the branch. I rode on five or six steps ahead of Dave and just as I got opposite the first trap I heard a rustling in the bushes within about five steps of me. I looked around and *pop, pop, pop* went the guns, covering me with smoke so close that I could see the blanket wads coming out of the muzzle. Well, sir, I wheeled and a ball hit Too Shebit in the neck and just touched the bone and we pitched heels over head, but Too Shebit raised runnin' and I on his back and the savages jist squattin' and grabbin' at me, but I raised a fog for about half a mile till I overtook Dave."

The foregoing story was corroborated by "Dave," a small, inoffensive man, who had come to the Rocky Mountains with General Ashley some fifteen years before and remained ever since, an excellent hunter and a good trapper. The next day we moved down the stream to its junction with Clark's Fork, within about three miles of the Yellowstone. On the following morning two men went to set traps down on the river and as they were hunting along the brushy banks for places to set, a party of sixty Blackfeet surrounded them, drove them into the river and shot after them as they were swimming across on their horses. One by the name of Howell was shot by two fusee balls through the chest, the other escaped unhurt. Howell rode within half a mile of the camp, fell and was brought in on a litter.

He lived about twenty hours and expired in the greatest agony imaginable. About an hour after he was brought in twenty whites and Delawares went to scour the brush along the river and fight the Blackfeet. Having found them they drove them on to an island and fought them until dark. The loss on our side during the battle was a Nez Perce Indian killed and one white slightly wounded in the shoulder. The Blackfeet, who were fortified on the island, drew off in the night, secreting their dead and carrying off their wounded. The next day we interred the remains of poor Howell at the foot of a large Cottonwood tree and called the place "Howell's Encampment," as a compliment to his memory.

11th—We travelled on to Prior's Fork and struck it where the Major's traps were setting, a distance of twenty-five miles southeast.

12th—Stopped at this place and gathered plums.

13th—Travelled east twelve miles to the left hand fork of the Prior.

14th—The snow fell all day and on the 15th it was fifteen inches deep.

16th—We returned to the west fork of the Prior and stopped the next day.

18th—The snow being gone, we returned to Clark's Fork.

19th—Seven of us left the camp and travelled to Rock Fork near the mountain, a distance of thirty-five miles, course southwest. We all kept together and set our traps on Rocky Fork near the mountain. We had been here five days when a party of Crow Indians came to us, consisting of forty-nine warriors. They were on their way to the Blackfoot village to steal horses. They staid with us two nights and then went to the camp which had come on to this stream about twenty miles below us.

28th—Another party of Crows came to us, consisting of no warriors. We went with them to the camp, which we found about ten miles below. They remained with the camp the next day and then left for the Blackfoot village, which they said was at the three forks of the Missouri.

30th—We travelled with the camp west on to the Rosebud.

Oct. 1st—The trappers scattered out in every direction to hunt beaver on the branches of the Rosebud and continued to the 10th, when we followed the camp down the Yellowstone, where Mr. Bridger had concluded to pass the winter. The small streams being frozen, trapping was suspended and all collected to winter quarters, where were thousands of fat buffalo feeding in the plains, and we had nothing to do but slay and eat.

Oct. 25—The weather becoming fine and warm, some of the trappers started again to hunt beaver. Myself and another started to Prior's Fork and set our traps on the east branch, where we staid six days. We then crossed a broken piece of country about twelve miles northeast and fell on to a stream running northeast into the Big Horn, called "Bovy's Fork." Here we set traps and staid ten days. This section of country was very uneven and broken, but abounded with buffalo, elk, deer and bear. Among other spontaneous productions of this country were hops, which grew in great abundance and of a superior quality. Thousands of acres along the small branches, the trees and shrubbery were completely entangled in the vines, nth—The weather becoming cold, the streams froze over again, and we started for camp, which we found on Clark's Fork about a mile above "Howell's Encampment."

The camp stopped at this place until Christmas, then moved down about four miles on to the Yellowstone. The bottoms along these rivers were heavily timbered with sweet Cottonwood, and our horses and mules were very fond of the bark, which we stripped from the limbs and gave them every night, as the buffalo had entirely destroyed the grass throughout this part of the country. We passed away the time very agreeably, our only employment being to feed our horses, kill buffalo and eat, that is to say, the trappers. The camp keepers' business in winter quarters is to guard the horses, cook and keep fires. We all had snug lodges made of dressed buffalo skins, in the centre of which we built a fire and generally comprised about six men to the lodge. The long winter evenings were passed away by collecting in some of the most spacious lodges and entering into debates, arguments or spinning long yarns until midnight, in perfect good humour, and I for one will cheerfully confess that I have derived no little benefit from the frequent arguments and debates held in what we termed "The Rocky Mountain College," and I doubt not but some of my comrades who considered themselves classical scholars have had some little added to their wisdom in the assemblies, however rude they might appear.

On the 28th of January myself and six more trappers concluded to take a cruise of five or six days after buffalo. The snow was about four inches deep and the weather clear and cold. We took seven loose animals to pack meat, and travelled up Clark's Fork about twelve miles, killed a cow and encamped. The next morning we started across toward Rock Fork and had gone about three miles over the smooth plain, gradually ascending to a range of hills which divided Clark's Fork from Rock, when, riding carelessly along with our rifles lying before us on the saddles, we came to a deep, narrow gulch, made by the water running from the hills in the spring season.

Behold, the earth seemed teeming with naked savages. A quick volley of fusees, a shower of balls and a cloud of smoke clearly bespoke their nation, tribe, manners and customs, and mode of warfare. A ball broke the right arm of one man and he dropped his rifle, which a savage immediately caught up and shot after us as we wheeled and scampered away out of reach of their guns. There were about eighty Indians, who had secreted themselves until we rode within fifteen feet of them. They got a rifle clear gain, and we had one man wounded and lost a rifle, so they had so much the advantage, and we were obliged to go to camp and study out some plan to get even, as by the two or three skirmishes we had fallen in their respect.

A few days afterwards a party of twenty were discovered crossing the plain to the river about six miles below us. Twenty men immediately mounted and set off and arrived at the place just as they had entered the timber. They ran into some old rotten Indian forts formed of small poles in a conical shape. The whites immediately surrounded and opened fire on them, which was kept up until darkness and the severity of the weather compelled them to retire. We had one man wounded slightly through the hip and one Delaware was shot in the leg by a poisoned ball which lodged under the knee cap. He lived four days and expired.

On examining the battleground next day, we found that three or four at least had been killed and put under the ice in the river. Seven or eight had been badly wounded, which they dragged away on trains to their village. We found that the old forts were not bullet proof in any place. Our rifle balls had whistled through them nearly every shot and blood and brains lay scattered about inside on the shattered fragments of the rotten wood.

CHAPTER 13

Brilliant Display of "Northern Lights"

February 22nd—Mr. Bridger, according to his usual custom, took his telescope and mounted a high bluff near the encampment to look out for "squalls," as he termed it. About one o'clock p.m. he returned appearing somewhat alarmed, and on being asked the cause he said the great plain below was alive with savages, who were coming across the hills to the timber about ten miles below us. From this place the river runs in a north-easterly direction, bearing east. On the north and west is a plain from six to ten miles wide, bordered by rough, broken hills and clay bluffs. On the south and east the river runs along the foot of a high range of steep bluffs, intersected by deep ravines and gulches. Along the river are large bottoms covered with large cottonwood timber and clear of uuderbrush. All hands commenced to build a breast works around the camp, which was constructed of logs and brush piled horizontally six feet high around the camp, inclosing about 250 feet square.

This being completed, at dark a double guard was mounted and all remained quiet, but it was a bitter cold night. I mounted guard from nine till twelve o'clock. The weather was clear, the stars shone with an unusual lustre and the trees cracked like pistols. At about ten o'clock the northern lights commenced streaming up, darting, flashing, rushing to and fro like the movements of an army. At length the shooting and flashing died away and gradually turned to a deep blood red, spreading over one-half the sky. This awful and sublime phenomenon (if I may be allowed to mingle such terms) lasted nearly two hours, then gradually disappeared, and being relieved by the morning guard, I went to bed and slept soundly till sunrise.

The next day we were engaged strengthening the fortress by cutting timber from twelve to eighteen inches in diameter, standing them inside on end, leaning them on the breastwork close together. This was completed about noon. About two o'clock Mr. Bridger and six men mounted and went to reconnoitre the enemy, but returned soon after with the intelligence that they were encamped about three miles below on the river and that there was a multitude of them on foot.

24th—The night passed without any disturbance and we began to fear we should not have a fight after all our trouble. About sunrise one solitary savage crept up behind the trees and shot about 200 yards at Mr. Bridger's cook as he was gathering wood outside the fort, then scampered off without doing any damage.

A Spaniard was ordered on to the bluff to look out, and found an Indian in the observatory built on the top, who waited until the Spaniard approached. The Indian then raised and the Spaniard wheeled and took to his heels. The Indian shot and the ball struck him in the heel as he made a fifty-foot leap down the bluff and slid down the snow to the bottom. In about half an hour the word was passed that they were coming on the ice, and presently they appeared coming round a bend of the river in close columns within 400 yards. They then turned off to the right into the plain and called a halt.

The chief, who wore a white blanket, came forward a few steps and gave us the signal that he should not fight, but return to his village. They then turned and took a northwest course across the plain toward the three forks of the Missouri. We came to the conclusion after numerous conjectures, that the wonderful appearance of the heavens a few nights previous, connected with our strong fortification, had caused them to abandon the ground without an attack, which is very probable, as all Indians are very superstitious. We supposed, on examining their camp next day, that their numbers must have been about eleven hundred, who had started from their village with the determination of rubbing us from the face of the earth, but that the Great Spirit had shown them that their side of the heavens was bloody, while ours was clear and serene.

February 28th we left our winter quarters on the Yellowstone and started for the Big Horn, the snow being six inches deep on an average. We travelled slowly and reached it in eight days at the mouth of Bovy Fork, about fifteen miles below the lower Big Horn mountain, and then began to slay and eat, but we slayed so much faster than we ate that our meat scaffolds groaned under the weight of fat buffalo meat. We remained here amusing ourselves with playing ball, hopping, wrestling, running foot races, etc., until the 14th of March, when we discovered the Crow village moving down the Big Horn toward us. Immediately all sports were ended. Some mounted horses to meet them, others fortified camp, ready for battle in case there should be a misunderstanding between us. The scouting party soon returned with some of the chiefs, accompanied by an American who was trading with them, in the employ of the American Fur Company.

The chiefs, after smoking and looking about for some time, returned to their village, which had encamped about three miles above on the river. The next morning they came and encamped within 300 yards of us. Their village contained 200 lodges and about 200 warriors. The Crows are a proud, haughty, insolent tribe, whenever their party is the strongest, but if the case is reversed they are equally cowardly and submissive. This village was called "Long Hair's" band, after their chief, whose hair was eleven feet six inches long, done up in an enormous queue about eighteen inches long and six inches thick, hanging down his back. He was about eighty years of age and seemed to be afflicted with the dropsy, the only case of the kind I ever knew among the mountain Indians. The village staid with us until the 25th of March and then moved down the river about six miles.

We left the Big Horn on the 1st of April and started on the spring hunt. On the 3rd up Bovy's Fork twenty miles.

4th—Up the same ten miles. After we had encamped four Delawares who were cruising about in the hills hunting buffalo, fell in with a party of ten or twelve Blackfeet, killed one on the spot and wounded several more. The Blackfeet then took to their heels and left the victorious Delawares without loss except one horse being slightly wounded in the neck.

10th—We arrived at "Howell's Encampment" at the mouth of Rocky Fork. The whole country here was filled with buffaloes, driven this way by the Crow village.

11th—We raised a *cache* of beaver and other articles which had been deposited in the ground in November previous.

14th—A party of twelve trappers and two camp keepers started to trap the "Mussel Shell" River, which heads in the mountain near "Twenty-five Yard" River, and runs into the Missouri on the south side above the mouth of the Yellowstone. Myself and three others started up Rocky Fork about twenty miles, .but found so much snow and ice that we could not set our traps for; beaver. We found a large cave on the southeast side of a perpendicular rock. In this we encamped six days, during which we made great havoc among the buffaloes. On the 23rd the camp moved up to our cave and the next day I went up the stream about twelve miles and set my traps and saw signs of several war parties of Blackfeet who were scouting about the country.

26th—I was cruising with another trapper through the timber and brush above where we had set our traps, when on a sudden we came within ten steps of two Blackfoot forts and saw the smoke ascending from the tops. As we saw no individuals we entered and found the Indians had been gone about half an hour.

28th—The party arrived from the Mussel Shell, having been defeated and lost one trapper and nearly all their horses and traps by the Blackfeet.

May 1st—All being collected, we left Rocky Fork close to the mountain and took around the foot in an easterly direction and encamped at a spring, where we staid the next day. The Blackfeet still continued dogging at our heels and to steal now and then a horse which might get loose in the night. There is a proverb among the mountaineers that "*it is better to count ribs than tracks.*" That is to say, it is better to fasten a horse at night until you can count his ribs from poverty than turn him loose to fatten and count his tracks after an Indian has stolen him.

3rd—Travelled on to Clark's Fork twelve miles southeast, and the. next day up the same fifteen miles south.

5th—Travelled to a small branch running into Stinking River, southerly direction fifteen miles.

6th—We encamped on Stinking River about fifteen miles below the forks, distance twelve miles, course southeast.

7th—We travelled from the river about twenty miles in a southerly direction and encamped at a spring.

8th— To the "Gray Bull" Fork of the Big Horn.

9th— To the Medicine Lodge Fork, twelve miles south.

10th—To the middle Fork of the Medicine Lodge, eight miles.

11th—To the South Fork of the Medicine Lodge, eight miles south. Here we staid two days.

14th—Travelled southeast to a small spring at the foot of the upper Big Horn mountain, distance twelve miles. The 15th travelled to the top of the Big Horn mountain and encamped on the divide. The country over which we had travelled since we left the "Stinking" was much broken by spurs of mountains and deep gullies, entirely destitute of timber except along the banks of the streams.

16th—Travelled down the mountain on the south side and encamped on a small branch of Wind River. This river loses its name whilst passing through the upper Big Horn mountains. From thence it takes the name of the Big Horn, derived from the vast numbers of mountain sheep or big horn inhabiting the mountains through which it passes.

17th—Over broken country south about fifteen miles.

18th—Encamped on the river after a march of ten miles south.

19th—The camp intending to stop here several days, I started with a raw son of Erin to hunt beaver on the headwaters of the river. We travelled up west about twenty-five miles to what was called the "Red Rock." Killed a sheep and encamped for the night where several branches of the river united.

20th—We took up a large branch about fifteen miles northwest, and found the water overflowing the banks of all the branches so much that it was impossible to catch beaver. We then altered our course northeast across the country in order to examine the small branches on our right, but finding all our efforts to trap useless and discovering that a war party consisting of eighty Blackfeet were in pursuit of us, we returned to the camp by a different route on the 23rd.

24th—Travelled with the camp to the North Fork of "Popo-azia" or Pope River, one of the principal branches of Wind River, distance twelve miles, course south.

25th—To the middle fork of the same stream, eight miles distance.

26th—To the oil spring on the South Fork of Popo-azia. This spring produced about one gallon per hour of pure oil or coal or rather coal tar, the scent of which is often carried on the wind five or six miles. The oil issues from the ground within thirty feet of the stream and runs off slowly into the water. Camp stopped here eight days. We set fire to the spring when there was two or three barrels of oil on the ground about it. It burned very quick and clear, but produced a dense column of thick, black smoke. The oil above ground being consumed, the fire soon went out. This was a beautiful country, thickly clothed with grass, intermingled with flowers of every hue. On the west rose the Wind River range of mountains abruptly from the smooth, rolling hills, until crowned with snow above the clouds. On the east stretched away the great Wind River plain and terminated at a low range of mountains rising between Wind and Powder Rivers. Buffalo, elk and sheep were abundant. Beds of iron and coal were frequently found in this part of the country.

June 5th we left the oil spring and took over a point of mountain about fifteen miles southwest and encamped on a small spring branch.

6th—Crossed the spurs of mountains due west twelve miles and encamped on a branch of Sweetwater.

7th—Travelled west about fifteen miles and encamped on "Little Sandy," a branch of Green River.

8th—Travelled north up the valley about eighteen miles and encamped on a stream called the New Fork of Green River where we staid the next day.

10th—Travelled west to the main river about twenty-five miles, and struck the river about twelve miles below the mouth of Horse Creek.

CHAPTER 14

The Arrival of Wagon Train and Supplies

Here we found the hunting parties all assembled waiting for the arrival of supplies from the States. Here presented what might be termed a mixed multitude. The whites were chiefly Americans and Canadian French, with some Dutch, Scotch, Irish, English, half-breed and full-blood Indians of nearly every tribe in the Rocky Mountains. Some were gambling at cards, some playing the Indian game of "hand" and others horse racing, while here and there could be seen small groups collected under shady trees relating the events of the past year, all in good spirits and health, for sickness is a stranger seldom met with in these regions. Sheep, elk, deer, buffalo and bear skins mostly supply the mountaineers with clothing, lodges and bedding, while the meat of the same animals supply them with food. They have not the misfortune to get any of the luxuries from the civilized world but once a year, and then in such small quantities that they last but a few days.

We had not remained in this quiet manner long before something new arose for our amusement. The Bannock Indians had for several years lived with the whites on terms partly hostile, frequently stealing horses and traps, and in one instance killed two white trappers. They had taken some horses and traps from a party of French trappers who were hunting Bear River in April previous, and they were now impudent enough to come with the village of sixty lodges and encamp within three miles of us in order to trade with the whites as usual, still having the stolen property in their possession and refusing to give it up. On the 15th of June four or five whites and two Nez Perce Indians went to their village and took the stolen horses (whilst the men were out hunting buffalo) and returned with them to our camp. About three o'clock p. m. of the same day thirty Bannocks came riding at full gallop up to the camp, armed with their war weapons.

They rode into the midst and demanded the horses which the Nez Perces had taken saying they did not wish to fight with the whites. But the Nez Perces, who were only six in number, gave the horses to the whites for protection, which we were bound to give, as they were numbered among our trappers and far from their own tribe. Some of the Bannocks, on seeing this, started to leave the camp. One of them as he passed me observed that he did not come to fight the whites; but another, a fierce looking savage, who still stopped behind, called out to the others, saying, "We came to get our horses or blood and let us do it."

I was standing near the speaker and understood what he said. I immediately gave the whites warning to be in readiness for an attack. Nearly all the men in camp were under arms. Mr. Bridger was holding one of the stolen horses by the bridle when one of the Bannocks rushed through the crowd, seized the bridle and attempted to drag it from Mr. Bridger by force, without heeding the cocked rifles that surrounded him any more than if they had been so many reeds in the hands of children. He was a brave Indian, but his bravery proved fatal to himself, for the moment he seized the bridle two rifle balls whistled through his body.

The others wheeled to run, but twelve of them were shot from their horses before they were ' out of reach of rifle. We then mounted horses and pursued them, destroyed and plundered their village, and followed and fought them three days, when they begged us to let them go and promised to be good Indians in future. We granted their request and returned to our camp, satisfied that the best way to negotiate and settle disputes with hostile Indians is with the rifle, for that is the only pen that can write a treaty which they will not forget. Two days after we left them three white trappers, ignorant of what had taken place, went into their village and were treated in the most friendly manner. The Indians said, however, they had been fighting with the Blackfeet.

July 5th a party arrived from the States with supplies. The cavalcade consisted of forty-five men and twenty carts drawn by mules, under the direction of Mr. Thomas Fitzpatrick, accompanied by Capt. William Stewart on another tour of the Rocky Mountains.

Joy now beamed In every countenance. Some received letters from their friends and relations; some received the public papers and news of the day; others consoled themselves with the idea of getting a blanket, a cotton shirt or a few pints of coffee and sugar to sweeten it just by way of a treat, gratis, that is to say, by paying 2,000 *per cent* on the first cost by way of accommodation. For instance, sugar $2 per pint, coffee the same, blankets $20 each, tobacco $2 per pound, alcohol $4 per pint, and common cotton shirts $5 each, etc. And in return paid $4 or $5 per pound for beaver. In a few days the bustle began to subside. The furs were done up in packs ready for transportation to the States and parties were formed for the hunting the ensuing year. One party, consisting of 110 men, was destined for the Blackfoot country, under the direction of L. B. Fontanelle as commander and James Bridger as pilot. I started, with five others to hunt the headwaters of the Yellowstone, Missouri and Big Horn Rivers, a portion of the country I was particularly fond of hunting.

CHAPTER 15

Back Again to the Hunting Grounds

On the 20th of July we left the rendezvous and travelled up Green River about ten miles.

21st—We travelled up Green River until noon, when we discovered a trail of eight or ten Blackfeet and a buffalo fresh killed and butchered, with the meat tied up in small bundles on the ground, which they had left on seeing us approach, and ran into the bushes. We, supposing them to be a small scouting party, tied their bundles of meat on to our saddles and still kept on our route but had not gone far before we discovered them secreted among some willows growing along a branch which crossed our trail. I was ahead leading the party when I discovered them. We stopped and one of my comrades, whose name was Allen, began to arrange the load on his pack mule. In the meantime I reined my horse to the left and rode onto a small hillock nearby and casting a glance towards the bushes, which were about 150 yards distant, I saw two guns pointed at me. I instantly wheeled my horse, but to no purpose. The two balls struck him, one in the loins and the other in the shoulder, which dropped him under me. The Indians at the same time jumped out of the bushes, sixty or seventy in number, and ran toward us, shooting and yelling. I jumped on a horse behind one of my comrades and we scampered away toward the rendezvous, where we arrived at dark.

25th—The parties started and all travelled with Mr. Fontanelle's party up Green River ten miles, intending to keep in their company five or six days and then branch off to our first intended route.

26th—We travelled twenty miles northwest across a low range of hills and encamped in a valley lying on a branch of Lewis Fork called "Jackson's Little Hole."

27th—We travelled down this stream 18 miles northwest. This stream ran through a tremendous mountain in a deep, narrow canyon of rocks. The trail ran along the cliffs from 50 to 200 feet above its bed and was so narrow in many places that only one horse could pass at a time for several hundred yards, and one false step would precipitate one into the chasm below. After leaving the canyon we encamped at a small spring in "Jackson's Big Hole," near the southern extremity.

28th—Travelled up the valley north fifteen miles and encamped. Killed some buffalo and staid next day.

30th—Left the camp in company with two trappers and one camp keeper. We received instructions from Mr. Fontanelle to meet the camp at the mouth of Clark's Fork of the Yellowstone on the 15th of the ensuing October, where they expected to pass the winter, but he said if he should conclude to change his winter quarters he would cause a tree to be marked at Howell's grave and bury a letter in the ground at the foot of it containing directions for finding the camp.

We travelled north till near sunset and encamped about forty miles from the main party.

31st—We travelled to the fork five miles below Jackson's Lake and ascended it in the same direction I had done the season before and encamped about fifteen miles from the valley.

August 1st—We reached the dividing spring about four o'clock p.m. and stopped for the night.

2nd—We encamped at the inlet of the Yellowstone Lake.

3rd—Travelled down the east shore of the lake and stopped for the night near the outlet at the steam springs.

4th—We took our course east northeast and after travelling all day over rugged mountains, thickly covered with pines and underbrush, we encamped at night about ten miles north of the secluded valley, on the stream which runs through it. After we had encamped we killed a deer, which came in good time, as we had eaten the last of our provisions the night previous at the Yellowstone Lake and the flies and mosquitoes were so bad and the underbrush so thick that we had not killed anything during the day.

5th—We travelled up a left hand branch of this stream northeast fifteen miles through the thick pines and brush until near the head, where we encamped in a beautiful valley about two miles in circumference, almost encircled with huge mountains whose tops were covered with snow, from which small rivulets were issuing clear as crystal, and, uniting in the smooth, grassy vale, formed the stream which we had ascended. We concluded to spend the next day at this place, as there were no flies or mosquitoes, for though warm and pleasant in the day, the nights were too cold for them to survive. The next day, after eating a light breakfast of roasted venison. I shouldered my rifle and ascended the highest mountain on foot.

I reached the snow in about an hour, when, seating myself upon a huge fragment of granite and having full view of the country around me in a few moments was almost lost in contemplation. This, said I, is not a place where heroes' deeds of chivalry have been achieved in days of yore, neither is it a place of which bards have sung until the world knows the precise posture of every rock and tree or the winding turn of every streamlet. But on the contrary those stupendous rocks whose surface is formed into irregular benches rising one above another from the vale to the snow, dotted here and there with low pines and covered with green herbage intermingled with flowers, with the scattered flocks of sheep and elk carelessly feeding or thoughtlessly reposing beneath the shade, having Providence for their founder and; Nature for shepherd, gardener and historian.

In viewing scenes like this the imagination of one unskilled in science wanders to the days of the Patriarchs and after numerous conjecturing returns without any fixed decision. Wonder is put to the test, but having no proof for its argument, a doubt still remains, but supposition steps forward and taking the place of knowledge, in a few words solves the mysteries of ages, centuries and eras. After indulging in such a train of reflections for about two hours, I descended to the camp, where I found my companions had killed a fat buck elk during my absence and some of the choicest parts of it were supported on sticks around the fire. My ramble had sharpened my appetite and the delicious flavour of roasted meat soon rid my brain of romantic ideas. My companions were men who never troubled themselves about vain and frivolous notions, as they called them. With them every country was pretty when there was weather, and as to beauty of nature or arts it was all a "humbug," as one of them, an Englishman, often expressed it. "Talk of a fine country," said he, "and beautiful places in these mountains. If you want to see a beautiful place, go to Highland and see the Duke of Rutland's place."

"Aye" says a son of Erin, who sat opposite with an elk rib in one hand and a butcher knife in the other, while the sweat rolling from his face mingled in the channels of grease which ran from the corners of his mouth, "Aye, an' ye would see a pretty place, go to old Ireland and: take a walk in Lord Farnham's domain. That is the place where ye can see plisure. Arrah, an' if I were upon that same ground this day I'd fill my body with good ould whisky."

"Yes," says the backwoods hunter on my left, as he cast away his bone and smoothed down his long auburn hair with his greasy hand, "Yes, you English and Irish are always talking about your fine countries, but if they are so mighty fine," said he with an oath, "why do so many of you run off and leave them and come to America to get a living?"

From this the conversation turned into an argument in which the hunter came off victorious, driving his opponents from the field.

Chapter 16

Thieving Indians Steal Most of the Horses

Aug. 7th—We travelled up the mountain in a southerly direction and fell into a smooth, grassy defile about 200 paces wide, which led through between two high peaks of rock. In this place we fell in with a large band of sheep, killed two ewes, packed the best meat on our horses and proceeded down the defile, which led us on to the head waters of "Stinking" River, about fifty miles from where it enters the plain. We travelled down the stream about ten miles south and encamped where we saw some signs of Snake Indians who inhabited these wilds. The next morning I arose about daybreak and went in search of our horses, which had been turned loose to feed during the night. I soon found all but three, and after hunting some time I discovered a trail made in the dew on the grass where an Indian had been crawling on his belly, and soon found where he had caught the horses. Two of us then mounted mules and followed the trail in a westerly direction up a steep, piney mountain until about ten o'clock, when we lost the trail among the rocks and were obliged to give up the pursuit. We then returned to camp and packed our remaining animals and travelled down the stream about ten miles.

9th—We left the main stream and ascended a small branch in a south southwest direction about eight miles, up a steep ascent, and encamped in a smooth, grassy spot near the head, where we concluded to stop the next day and hunt beaver. Early the next morning a few of the "Mountain Snakes" came to our camp, consisting of three men and five or six women and children. One of them told me he knew the Indians who had stolen our horses; that they lived in the mountains between Stinking River and Clark's Fork, and said that he would try to get them. After trading some beaver and sheep skins from them, talking, smoking, etc., about an hour, I mounted my mule with six traps and my rifle, and one of my comrades did the same, and we started to hunt beaver. We left the camp in a southwest direction and travelled about eight miles over a high, craggy mountain, then descended into a small circular valley about a mile in circumference, which was completely covered with logs, shattered fragments of trees and splinters four or five feet deep. There had been trees two and three feet in diameter broken off within two feet of the ground and shivered into pieces small enough for a kitchen fireplace.

This, in all probability, was the effect of an avalanche about two years previous, as the tall pines had been completely cleared for the space of 400 yards wide and more than two miles up the side of the mountain. Finding no beaver on the branches of this stream, we returned to camp at sunset. Our camp keeper had prepared an excellent supper of grizzly bear meat and mutton, nicely stewed and seasoned with salt and pepper, which, as the mountain saying goes, is not bad to take upon an empty stomach after a hard day's riding and climbing over the mountains and rocks.

Aug. 11th—We returned to the river and travelled up about four miles, then left it and travelled up a branch in a due east direction about six miles, killed a couple of fat doe elk and encamped.

12th—Myself and Allen (which was the name of the backwoodsman) started to hunt the small streams in the mountains to the west of us, leaving the Englishman, who was the other trapper, to set traps about the camp. We hunted the branches of this stream, then crossed the divide to the waters of the Yellowstone Lake, where we found the whole country swarming with elk. We killed a fat buck for supper and encamped for the night. The next day Allen shot a grizzly bear and bursted the percussion tube of his rifle, which obliged us to return to our comrades on the 13th and make another tube. The next day we returned to Stinking River and travelled up about ten miles above where we first struck it.

15th—It rained and snowed all day and we stopped in camp.

16th—Took a northeast course up the mountain and reached the divide about noon, then descended in a direction nearly east and encamped in a valley on the head of Clark's Fork. This valley is a prairie about thirty miles in circumference, completely surrounded by high mountains. The stream, after passing southeast, falls into a tremendous canyon just wide enough to admit its waters between rocks from 300 to 500 feet perpendicular height, extending about twelve miles to the great plain.

18th—We moved up the stream to the head of the valley and encamped. Here the stream is formed of two forks nearly equal in size. The right hand fork falls into the left from off a bench upwards of 700 feet high, nearly perpendicular. The view of it at a distance of eight or ten miles resembles a bank of snow.

19th—Travelled up the west branch about ten miles northwest through thick pines and fallen timber, then leaving the stream to our right turned into a defile which led us on to the waters of the Yellowstone in about eight miles, where we stopped, set traps for beaver and staid next day.

21st—We travelled down this stream, which runs west through a high range of mountains about twenty-five miles.

22nd—Travelled down the stream about fifteen miles west and encamped in the secluded valley, where we staid two days.

25th—Travelled down the valley to the north and crossed a low space about four miles north and fell on to a stream running into the one we had left. Here we set traps and staid until the 2nd of September.

3rd—Travelled over a high, rugged mountain about twenty miles northwest and camped in a beautiful valley on a small stream running into the one we had left in the morning.

4th—Travelled fifteen miles northwest over a high, piney mountain and encamped on a stream running south into the Yellowstone, where we staid and trapped until the 13th. We then travelled up the stream northeast about eight miles.

14th—Travelled up the stream twelve miles in the same direction.

15th—We crossed the divide of the main range north towards the Big Plains. We found the snow belly deep to our horses. After leaving the snow we travelled about eight miles north and encamped on the head branch of the cross creek running north into the Yellowstone about twelve miles below the mouth of "Twenty-five Yard" River.

Here a circumstance occurred which furnished the subject for a good joke upon our green Irish camp keeper. The Englishman had stopped on the mountain to hunt sheep, while we descended to the stream and encamped on a prairie about two miles in circumference. It was the commencement of the rutting season with the elk, when the bucks frequently utter a loud cry resembling a shrill whistle, especially when they see anything of a strange appearance. We had made our beds at night on a little bench between two small, dry gullies. The weather was clear and the moon shone brightly. About ten o'clock at night, when I supposed my comrades fast asleep, an elk blew his shrill whistle within about 100 yards of us. I took my gun, slipped silently into the gully and crept toward the place where I heard the sound, but I soon found he had been frightened by the horses and ran off up the mountain.

On turning back I met Allen, who, hearing the elk, had started to get a shot at him in the same manner I had done without speaking a word. We went back to camp, but our camp keeper was nowhere to be found. We searched the bushes high and low, ever and *anon* calling for "Conn," but no "Conn" answered. At length Allen, cruising through the brush, tumbled over a pile of rubbish, when lo! Conn was beneath, nearly frightened out of his wits. "Arrah! An' is it' you, Allen?" said he trembling as if an ague fit was shaking him. "But I thought the whole world was full of the spalpeens of savages. And where are they gone?" It was near an hour before we could satisfy him of his mistake, and I dare say his slumbers were by no means soft or smooth during the remainder of the night.

Chapter 17

Stampeded Buffalo

16th—The Englishman arrived and we travelled down this stream about ten miles, where we staid the next day, as it snowed very hard.

18th—Travelled down about twenty miles and on the 19th came to the plains in about ten miles travel, where we encamped. Here we found the country filled with buffalo as usual.

20th—We shaped our course northeast and travelled about twenty-five miles across the spurs of the mountain, fell on to the north fork of the Rosebud, where we staid the next day, as it rained.

22nd—We travelled south along the foot of the mountain for twenty miles, keeping among the low spurs which project into the plain, in order to prevent being discovered by any straggling parties of Blackfeet which might chance to be lurking about the country. The plains below us were crowded with buffalo, which we were careful not to disturb for fear of being discovered. We stopped and set our traps on the small branches of the Rosebud until the 11th of October, then travelled to Rocky Fork and went up it into the mountains and encamped. On the 13th myself and Allen started to hunt Mr. Fontanell's party, leaving our comrades in the mountains to await our return. We travelled down Rocky Fork all day amid crowds of buffalo and encamped after dark near the mouth.

The next morning we went to "Howell's Encampment," but found no tree marked, neither had the earth been disturbed since we had closed it upon the remains of the unfortunate Howell. We now sat down and consulted upon the best course to pursue. As winter was approaching we could not think of stopping in this country, where parties of Blackfeet were ranging at all seasons of the year. After a few moments' deliberation, we came to the conclusion, and I wrote a note, enclosed it in a buffalo horn, buried it at the foot of the tree, and then marked the tree with my hatchet. This being done we mounted our mules and started back to the mountains. We travelled about six miles and then stopped and killed a cow. As we were lying within about sixty paces of the band, which contained about 300 cows, Allen made an observation which I shall never forget. Said he, "I have been watching those cows some time and I can see but one that is poor enough to kill, for," said he, "it is a shame to kill one of those large, fat cows merely for two men's supper." So saying he levelled his rifle on the poorest and brought her down.

She was a heifer about three years old and but an inch of fat on her back. After cooking and eating we proceeded on our journey until some time after dark, when we found ourselves on a sudden in the midst of an immense band of buffaloes, which, getting the scent of us, ran helter-skelter around us in every direction, rushing to and fro like the waves of the ocean, approaching sometimes within ten feet of us. We stood still, for we dared not retreat or advance until this stream of brutes took a general course and rolled away like distant thunder, and then we hurried on through Egyptian darkness a few hundred paces, where we found a bunch of willows and concluded to stop for the night rather than risk our lives any further among such a whirlwind of beef.

15th—We reached the camp about ten o'clock a.m. We staid on Rocky Fork and its branches trapping until the 27th of October, when we concluded to go to a small fork running into Wind River on the east side above the upper Big Horn mountain, and there pass the winter unless we should hear from the main party.

28th—We travelled to Clark's Fork and the next day to Stinking River, east southeast direction.

30th—We crossed Stinking River and travelled in the same direction over a broken, barren tract of country about thirty-five miles, whilst the rain poured all day in torrents. About sun an hour high we stopped and the weather cleared up. We encamped for the night in a small ravine, where some water was standing in a puddle, but there was no wood save a lone green Cottonwood tree which had supported a bald eagle's nest probably more than half a century.

31st—We travelled over ground similar to that of the day before, shaping our course more easterly until night.

Nov. 1st—After travelling about ten miles we reached the Big Horn River and stopped and commenced setting traps. The river at this place was bordered with heavy cottonwood timber with little or no brush beneath.

Chapter 18

Threatened and Robbed by the Crow Indians

Along towards night a party of Crow Indians came to us on foot, armed as if going to war. After smoking and eating they told us they were on their way to the Snakes to steal horses and intended to stay all night with us and leave the next morning. They told us the village to which they belonged was nearly a day's travel below on the river and that Long Hair's village was on Wind River above the mountain, but could give us no information of Mr. Fontanell or his party. They were very insolent and saucy, saying we had no right in their country, and intimated they could take everything from us if they wished. The next morning after eating breakfast they said if we would give them some tobacco and ammunition they would leave us, so we divided our little stock with them. They then persisted in having all, and when we refused them, telling them we could not spare it, one of them seized the sack which contained it, while another grasped the Englishman's rifle. We immediately wrenched them out of their hands and told them if they got more they should fight for it.

During the scuffle they had all presented their arms, but when we gained possession of the rifle and the sack, they put down their arms and told us, with an envious savage laugh, they were only joking, but we were too well acquainted with the Crows to relish such capers as mere jokes and wished to get out of their power the easiest way possible, as their villages were on either side of us. We then packed up our horses and forded the river and travelled up about six miles and encamped. At the same time the Indians were mounted on our pack horses and riding animals trailing us and the remainder on foot, except one who returned towards the village crying.

After we had stopped they made a sort of shelter, as it looked likely for rain, and at night ordered us to go into it and sleep, but we bluntly refused and removed our baggage about thirty paces from them. Sitting down reclining against it, one of them had taken the only blanket I possessed off my riding saddle and put an old worn out coat in its place, with a hint that exchanging was not robbing. They laid down in their shelter and continued to sing their noisy and uncouth war songs until near midnight, when they ceased and all became silent.

The night was dark with a sprinkling of rain. We lay without hearing any disturbance until daybreak, when we began to look around, but could find neither Indians nor horses, though we soon found their trail going down the river. We then set about burning our saddles, robes, etc., and *caching* our beaver in the ground, intending after making a few deposits and bonfires to shoulder our rifles and travel to Fort William at the mouth of Savorney's Fork of the Platte.

Our saddles, *epishemores*, ropes, etc., were scarcely consumed when we saw five or six Indians on horseback coming toward us at full gallop and presently fifteen or twenty more appeared following them. They rode up, alighted from their horses and asked for tobacco to smoke. We gave them some. They formed a circle and sat down. I was not acquainted with any of them except the chief, who was called the "Little Soldier." He spoke to me in the Snake language and said he wished me to smoke with them, but the manner in which they had formed the ring and placed their war weapons excited suspicion, and Allen immediately declined, as he had lived with the Crows two winters and said he knew that thieving and treachery were two of the greatest virtues the nation could boast of, and we quickly resolved to leave them at all hazards. So we shouldered our rifles and those who had blankets took them and began to travel.

The Indians looked at us with pretended astonishment and asked what was the matter. Allen told them that he was aware that they wanted to rob us and were laying plans to do it without danger to themselves, but, said he, "if you follow us or molest us we will besmear the ground with blood and guts of Crow Indians, and do not speak to me more," said he, "for I despise the odious jargon of your nation." So saying he wheeled around and we marched away in a southerly direction toward the mountain. We had not gone far before two of them came after us. We stopped and turned round, when one of them stopped within 300 paces of us, while the other, who was the chief, advanced slowly unarmed.

When he came up he addressed me in the Snake language, for knowing the disposition of Allen, he did not wish to trifle with his own life so much as to begin a conversation with him in his own language. Taking me by the hand as he spoke, he said, "My friends, you are very foolish. You do not know how bad my heart feels to think that you have been robbed by men belonging to my village; but they are not men, they are dogs who took your animals. The first I knew of your being in this country, about midnight a young man came to the village crying and told me of their intention. I immediately mounted my horse and hastened to your assistance, but arrived too late, but if you will go with me I will get your animals and give you some saddles and robes and fit you out as well as I can. You can then stay with me until the blanket chief comes" (the name they gave Mr. Bridger).

I interpreted what he had said to my comrades, but they said tell him we will not go to the Crow village; we will not trust our lives among them. When I told him this, he replied, "I am very sorry. What shall I say to the blanket chief? How can I hold up my head when I shall meet him, and what shall I do with the things you have left behind?" I told him to give them to the blanket chief. He then turned and left us, slowly and sadly, but I am well aware that a Crow Indian can express great sorrow for me and at the same time be laying a plan to rob me or secretly take my life. After he had left us we travelled on towards the mountains about ten miles, stopped, killed a cow and ate supper, and then travelled until about midnight, when, it being dark and cloudy, we stopped and kindled a fire with sage and weeds which we gathered about us, and sat down to wait for daylight.

Sleep was far from us. Our minds were so absorbed in the reflections on the past that few were the words that passed among us during the night. A short time after we stopped it commenced snowing very fast and we were obliged to hover over our little fire to keep it from being extinguished. The day at length appeared and we proceeded on our journey toward the mountains, while it still continued to snow. As we began to ascend the mountain the snow grew deeper, and about noon was up to our knees. We travelled on until sun about an hour high, and stopped at some scrubby cedars and willows which grew around a spring. After scraping away the snow we built a fire, broke some cedar boughs, spread them on the ground and laid down, weary and hungry, but we had meat enough with us for supper. Three of us, myself, Allen and Greenberry, had been more or less inured to the hardships of a hunter's life, but our camp keeper, John Conn, could not relish the manner in which he was treated in a country that boasted so much of its freedom and independence, and often wished himself back on the shamrock shore.

Myself and Allen had one blanket between us, the others had a blanket each. The wind blew cold and the snow drifted along the brow of the mountains around us. When we arose in the morning our fire had gone out, the snow was three inches deep oh our covering, and it still kept snowing. Allen killed a black-tailed deer close by and we concluded to stop all day at this place.

Nov. 6th—The sun rose clear and we started up the mountain, keeping on the ridges where the wind had driven off the snow, and arrived at the top about ten o'clock a.m. From this elevation we could see the Wind River plains, which were dry and dusty, whilst we were in snow up to the middle. We killed some sheep which were in large numbers about us, cooked some of the best meat over a slow fire, packed it on our backs and proceeded down the mountain south and slept on bare ground that night.

Nov. 7th—We arose and found ourselves much refreshed by our night's rest. We travelled nearly east all day, ascending a gradual smooth slope of country which lies between Wind and Powder Rivers, and stopped at night on the divide, where we found the snow hard and about two inches deep and the weather cold and windy, whilst not a stick of wood or a drop of water were to be found within ten miles of us. We found a place washed out by the water in the spring of the year. It was the only shelter to be had, and digging down to the dry earth, scattered some branches of sage upon it to lie upon. I then went in search of a rock in order to heat it and melt snow in my hat, but I could not find so much as a pebble, so we kindled a little fire of sage and sat down with a piece of mutton in one hand and a piece of snow in the other.

Eating meat and snow in this manner we made out our supper and laid down to shake, tremble and suffer with the cold till daylight, when we started and travelled as fast as our wearied limbs would permit in the same direction we had travelled the day before, descending a gradual slope toward the head of Powder River, until near night, when finding some water standing in a puddle, with large quantities of sage about it, we killed a bull near by, and taking his skin for a bed and some of the best meat for supper, we passed the night very comfortably. We were now in sight of the red buttes on the River Platte, which appeared about forty miles distant southeast.

The next morning we found the weather foggy, with sleet and snow falling. I tried to persuade my comrades to stop until it should clear away, urging the probability of our steering a wrong course, as we could not see more than 200 paces, but they concluded we could travel by the wind, and after making several objections to travelling by such an uncertain guide to no purpose, I gave up the argument and we started and travelled about east southeast for three hours as we supposed, then stopped a short time and built a fire of sage, while it continued to rain and snow alternately, and seeing no signs of the weather clearing, we started again and went on until near night, when, the sun coming out, we found that instead of travelling south southeast our course had been north northeast and we were as far from the Platte as we were in the morning, with the country around us very broken and intersected with deep ravines and gullies. We saw some bulls three or four miles ahead and we started for them.

After the sun had set it clouded up and began to rain. We reached the bulls about an hour after dark. Allen crawled close to them, shot and killed one, took off the skin and some of the meat, whilst myself and the others were groping about in the dark hunting a few bits of sage and weeds to make a fire, and after repeated unsuccessful exertions we at last kindled a blaze. We had plenty of water under, over and all around us, but could not find a stick for fuel bigger than a man's thumb. We sat down around the fire with each holding a piece of beef over it on a stick with one hand while the other was employed in keeping up the blaze by feeding it with sage and weeds until the meat was warmed through, when it was devoured, with an observation that "bull meat was dry eating when cooked too much."

After supper (if I may be allowed to disgrace the term by applying it to such a wolfish feast) we spread the bull skin down in the mud in the driest place we could find, and laid down upon it. Our fire was immediately put out by the rain and all was Egyptian darkness. We lay tolerably comfortable while the skin retained its animal warmth and remained above the surface, but the mud being soft, the weight of our bodies sunk it by degrees below the water level, which ran under us on the skin. We concluded it was best to lie still and keep the water that was about us warm, for if we stirred we let in the cold water and if we moved our bed we were more likely to find a worse, instead of a better, place, as it rained hard all night.

At daylight we arose, bid *adieu* to our uncomfortable lodgings, and left as fast as our legs would carry us through the mud and water, and after travelling about twelve miles south course, we stopped, killed a bull, and took breakfast. After eating, we travelled south until sunset. The weather was clear and cold, but we found plenty of dry sage to make a fire and dry weeds for a bed.

11th—The ground was frozen hard in the morning and the wind blew cold from the north.

We travelled until about noon, when we fell in with large bands of buffalo, and seeing the red buttes about five or six miles ahead we killed two fat cows and took as much of the meat as we could conveniently carry and travelled to the Platte, where we arrived about the middle of the afternoon, weary and fatigued. Here we had plenty of wood, water, meat and dry grass to sleep on, and taking everything into consideration, we thought ourselves comfortably situated—comfortably, I say, for mountaineers, not for those who never repose on anything but a bed of down or sit or recline on anything harder than silken cushions, for such would spurn the idea of a hunter talking about comfort and happiness.

But experience is the best teacher, hunger good sauce, and I really think to be acquainted with misery contributes to the enjoyment of happiness, and to know one's self; greatly facilitates the knowledge of mankind. One thing I often console myself with, and that is, the earth will lie as hard upon the monarch as it will upon the hunter, and I have no assurance that it; will lie upon me at all. My bones may, in a few years, or perhaps I days, be bleaching upon the plains in these regions, like many of my I occupation, without a friend to turn even a turf upon them after a hungry wolf has finished his feast.

Chapter 19

Fort William

12th—The sun rose clear and warm and we found ourselves much refreshed by our night's rest. We travelled down the river about five miles, waded across it and stopped the remainder of the day. I had a severe attack of rheumatism in my knees and ankles, but this was no place to be sick, so we jogged along over the Black Hills, having plenty of wood, water and fresh buffalo meat every night, until the 18th, when we reached Fort William. When I entered this fort I was met by two of my old messmates, who invited me to their apartments. I now felt myself at home, as Mr. Fontanell was one of the chief proprietors of the establishment, and who had been partly, and I may say wholly, the cause of our misfortunes. At night I lay down, but the pains in my legs and feet drove sleep from me.

The next day I walked around the fort as well as I could in order to get my joints limber, and on the third day after our arrival I felt quite recovered and at breakfast I asked my messmates where the man was who had charge of the fort. They replied he was in his house, pointing across the square. I inquired if he was sick, for I had not seen him. They said he was unwell, but not so as to confine him to his room. I observed I must go and see him, as I discovered he was not coming to see me, so saying, Allen and myself started across the square and met him on the way from the storehouse to his dwelling room. We bid him "good morning," which he coldly returned and was on the point of turning carelessly away, when we told him we would like to get some robes for bedding, likewise a shirt or two and some other necessary articles.

"Well," said he, "as for blankets, shirts or coats, I have none, and Mr. Fontanell has left no word when there will be any come up."

"If that is the case," I replied, "you can let us have some buffalo robes and *epishemores*."

"Yes," said he, "I believe I can let you have an *epishemore* or two. Here, John, go up into yonder bastion and show these men those *epishemores* that were put up there some time ago."

"I don't think there are any there," replied John, "but some old ones, and them the rats have cut all to pieces."

"Oh, I guess you can find some there that will do," he replied, turning around and swinging a key on his thumb as the insignia of his dignified position and with a stiff stride walked to his apartments, while we followed the *major domo* of this elevated quadruped to the bastion, where I took the best *epishemore* I could find, which was composed of nine pieces of buffalo skin sewed together. But necessity compelled me to take it, knowing at the same time there were more than 500 new robes in the warehouse which did not cost a pint of whisky each. But they were for the people in the U. S. and not for trappers.

This was the 21st day of November, 1837. I never shall forget the time, place nor circumstance, but shall always pity the being who held imperial sway over a few sticks of wood, with five or six men to guard them. It was not his fault, for how should he depart from the way in which he had been brought up? And what is more, trappers have no right to meet with bad luck, for it is nothing more nor less than the result of bad management. This is the literal reasoning of bandbox and counter-hopping philosophers, consoling the unfortunate by enumerating and multiplying their faults, which are always the occasion of their misfortune and so clearly to be seen after the event has occurred. I would rather at any time take an emetic than to be compelled to listen to the advice of such predicting and freakish counsellors. If I must be told of something I already know, let it be that I have learned another lesson by experience and then give me advice for the future. I have often derived a good deal of information from a person who kept silent in the crowd, and it is well known that a certain class of individuals display the most wisdom when they say the least.

On the fourth day after our arrival a large Sioux Indian, arrayed in the costume of the whites, with a sword suspended by his side, entered the lodging where I staid and looked round on the whites for some time without speaking a word. At length he gave me a signal to follow him, and conducted me to his lodge, which I found had been prepared for the reception of a stranger. The *epishemores* and robes had been arranged in the back part of the lodge. I was invited to sit by my mute conductor, who, being the proprietor, seated himself on my right. The big pipe went round with the usual ceremonies and the necessary forms of Indian etiquette being complied with, mine host commenced asking questions by signs without moving his lips, and having acquired the knowledge of conversation by signs without uttering a word. It is impossible for a person not acquainted with the customs of Indians to form a correct idea in what way a continuous conversation is held for hours between two individuals who cannot understand each other's language, but frequent practice renders it faultless and I have often seen two Americans conversing by signs by way of practice.

But to return to my story. My inquisitive host gathered in the course of an hour the minute details of my defeat by the Crows, with my tedious journey to the fort, and in return gave me a brief history of his life and intercourse with the whites since he had first seen them, minutely describing the battles he had been in with the Crows, the places where they were fought and their results, particularly the rank of the killed and wounded on both sides. After an hour's dumb conversation a dish of roasted buffalo tongues was set before me, accompanied by a large cake made of dried meat and fruit pounded together, mixed with buffalo marrow. It is considered an insult by an Indian for a stranger, whether white man or Indian, to return any part of the food which is set before him to eat. If there is more than he wishes to eat at one time he must, to avoid giving offense, take the remainder with him when he leaves the lodge. It is their general custom to set the best victuals their lodge affords before a stranger to eat.

On the 22nd of November a small trapping party arrived, under the direction of Mr. Thomas Biggs, who intended to remain in the vicinity of the fort until he received further orders from Mr. Fontanell. On alighting from his horse, he directed his course to our lodgings. "Well, boys," said he on entering the door, "the Crows found you, did they, and could not let you go without bestowing some of their national favours upon you?"

"Yes," I observed, "and we have not mended matters much by coming to this place," and related what had passed between me and the fort superintendent.

"Well," said he, after I had done, "that is too ridiculous. I thought before that Mr. —— had a soul. But I am glad I have found you here. I will see that you get such articles as you want if they can be had at this place, and you must go with me. I shall go up about fifteen miles on the Platte and encamp. I have 200 pounds of lead and powder to shoot it, and about thirty of the company's horses, which you well know were left after more than 200 were chosen out of the band to go into the Blackfoot country, and I have not one which has not from one to three of his legs standing awry, but such as they are, you are welcome to them or anything there is in the camp, even to the half of tobacco. Nearly all of my men are French and but little company for me, and I want to see you slay the fat cows and eat." So saying, he turned and walked to the apartments of his wisdom, the overseer.

Presently one of the interpreters came and told us that Mr. —— wished us to come and get our things. "Oh," said Allen, "he has got 'things,' has he, and has found out the company is owing us money? He is afraid of getting turned out of his employment by his superior. Well, let us go and get some of his things and yet inform Mr. Fontanell of his conduct."

After getting our things we went to Mr. Biggs' camp as soon as possible. Then I felt a little more independent. The rheumatism had left me and I felt as though I had rather walk than ride a poor horse. This section of country, which was called the "Black Hills," was always celebrated for the game with which it abounded. I passed most of my time hunting black tailed deer among the hills on foot, which has always been my favourite sport. One day as myself and one of my fellow hunters were travelling through the hills, coming toward us at full speed, was an immense herd of these animals. We stopped and they passed within eighty yards of us without making a halt. We shot the charges that were in our rifles, loaded and shot two more each before they had all passed by. As the hindmost were passing I could see the foremost passing over a ridge covered with snow more than three miles distant, apparently at the same rate they had passed us. They made a trail about thirty paces wide and went in as compact a body as they consistently could. They consisted mostly of females.

CHAPTER 20

Leave for Powder River with Supplies

On the 20th day of December, 1837, Mr. Fontanell arrived at the camp with fifteen men, bringing the furs he had collected during the hunt, for the purpose of depositing them at the fort. He informed us he had left the main party on Powder River and expressed his sorrow that he had been the cause of our misfortune. He had mistaken the day agreed upon to meet at Clark's Fork, and sent two men to the place on the 18th of November, who found the note I had left. "But," said he, "I have met with that village of Crows and recovered all your property that could be identified. I told them, when I heard the circumstances, that if they did not produce your property forthwith, their heads would pay for it within twenty-four hours."

On hearing this they immediately gave up, as they repeatedly affirmed, all except the beaver skins, which they had traded to a Portuguese by the name of Antonio Montaro, who had built some log cabins on Powder River for the purpose of trading with the Crows." He immediately continued: "We went to the cabins and asked Mr. Montaro what right he had to trade beaver skins from Indians with white men's names marked upon them, knowing them to be stolen or taken by force from the whites, and asked him to deliver them to me, which he refused to do. I then ordered him to give me the key to his warehouse, which he reluctantly did. I then ordered my clerk to go in and take all the beaver skins he could find with your names marked upon them, and have them carried to my camp, which was done without further ceremony."

Here, then, was the sum and substance of the sorrows expressed by the Crow chief, whose feelings were so much hurt to think that we were robbed by men, or dogs, belonging to his village, yet I have no doubt if we had gone with him we would have received our things and fared better than we did by the course we pursued. However, we were like all mortals of the present day—destitute of foreknowledge.

On the 28th of January the party started for Powder River with supplies for the main camp, leaving Mr. Fontanell at the fort. The weather being cold, we were compelled to travel on foot most of the time to keep ourselves from freezing. The snow was about ten inches deep generally, but drifted very much in many places. On the 7th of February we reached the encampment, all in good health, fine spirits, and with full stomachs. Here we found the camp living on the fat of the land. The bottoms along Powder River were crowded with buffaloes, so much so that it was difficult keeping them from among the horses, which were fed upon sweet cottonwood bark, as the buffaloes had consumed everything in the shape of grass along the river.

We passed the remainder of the winter very agreeably until the 15th of March, when the winter began to break, the buffaloes to leave the stream and scatter among the hills and the trappers to prepare for the spring hunt.

CHAPTER 21

Spring Hunt

After making the usual arrangements we started on the 29th down Powder River, making short marches, as our animals were very poor. On the 3rd of April we left the river and travelled across the country, which was generally comprised of rolling hills, in a northerly direction until the 18th, when we reached the Little Horn River and travelled down it to the forks. This river empties into the Big Horn about forty miles below the lower mountain. April 21st we left the forks and travelled nearly west over a broken and uneven country, about eighteen miles, and encamped on a small spring branch.

After we had encamped the trappers made preparations for starting the next day to hunt beaver, as we had set but few traps since we left winter quarters, for the Crows had destroyed nearly all the beaver in the part of the country through which we had been travelling. Early next morning about thirty of us were armed, equipped and mounted, as circumstances required. A trapper's equipment in such cases is generally one animal upon which is placed one or two *epishemores*, a riding saddle and bridle, a sack containing six beaver traps, a blanket with an extra pair of *moccasins*, his powder horn and bullet pouch, with a belt to which is attached a butcher knife, a wooden box containing bait for beaver, a tobacco sack with a pipe and implements for making fire, with sometimes a hatchet fastened to the pommel of his saddle. His personal dress is a flannel or cotton shirt (if he is fortunate enough to obtain one, if not antelope skin answers the purpose of over and undershirt), a pair of leather breeches with blanket or smoked buffalo skin leggings, a coat made of blanket or buffalo robe, a hat or cap of wool, buffalo or otter skin, his hose are pieces of blanket wrapped around his feet, which are covered with a pair of *moccasins* made of dressed deer, elk or buffalo skins, with his long hair falling loosely over his shoulders, completes his uniform.

He then mounts and places his rifle before him on his saddle. Such was the dress equipage of the party, myself included, now ready to start. After getting the necessary information from Mr. Bridger concerning the route he intended to take with the camp, we all started in a gallop in a westerly direction and travelled to the Big Horn and there commenced separating by twos and threes in different directions. I crossed the river with the largest party, still keeping a west course, most of the time in a gallop, until sun about an hour high at night, when we killed a bull and each taking some of the meat for supper proceeded on our journey till sunset, when I found myself with only one companion. All had turned to the right or left without once hinting their intentions, for it was not good policy for a trapper to let too many know where he intended to set his traps, particularly if his horse is not as fast as those of his companions.

I am sure my remaining companion, who was a Canadian Frenchman, knew not where I intended to set until I stopped my horse at a beaver dam between sunset and dark. We set three traps each and went down the stream half a mile and encamped some time after dark. This day I had travelled about forty miles with a poor horse, over a rough and broken country, intersected with deep ravines. The next morning we set the remainder of our traps and started down the stream about a mile, where we found two more trappers. We encamped with them, hobbled our horses and turned them out to feed, and before night our numbers had increased to twelve men. The camp came to us on the 26th of April, and found us nearly all together. We raised our traps and moved on with them to the West Fork of Prior's River, where we arrived on the 29th. The next morning we made another start, as formerly. My intentions were to set my traps on Rocky Fork, which we reached about three o'clock p. m., our party having diminished to three men beside myself.

In the meanwhile it began to rain and we stopped to approach a band of buffaloes, and as myself and one of my comrades (a Canadian) were walking along, half bent, near some bushes, secreting ourselves from the buffalo, a large grizzly bear, which probably had been awakened from his slumbers by our approach, sprang upon the Canadian, who was five or six feet before me, and placing one fore paw upon his head and the other on his left shoulder, pushed him to one side about twelve feet with as little ceremony as if he had been a cat, still keeping a direct course as though nothing had happened. I called to the Canadian and soon found the fright exceeded the wound, as he had received no injury except what this impudent stranger had done by tearing his coat, but it was hard telling which was the most frightened, the man or the bear. We reached Rocky Fork about sunset and going along the edge of the timber saw another bear lying down with a buffalo calf which he had already killed between his forepaws, while the mother was standing about twenty paces distant, moaning very pitifully for the loss of her young. The bear, on seeing us, dropped the calf and took to his heels into the brush.

The next day we travelled up Rocky Fork till about eleven o'clock, when I discovered there were trappers ahead of me. I then altered my course, leaving the stream at right angles in a westerly direction, and travelled across the country, parallel with the mountain, in company with a Canadian, for about ten miles, set my traps on a stream called Bodair's Fork (named after a Canadian who was killed by the Blackfeet in 1836). After setting our traps we travelled down the stream, encamped, and before night our party consisted of fifteen men who had set their traps and come to this place to spend the night without any previous arrangement whatever. But an old trapper can form some idea where his companions will encamp, though they seldom tell before their traps are set. I stopped at this place until the 6th of May, when, learning that the camp had arrived on Rocky Fork below, I left my traps and went to it to get a fresh horse.

On the 7th the camp moved near to where my traps were set and the next day moved on to the right hand fork of the Rosebud.

9th—I raised my traps and overtook them at the junction of the three forks of the Rosebud. The next day I started with two more to trap the head streams of this river. We travelled up the middle fork to the mountains, where we found signs of four or five trappers before us, and to follow a fresh horse track in trapping time is neither wise nor profitable with such a number of trappers as our camp contained. On the 14th we started to the camp, which we found on the Yellowstone at the mouth of the cross creeks. The next day the camp crossed the Yellowstone and moved up the north side to the mouth of "Twenty-five Yard" River. There I stopped with the camp till the 19th, when I started again with three others. Travelled up "Twenty-five Yard" River about twenty-five miles in a northerly direction, then left it and took around a low point of mountains in a westerly direction and fell on to a branch of the same river which forms a half circle from the north point of the mountain from where we first struck the river. We found this part of the country had been recently trapped by the Blackfeet.

The next morning. May 20th, two of my comrades returned to the camp, as it rained very hard. The other asked me which way I was going. I replied, "To hunt beaver," and started off as I spoke. He mounted his horse and followed me without further ceremony. We left the stream and took up the mountain in a south-westerly direction. After travelling about six miles we fell into a defile running through the mountains on to Cherry River, a branch of the Yellowstone. We travelled down this branch until near night and encamped. The next day continued down the stream and reached the plains about three o'clock p.m., within about twenty-five miles of the junction of the three forks of the Missouri. We here left the stream we had descended and took up a small right hand fork of it in an easterly direction, where we remained until the camp arrived on the 25th.

27th—We moved with the camp to the Gallatin Fork the next day. We crossed it with some difficulty but without accident, except the loss of three rifles. The current ran so swift that several horses lost their footing and were washed down the stream, which compelled their riders to abandon both horses and guns and swim ashore.

May 29th—Travelled up this stream to the mountain, about fifteen miles, and encamped. This valley is the largest in the Rocky Mountains, except the valley of the Snake River, but far smoother than the latter and more fertile.

May 30th—Travelled up the Gallatin Fork about ten miles into the mountains and encamped.

31st—We travelled up a small branch in a westerly direction about twenty-five miles.

June 1st—We crossed the mountains in the same direction and encamped in the valley on the Madison Fork which, after leaving the valley, runs through a deep, rocky canyon into the plains below.

CHAPTER 22

Battle With the Blackfeet

June 2nd—We crossed this fork and travelled up on the west side about fifteen miles, on a trail made by a village of Blackfeet which had passed up three or four days previously. They were, to all appearances, occasionally dying of the smallpox, which had made terrible havoc among the Blackfeet during that winter. That day we passed an Indian lodge standing in the prairie near the river, which contained nine dead bodies.

3rd—Continued up the stream on their trail until ten o'clock a.m., when Mr. Bridger, having charge of the camp, tried to avoid them by taking into the mountains, but the majority of the men remonstrated so hard against trying to avoid a village of Blackfeet which did not contain more than three times our number, that he altered his course, and turned back toward the Madison and encamped about two miles from the river on a small spring branch.

This branch ran through a ridge in a narrow passage of rocks, a hundred feet perpendicular on both sides, about a quarter of a mile from the Madison. The next morning as we were passing over the ridge around this place, we discovered the village about three miles above us on the river. We immediately drove into the canyon with the camp and prepared for battle.

Our leader was no military commander, therefore no orders were given. After the company property was secured about fifteen men mounted horses and started for the village in order to commence a skirmish. The village was situated on the west bank of the river. About thirty rods behind it arose a bench of land 100 feet high, running parallel with the river and gradually ascending to the westward until it terminated in a high range of mountains about two miles distant.

While our men were approaching the village I took a telescope and ascended the highest point of rocks which overhung the camp, to view the manoeuvres. They rode within a short distance of the edge of the bench, then dismounted and crept to the edge and opened fire on the village, which was the first the Indians knew of our being in the country. They fired three or four rounds each before the Indians had time to mount their horses and ascend the bluff 150 yards above them. The whites then mounted their horses and returned towards the camp before about five times their number. A running fire was kept up on both sides until our men reached the camp, when the Indians took possession of an elevated point formed of broken rock, about 300 paces distant on the south side of the camp, from which they kept shooting at intervals for about two hours without doing any damage. Presently one of them called to us in the Flathead tongue and said that we were not men, but women, and had better dress ourselves as such, for we had bantered them to fight and then crept into the rocks like women.

An old Iroquois trapper who had been an experienced warrior, trained on the shores of Lake Superior, understanding this harangue, turned to the whites about him and made a speech in imperfect English nearly as follows: "My friends, you see dat Ingun talk? He no talk good, he talk berry bad. He say you, me, all same like squaw. Dat no good. 'Spose you go wid me. I make him no talk dat way." On saying this he stripped himself entirely naked, throwing his powder horn and bullet pouch over his shoulder, and taking his rifle in his hand, began to dance and utter the shrill war-cry of his nation. Twenty of us who stood around and near him cheered the sound which had been the death warrant of so many whites during the old French war. He started and we followed, amid a shower of balls.

The distance, as I said before, was about 300 yards up a smooth and gradual ascent to the rocks where the Blackfeet had secreted themselves to the number of 150. The object of our leader was to make an open charge and drive them from their position, which we effected without loss, under an incessant storm of fusee balls. When we reached the rocks we stopped to breathe for about half a minute, not having as yet discharged a single gun. We then mounted over the piles of granite and attacked them muzzle to muzzle.

Although seven or eight times our number, they retreated from rock to rock like hunted rats among the ruins of an old building, whilst we followed close at their heels, loading and shooting, until we drove them entirely into the plain where their horses were tied. They carried off their dead, with the exception of two, and threw them into the river. They placed their wounded on horses and started slowly towards their village with a mournful cry. We then packed our animals and followed them with the camp within a quarter of a mile of the village, where we stopped for the night. During the night they moved the village up about three miles further.

Next morning we ascended the bench, intending to pass with the camp by the village. We soon found, however, that they had formed a line of mounted warriors from the river to the thick pines which grew on the mountain. About thirty of us concluded to try the bravery of those cavaliers on the field, leaving the remainder of the camp to bring up the rear. Under cover of the camp we rode into a thicket, out of their sight, and turned into a deep ravine, which led us, undiscovered, within twenty or thirty paces of their line. They, in the meantime, were watching the motions of the camp, intending to attack it while crossing the ravine. We approached nearly to the top of the bank, where we concluded to rest our horses a moment and then charge their line in front near the left wing. We were close enough to hear them talking as they pranced back and forth on the bench above us.

After tightening our girths and examining our arms, each of us put four or five bullets in our mouths and mounted without noise. Our leader (the same old Iroquois) sallied forth with a horrid yell, and we followed. The Indians were so much surprised with such a sudden attack that they made no resistance whatever, but wheeled and took toward the village as fast as their horses could carry them, whilst we pursued close at their heels until within about 300 yards of their lodges, where we made a halt and stopped until the camp had passed, then rode quietly away to our own party.

After leaving them we travelled up the Madison about eight miles and encamped near the place where we had fought the Blackfeet in September, 1835. Madison, after leaving the mountains, runs westerly to this place, forms a curve, and, turning east of north, in which direction it runs, to the junction of the three forks. The next day, June 6th, we left the Madison and travelled south over an undulating plain, about fifteen miles, and encamped at Henry Lake. This lake is about thirty miles in circumference, surrounded by forests of pine, except on the southeast side, where there is a small prairie about one mile wide and two long, terminating almost to a point at the two extremities.

Here we discovered another village of Blackfeet of about fifteen lodges, who were encamped on our route at the southeast side of the lake. The next morning we concluded to move camp to the village and smite it, without leaving one to tell their fate, but when within about two miles of the village we met six of them coming to us unarmed, who invited us in the most humble and submissive manner to their village to smoke and trade. This proceeding conquered the bravest in our camp, for we were ashamed to think of fighting a few poor Indians, nearly dwindled to skeletons by the smallpox, and approaching us without arms. We stopped, however, and traded with them and then started on our journey, encamping at night in the edge of the pine woods.

June 8th—We commenced our march through the pine woods by the lower track, which runs south nearly parallel with the course of Henry's Fork, and on the 11th we emerged from the pine woods into the plains of Snake River, where we stopped and trapped until the 14th. From thence we went to Pierre's Hole, where we found a party of ten trappers who had left the party at the mouth of Twenty-five Yard River. They had been defeated by the Blackfeet, lost most of their horses, and one man was wounded in the thigh by a fusee ball.

CHAPTER 23

Fall Hunt

June 18th—We left Pierre's Hole and crossed the mountain to Jackson's Big Hole. The next day myself and another trapper left the camp, crossed Lewis Fork and travelled down the valley to the south end. The next day we travelled in a southwest direction over high and rugged spurs of mountain and encamped on a small stream running into Gray's River, which empties into Lewis Fork above the mouth of Salt River.

21st—Travelled down the stream to Gray's River and set traps. We remained hunting the small streams which ran into this river until the 28th of June, then crossed the mountains in a southeast direction and fell on to a stream running into Green River, about thirty-five miles below the mouth of Horse Creek, called Seborges Fork.

July 1st—We travelled down this stream to the plains and steered our course northeast towards Horse Creek, where we expected to find the rendezvous. The next day we arrived at the place, but instead of finding the camp we found a large band of buffaloes near the appointed place of meeting. We rode up to an old log building which was formerly used as a store house during the rendezvous, where I discovered a piece of paper fastened upon the wall, which informed me that we should find the whites at the forks of Wind River. This was unwelcome news to us, as our animals were very much jaded. We then went down Green River, crossed and encamped for the night. The next day we travelled to Little Sandy.

3rd—We camped on the point of the mountain on a branch of Sweetwater. 4th—We encamped at the Oil Spring on Popo-azia, and the next day we arrived at the camp. There we found Mr. Dripps from

St. Louis, with twenty horse carts loaded with supplies, and again met Captain Stewart, likewise several missionaries with their families on their way to the Columbia River. On the 8th Mr. F. Ermatinger arrived with a small party from the Columbia, accompanied by the Rev. Jason Lee, who was on his way to the United States. On the 20th of July the meeting broke up and the parties again dispersed for the fall hunt.

I started, with about thirty trappers, up Wind River, expecting the camp to follow in a few days. During our stay at the rendezvous it was rumoured among the men that the company intended to bring no more supplies to the Rocky Mountains, and discontinue all further operations. This caused a great deal of discontent among the trappers and numbers left the party.

21st—We travelled up Wind River about thirty miles and encamped.

22nd—Continued up the river till noon, then left it to our right, travelled over a high ridge covered with pines, in a westerly direction about fifteen miles, and fell on to the Grosvent Fork. Next day we travelled about twenty miles down Grosvent Fork.

24th—Myself and another crossed the mountain in a northwest direction, fell on to a stream running into Lewis Fork, about ten miles below Jackson's Lake. Here we staid and trapped until the 29th. Then we started back to the Grosvent Fork, where we found the camp, consisting of about sixty men, under the direction of Mr. Dripps, with James Bridger pilot.

The next day the camp followed down the Grosvent Fork to Jackson's Hole. In the meantime myself and comrade returned to our traps, which we raised, and took over the mountain in a southwest direction and overtook the camp on Lewis Fork. The whole company was starving. Fortunately I had killed a deer in crossing the mountain, which made supper for the whole camp.

Aug. 1st—We crossed Lewis Fork and encamped and staid the next day.

3rd—Camp crossed the mountain to Pierre's Hole and the day following I started with my former comrade to hunt beaver on the streams which ran from the Yellowstone. About the middle of the afternoon, as we were winding down a steep declivity which overhung a precipice of rock nearly 200 feet perpendicular, my horse slipped and fell headlong down and was dashed to pieces.

6th—I returned to camp in Pierre's valley. On the next day made another start with the same comrade. After leaving camp we travelled in a southwest direction across the valley, then took over low hills, covered with pines until sun about an hour high, when we stopped and set our traps. On the 8th we travelled down the stream about three miles and then ascended a left hand branch in a north-easterly direction. After travelling about ten miles we fell into a valley surrounded by high mountains, except on the southwest side. This valley was about four miles long and one mile wide, whilst the huge piles of rock reaching above the clouds seemed almost to overhang the place on the north and east sides. We stopped here on the 9th and on the 10th returned to hunt the camp.

When leaving we took up the valley in a westerly direction and from thence travelled a northwest course through dense forests of pines about fifteen miles, when we struck the trail of the camp going north. We followed the track, which still led us through the forest, about twelve miles, when we came to a prairie about five miles in circumference in which the camp had stopped the night previous. We stopped here a few minutes, then resumed our journey on the trail, and after winding about among the fallen trees and rocks about six miles, we fell on to the middle branch of Henry's Fork, which is called by hunters "The Falling Fork," from the numerous cascades it forms whilst meandering through the forest previous to its junction with the main river.

At the place where we struck the fork is one of the most beautiful cascades I have ever seen. The stream is about sixty yards wide and falls over the rocks in a straight line about thirty feet perpendicular. It is very deep and still above where it breaks, and it gradually shallows to the depth of three feet on the brink. It is also very deep below and almost dead, except the motion caused by the waters falling into the deep, pond-like stream and boiling from the bottom, rolling off into small riffles and dying away into a calm, smooth surface.

We ascended this stream, passing several beautiful cascades, for about twelve miles, where the trail led us into a prairie seven or eight miles in circumference, in which we found the camp just as the sun was setting.

The next morning, August 11th, we bid *adieu* to the camp and started on the back track to trap the stream we had left the day previous. However, we took a nearer route and reached the little valley, where we staid until the 25th. This day we had a tremendous thunder storm, which broke in peals against the towering rocks above us with such dreadful clashing that it seemed as if they would have been torn from their foundations and hurled into the valley upon our heads. Such storms are very frequent about these mountains and often pass over without rain.

27th—We left the valley and ascended the mountain southwest and travelled about fifteen miles to a branch of Henry's Fork. Here we staid until the 7th of September, and then started down Henry's Fork southwest. After travelling about twelve miles we left the pines and travelled parallel with the stream over rolling ridges among scattered groves of quaking asps, when we arrived at the edge of the plains in travelling about eight miles. Here we discovered a trail made by a war party of Blackfeet, evidently the night previous. We then took a course south and travelled our horses in a trot all day and encamped an hour after dark on Lewis Fork, about fifteen miles above the junction. The next day we travelled to Blackfoot Creek and the day following to Fort Hall. We remained at the fort until the 20th, and then started down Snake River trapping, with a party of ten men beside ourselves.

CHAPTER 24

Spring Hunt

22nd—We arrived at a stream called Cozzu (or Raft River). This we ascended and hunted until the 5th of October, when, finding the country had been recently hunted, we returned to Fort Hall. From thence we started on the 18th with the fort hunter and six men to kill and dry buffalo meat for the winter. We cruised about on the Snake River and its waters until the 23rd of November, when the weather becoming very cold, and snow about fifteen inches deep, we returned with our horses loaded with meat to Fort Hall. We stopped here until the 1st of January, 1839, when we began to be tired of dried meat, and concluded to move up the river to where Lewis Fork leaves the mountain and there spend the remainder of the winter, killing and eating mountain sheep.

There were six in the company and we started on the 2nd travelling slowly, as the snow was deep and the weather cold, and arrived at the destined place on the 20th of January. We were followed by seven lodges of Snake Indians. We found the snow shallow about the foot of the mountain, with plenty of sheep, elk and some few bulls among the rocks and low spurs.

26th—I, with two white men and several Indians, started through the canyon to hunt elk. After travelling about four miles, I left the party and took up the river on the north side, whilst the remainder crossed the river on the ice to follow the trail of some bulls. I ascended the river, travelling on the ice and land alternately, about four miles further and encamped for the night. This was a severe, cold night, but I was comfortably situated with one blanket and two *epishemores* and plenty of dry wood to make a fire. When I arose in the morning I discovered a band of elk about half a mile up the mountain. I took my rifle and went to approach them through the snow three feet deep, and when within about 250 paces of them they took the wind of me and ran off, leaving me to return to my encampment with the consolation that this was not the first time the wind had blown away my breakfast. When I arrived at my camp, I found plenty of fresh buffalo meat hanging on the bushes near where I had slept. I immediately began to roast and eat, as twenty-four hours' fasting would naturally dictate. Presently a Snake Indian arrived to whom the meat belonged.

Near where I was encamped was a small stream which ran from a spring about 100 paces distant and emptied into the river. The water was a little more than blood warm. The beaver had taken advantage of the situation, dammed it up at the mouth and built a large lodge on the bank. At sunrise I discovered three of them swimming and playing in the water.

The next day I killed a bull and returned, through the canyon, to our camp.

On the 30th I started, with my old comrade (Elbridge), back with our traps to try the beaver. The snow was about two feet deep on the level plain and it took us till near night to reach the place. We encamped in a cave at the foot of the mountain near by and I set four traps. The weather was extremely cold, but I felt very comfortable while walking around in the warm water. On coming out and running as fast as I could to the camp, forty rods distant, both my feet were frozen. I soon drew out the frost, however, by stripping them and holding them in the cold snow. Next morning I found four large, fat beavers in my traps, and on the 2nd day of February we returned to camp with twelve beavers.

February *10th*—Moved with the camp up the river to where we had caught the beaver and encamped. Lewis Fork comes through this canyon for about twelve miles, where the rock rises 200 or 300 feet, forms a bench and ascends gradually to the mountain, which approaches very close on the north side, and on the south side is about three or four miles distant. An occasional ravine running from the mountain to the river through the rocks on the north side forms convenient places for camping, as the bench and low spurs are well clothed with bunch grass. Here we found immense numbers of mountain sheep, which the deep snows had driven down to the low points of rock facing the south near the river. We could see them nearly every morning from our lodges, standing on the points of rock jutting out so high in the air that they appeared no larger than weasels.

It is in this position that a hunter delights to approach them from behind and shoot, whilst their eyes are fixed on some object below. It is an exercise which gives vigour, health and appetite to the hunter, to shoulder his rifle at daybreak on a clear, cold morning and wind his way up a rugged mountain, over I rocks and crags, at length killing a fat old ewe and taking the meat to camp on his back. This kind of exercise gives him an appetite for his breakfast. But hunting sheep is attended with great danger in many places, especially when the rocks are covered with sleet and ice. I have often passed over places where I have had to cut steps in the ice with my butcher knife in which to place my feet, directly over the most frightful precipices, but being excited in the pursuit of game, I would think but little of danger until I had laid down to sleep at night. Then it would make my blood run cold to meditate upon the scenes I had passed through during the day, and often have I resolved never to risk myself in such places again and as often broken the resolution. The sight of danger is less hideous than the thought of it.

On the 18th of March the winter commenced breaking up with a heavy rain, and four of us started up the river to commence the spring hunt, whilst the remainder of the party returned to the fort. After travelling through the canyon we found the ground bare in many places, whilst it still continued to rain. On the 30th of March we travelled to the mouth of Muddy. This we ascended and crossed the mountain with some difficulty, as the snow was very deep, on to the head waters of Gray's Creek. There two of our party (who were Canadians) left us and struck off for themselves. Our camp then consisted of myself and my old comrade, Elbridge. I say old comrade because we had been some time together, but he was a young man, from Beverly, Mass., and being bred a sailor, he was not much of a landsman, woodsman or hunter, but a great, easy, good-natured fellow, standing five feet ten inches and weighing 200 pounds.

On the 20th of April we crossed a high ridge in a north direction and encamped on a stream that sinks in the plain soon after leaving the mountain. Here we set our traps for beaver, but their dams were nearly all covered with ice, excepting some few holes which they had made for the purpose of obtaining fresh provisions. We stopped on this stream until the 26th of April and then travelled out by the same way which we came.

26th—We travelled in a southerly direction about twenty-five miles, crossing several of the head branches of Gray's Creek. On the 1st of May we travelled about ten miles east course and the next day went to the head of Gray's marsh, about twenty miles south course. There we deposited the furs we had taken, and the next day started for Salt River to get a supply of salt. We took an easterly direction about six miles and fell on to Gardner's Fork, which we descended to the valley, and on the 6th arrived at the Salt Springs on Scott's Fork of Salt River. Here we found twelve of our old comrades who had come, like ourselves, to gather salt. We staid two nights together at this place, when Elbridge and myself took leave of them and returned to Gray's marsh. From there we started toward Fort Hall, travelling one day and laying by five or six to fatten our horses, and arrived at the fort on the 5th of June.

CHAPTER 25

Another Viewpoint

This fort now belonged to the British Hudson Bay Company, who obtained it by purchase from Mr. Wyeth in the year 1837. We stopped at the fort until the 26th of June, then made up a party of four for the purpose of trapping in the Yellowstone and Wind Mountains, and arrived at Salt River valley on the 28th.

29th—We crossed the valley northeast, then left it, ascending Gray's River in an easterly direction about four miles, into a narrow, rugged pass, encamped and killed a sheep.

30th—We travelled up this stream thirty miles east and encamped in a small valley and killed a bull, and the next day we encamped in the south end of Jackson's Hole.

July 2nd—We travelled through the valley north until night, and the next day arrived at Jackson's Lake, where we concluded to spend the Fourth of July at the outlet.

July 4th—I caught about twenty very fine silver trout, which, together with fat mutton, buffalo beef and coffee, and the manner in which it was ground up, constituted a dinner that ought to be considered independent, even by Britons.

July 5th—We travelled north parallel with the lake, on the east side, and the next day arrived at the inlet or northern extremity.

7th—We left the lake and followed up Lewis Fork about eight miles in a north-easterly direction and encamped. On the day following we travelled about five miles, when we came to the junction of two equal forks. We took up the left hand on the west side, through the thick pines, and in many places so much fallen timber that we frequently had to make circles of a quarter of a mile to gain a few rods ahead, but our general course was north, and I suppose we travelled about sixteen miles in that direction. At night we encamped at a lake about fifteen miles in circumference, which formed the stream we had ascended.

July 9th—We travelled round this lake to the inlet on the west side, and came to another lake about the same size. This had a small prairie on the west side, whilst the other was completely surrounded by thick pines. The next day we travelled along the border of the lake till we came to the northwest extremity, where we found about fifty springs of boiling hot water. We stopped here some hours, as one of my comrades had visited this spot the year previous and wished to show us some curiosities. The first spring we visited was about ten feet in diameter, which threw up mud with a noise similar to boiling soap. Close about this were numerous springs similar to it, throwing up mud and water five or six feet high. About thirty or forty paces from these, along the side of a small ridge, the hot steam rushed forth from holes in the ground, with a hissing noise which could be heard a mile distant.

On a near approach we could hear the water bubbling underground, some distance from the surface. The sound of our footsteps over this place was like thumping over a hollow vessel of immense size. In many places were peaks from two to six feet high formed of limestone, which appeared of a snowy whiteness, deposited by the boiling water. The water, when cold, was perfectly sweet, except having a fresh limestone taste. After surveying these natural wonders for some time my comrade conducted me to what he called the "Hour Spring." At that spring the first thing which attracted the attention was a hole about fifteen inches in diameter in which the water was boiling slowly about four inches below the surface.

At length it began to boil and bubble violently and the water commenced raising and shooting upwards until the column arose to the height of sixty feet, from whence it fell to the ground in drops in a circle about thirty feet in diameter, perfectly cold when it struck the ground. It continued shooting up in this manner five or six minutes and then sank back to its former state of slowly boiling for an hour and then it would shoot forth again as before. My comrade said he had watched the motions of this spring for one whole day and part of the night the year previous and found no irregularity whatever in its movements.

After surveying these wonders for a few hours we left the place and travelled north about three miles over ascending ground, then descended a steep and rugged mountain four miles in the same direction and fell on to the head branch of the Jefferson branch of the Missouri. The whole country was still thickly covered with pines except here and there a small prairie. We encamped and set some traps for beaver and staid four days. At this place there was also a large number of hot springs, some of which had formed cones of limestone twenty feet high of a snowy whiteness, which makes a splendid appearance standing among the evergreen pines. Some of the lower peaks are very convenient for the hunter in preparing his dinner when hungry, for here his kettle is always ready and boiling. His meat being suspended in the water by a string is soon prepared for his meal without further trouble.

Some of these spiral cones are twenty feet in diameter at the base and not more than twelve inches at the top, the whole being covered with small, irregular semicircular ridges about the size of a man's finger, having the appearance of carving in has relief, formed, I suppose, by the waters running over it for ages unknown. I should think this place to be 3,000 feet lower than the springs we left on the mountain. Vast numbers of black tailed deer are found in the vicinity of these springs and seem to be very familiar with hot water and steam, the noise of which seems not to disturb their slumbers, for a buck may be found carelessly sleeping where the noise will exceed that of three or four engines in operation. Standing upon an eminence and superficially viewing these natural monuments, one is half inclined to believe himself in the neighbourhood of the ruins of some ancient city, whose temples had been constructed of the whitest marble.

July 15th—We travelled down the stream northwest about 12 miles, passing on our route large numbers of hot springs with their snow white monuments scattered among the groves of pines. At length we came to a boiling lake about 300 feet in diameter, forming nearly a complete circle as we approached on the south side. The steam which arose from it was of three distinct colours. From the West side for one-third of the diameter it was white, in the middle it was pale red, and the remaining third on the east, light sky blue. Whether it was something peculiar in the state of the atmosphere, the day being cloudy, or whether it was some chemical properties contained in the water which produced this phenomenon, I am unable to say, and shall leave the explanation to some scientific tourist who may have the curiosity to visit this place at some future period. The water was of deep indigo blue, boiling like an immense cauldron, running over the white rock which had formed around the edges to the height of four or five feet from the surface of the earth, sloping gradually for sixty or seventy feet. What a field of speculation this presented for chemist and geologist.

The next morning we crossed the stream, travelled down the east side about five miles, then ascended another fork in an easterly direction about ten miles and encamped. From where we left the main fork it runs in a northwest direction about forty miles before reaching the Burnt Hole.

July 17th—We travelled to the head of this branch, about twenty miles, east direction.

18th—After travelling in the same direction about seven miles over a low spur of the mountains, we came into a large plain on the Yellowstone River, about eight miles below the lake, and followed up the Yellowstone to the outlet of the lake and encamped and set our traps for beaver. We stopped here trapping until the 28th and from thence we travelled to the "Secluded Valley," where we staid one day. From there we travelled east to the head of Clark's Fork, where we stopped and hunted the small branches until the 4th of August, and then returned to the valley. On the 9th we left the valley and travelled two days over the mountain, northwest and fell on to a stream running south into the Yellowstone, where we staid until the 16th, and then crossed the mountain, in a northwest direction, over the snow, and fell on to a stream running into the Yellowstone plains and entering that river about forty miles above the mouth of Twenty-five Yard River.

18th—We descended this stream within about a mile of the plain and set our traps.

The next day my comrades started for the plains to kill some buffalo cows. I remonstrated very hard against them going into the plains and disturbing the buffaloes in such a dangerous part of the country, when we had plenty of fat deer and mutton, but to no purpose. Off they started and returned at night with their animals loaded with cow meat. They told me they had seen where a village of 300 or 400 lodges of Blackfeet had left the Yellowstone in a north-westerly direction but three or four days previous.

Aug. 22nd—We left this stream and travelled along the foot of the mountains at the edge of the plain, about twenty miles west course, and encamped at a spring. The next day we crossed the Yellowstone River and travelled up the river on the west side to the mouth of Gardner's Fork, where we staid the next day.

25th—We travelled to "Gardner's Hole," then altered our course southeast, crossing the eastern point of the valley, and encamped on a small branch among the pines.

26th—We encamped on the Yellowstone in the big plain below the lake. The next day we went to the lake and set our traps on a branch running into it, near the outlet on the northeast side.

CHAPTER 26

Wounded by Arrows of Blackfeet

28th—After visiting my traps I returned to the camp, where, after stopping about an hour or two, I took my rifle and sauntered down the shore of the lake among the scattered groves of tall pines until tired of walking about (the day being very warm), I took a bath in the lake, probably half an hour, and returned to the camp about four o'clock p.m. Two of my comrades observed, "Let us take a walk among the pines and kill an elk," and started off, whilst the other was lying asleep. Some time after they were gone I went to a bale of dried meat which had been spread in the sun thirty or forty feet from the place where we slept. Here I pulled off my powder horn and bullet pouch, laid them on a log, drew my butcher knife and began to cut. We were encamped about a half mile from the lake on a stream running into it in a southwest direction through a prairie bottom about a quarter of a mile wide. On each side of this valley arose a bench of land about twenty feet high, running parallel with the stream and covered with pines.

On this bench we were encamped on the southeast side of the stream. The pines immediately behind us were thickly intermingled with logs and fallen trees. After eating a few minutes I arose and kindled a fire, filled my tobacco pipe and sat down to smoke. My comrade, whose name was White, was still sleeping. Presently I cast my eyes toward the horses, which were feeding in the valley, and discovered the heads of some Indians who were gliding round under the bench within thirty steps of me. I jumped to my rifle and aroused White. Looking towards my powder horn and bullet pouch, it was already in the hands of an Indian, and we were completely surrounded. We cocked our rifles and started through their ranks into the woods, which seemed to be completely filled with Blackfeet, who rent the air with their horrid yells.

On presenting our rifles, they opened a space about twenty feet wide, through which we plunged. About the fourth jump an arrow struck White on the right hip joint. I hastily told him to pull it out and as I spoke another arrow struck me in the same place, but this did not retard our progress. At length another arrow struck through my right leg beneath the flesh and above the knee, so that I fell with my breast across a log. The Indian who shot me was within eight feet of me and made a spring toward me with his uplifted battle axe. I made a leap and dodged the blow and kept hopping from log to log through a shower of arrows which flew around us like hail, lodging in the pines and logs. After we had passed them about ten paces we wheeled and took aim at them. They began to dodge behind the trees and shoot their guns.

We then ran and hopped about fifty yards further in the logs and bushes and made a stand. I was very faint from the loss of blood and we sat down among the logs, determined to kill the two foremost when they came up and then die like men. We rested our rifles across a log. White aiming at the foremost and myself at the second. I whispered to him that when they turned their eyes toward us to pull trigger. About twenty of them passed by us within fifteen feet without casting a glance toward us. Another file came round on the opposite side within twenty or thirty paces, closing with the first few a few rods beyond us and all turning to the right, the next minute were out of sight among the bushes. They were well armed with fusees, bows and battle axes. We sat until the rustling among the bushes had died away, then arose, and after looking carefully around us, White asked in a whisper how far it was to the lake. I replied, pointing to the southeast, about a quarter of a mile.

I was nearly fainting from the loss of blood and the want of water. We hobbled along forty or fifty rods and I was obliged to sit down a few minutes, then go a little further and rest again. We managed in this way until we reached the bank of the lake. Our next object was to obtain some of the water, as the bank was very steep and high. White had been perfectly calm and deliberate until now. His conversation became wild, hurried and despairing. He observed, "I cannot go down to that water, for I am wounded all over. I shall die." I told him to sit down while I crawled down and brought some in my hat. This I effected with a great deal of difficulty.

We then hobbled along the border of the lake for a mile and a half, when it grew dark and we stopped. We could still hear the shouting of the savages over their booty. We stopped under a large pine tree near the lake, and I told White I could go no further.

"Oh," said he, "let us go into the pines and find a spring." I replied there was no spring within a mile of us, which I knew to be a fact. "Well," said he, "if you stop here I shall make a fire."

"Make as much as you please," I replied angrily. "This is a poor time now to undertake to frighten me." I then started to the water, crawling on my hands and one knee, and returned in about an hour with some in my hat.

While I was at this he had kindled a small fire, and taking a draught of water from the hat he exclaimed, "Oh, dear, we shall die here; we shall never get out of these mountains."

"Well," said I, "if you persist in thinking so you will die, but I can crawl from this place on my hands and one knee and kill two or three elk and make a shelter of the skins, dry the meat, until we get able to travel." In this manner I persuaded him that we were not in half so bad a situation as we might be, although he was not in half so bad a situation as I expected, for, on examining I found only a slight wound from an arrow on his hip bone. But he was not so much to blame, as he was a young man who had been brought up in Missouri, the pet of the family, and had never done or learned much of anything but horse racing and gambling whilst under the care of his parents (if care it could be called) . I pulled off an old piece of a coat made of blanket (as he was entirely without clothing except his hat and shirt), set myself in a leaning position against a tree, ever and *anon* gathering such branches and rubbish as I could reach without altering the position of my body, to keep up a little fire, and in this manner miserably spent the night.

The next morning, August 29, I could not arise without assistance, when White procured a couple of sticks for crutches, by the help of which I hobbled to a small grove of pines about sixty yards distant. We had scarcely entered the grove when we heard a dog barking and Indians singing and talking. The sound seemed to be approaching us. They at length came near to where we were, to the number of sixty. Then they commenced shooting at a large band of elk that was swimming in the lake, killed four of them, dragged them to the shore and butchered them, which occupied about three hours. They then packed the meat in small bundles on their backs and travelled up along the rocky shore about a mile and encamped. We then left our hiding place and crept into the thick pines about fifty yards distant and started in the direction of our encampment in the hope of finding our comrades.

My leg was very much swollen and painful, but I managed to get along slowly on my crutches by White carrying my rifle. When we were within about sixty rods of the encampment we discovered the Canadian hunting around among the trees as though he was looking for a trail. We approached him within thirty feet before he saw us, and he was so much agitated by fear that he knew not whether to run or stand still. On being asked where Elbridge was, he said they came to the camp the night before at sunset. The Indians pursued them into the woods, where they separated, and he saw him no more.

At the encampment I found a sack of salt. Everything else the Indians had carried away or cut to pieces. They had built seven large conical forts near the spot, from which we supposed their numbers to have been seventy or eighty, part of whom had returned to their village with the horses and plunder. We left the place, heaping curses on the head of the Blackfoot nation, which neither injured them nor alleviated our distress.

We followed down the shores of the lake and stopped for the night. My companions threw some logs and rubbish together, forming a kind of shelter from the night breeze, but in the night it took fire (the logs being of pitch pine) and the blaze ran to the tops of the trees. We removed a short distance, built another fire and laid by it until morning. We then made a raft of dry poles and crossed the outlet upon it. We then went to a small grove of pines near by and made a fire, where we stopped the remainder of the day in hopes that Elbridge would see our signals and come to us, for we left directions on a tree at the encampment which route we would take. In the meantime the Canadian went to hunt something to eat, but without success. I had bathed my wounds in salt water and made a salve of beaver's oil and *castorium*, which I applied to them. This had eased the pain and drawn out the swelling in a great measure.

The next morning I felt very stiff and sore, but we were obliged to travel or starve, as we had eaten nothing since our defeat and game was very scarce on the west side of the lake. Moreover the Canadian had got such a fright we could not prevail on him to go out of our sight to hunt. So on we trudged slowly, and after getting warm I could bear half my weight on my lame leg, but it was bent considerably and swelled so much that my knee joint was stiff. About ten o'clock the

Canadian killed a couple of small ducks, which served us for breakfast. After eating them we pursued our journey. At twelve o'clock it began to rain, but we still kept on until the sun was two hours high in the evening, when the weather clearing away, we encamped at some hot springs and killed a couple of geese.

Whilst we were eating them a deer came swimming along in the lake within about 100 yards of the shore. We fired several shots at him, but the water glancing the balls, he remained unhurt and apparently unalarmed, but still kept swimming to and fro in the lake in front of us for an hour and then started along up close to the shore. The hunter went to watch it in order to kill it when it should come ashore, but as he was lying in wait for the deer a doe elk came to the water to drink and he killed her, the deer being still out in the lake swimming to and fro until dark.

Now we had plenty to eat and drink but were almost destitute of clothing. I had on a pair of trousers and a cotton shirt which were completely drenched with the rain. We made a sort of shelter from the wind out of pine branches and built a large fire of pitch knots in front of it, so that we were burning on one side and freezing on the other, alternately, all night. The next morning we cut some of the elk meat in thin slices and cooked it slowly over a fire, then packed it in bundles, strung them on our backs and started. By this time I could carry my own rifle and limp along half as fast as a man could walk, but when my foot touched against the logs or brush the pain in my leg was very severe. We left the lake at the hot springs and travelled through the thick pines, over a low ridge of land, through the snow and rain together, but we travelled by the wind about eight miles in a southwest direction, when we came to a lake about twelve miles in circumference, which is the head spring of the right branch of Lewis Fork. Here we found a dry spot near a number of hot springs, under some thick pines.

Our hunter had killed a deer on the way and I took the skin, wrapped it around me and felt prouder of my mantle than a monarch with his imperial robes. This night I slept more than four hours, which was more than I had slept at any one time since I was wounded, and arose the next morning much refreshed. These springs were similar to those on the Madison, and among these, as well as those, sulphur was found in its purity in large quantities on the surface of the ground. We travelled along the shore on the south side about five miles in an easterly direction, fell in with a large band of elk, killed two fat does and took some of the meat.

We then left the lake and travelled due south over a rough, broken country, covered with thick pines, for about twelve miles, when we came to the fork again, which ran through a narrow prairie bottom, followed down it about six miles and encamped at the forks. We had passed up the left hand fork on the 9th of July on horseback, in good health and spirits, and down on the right bank on the 31st of August on foot, with weary limbs and sorrowful countenances. We built a fire and laid down to rest, but I could not sleep more than fifteen or twenty minutes at a time, the night being so very cold. We had plenty of meat, however, and made moccasins of raw elk hide. The next day we crossed the stream and travelled down near to Jackson's Lake on the west side, then took up a small branch in a west direction to the head. We then had the Teton mountain to cross, which looked like a laborious undertaking, as it was steep and the top covered with snow. We arrived at the summit, however, with a great deal of difficulty, before sunset, and after resting a few moments, travelled down about a mile on the other side and stopped for the night.

After spending another cold and tedious night, we were descending the mountain through the pines at daylight and the next night we reached the forks of Henry's Fork of Snake River. This day was very warm, but the wind blew cold at night. We made a fire and gathered some dry grass to sleep on and then sat down and ate the remainder of our provisions. It was now ninety miles to Fort Hall and we expected to see little or no game on the route, but we determined to travel it in three days. We lay down and shivered with the cold till daylight, then arose and again pursued our journey toward the fork of Snake River, where we arrived sun about an hour high, forded the river, which was nearly swimming, and encamped. The weather being very cold and fording the river so late at night, caused me much suffering during the night.

Sept. 4th—We were on our way at daybreak and travelled all day through the high sage and sand down Snake River. We stopped at dark, nearly worn out with fatigue, hunger and want of sleep, as we had now travelled sixty-five miles in two days without eating. We sat and hovered over a small fire until another day appeared, then set out as usual and travelled to within about ten miles of the fort, when I was seized with a cramp in my wounded leg, which compelled me to stop and sit down every thirty or forty rods. At length we discovered a half breed encamped in the valley, who furnished us with horses and went with us to the fort, where we arrived about sun an hour high, being naked, hungry, wounded, sleepy and fatigued. Here again I entered a trading post after being defeated by the Indians, but the treatment was quite different from that which I had received at Savonery's Fork in 1837, when I had been defeated by the Crows.

The fort was in charge of Mr. Courtney M. Walker, who had been lately employed by the Hudson Bay Company for that purpose. He invited us into a room and ordered supper to be prepared immediately. Likewise such articles of clothing and blankets as we called for. After dressing ourselves and giving a brief history of our defeat and sufferings, supper was brought in, consisting of tea, cakes, buttermilk, dried meat, etc. I ate very sparingly, as I had been three days fasting, but drank so much strong tea that it kept me awake till after midnight. I continued to bathe my leg in warm salt water and applied a salve, which healed it in a very short time, so that in ten days I was again setting traps for beaver. On the 13th of September Elbridge arrived safe at the fort. He had wandered about among the mountains several days without having any correct knowledge, but at length accidentally falling on to the trail which we had made in the summer, it enabled him to reach the plains and from there he travelled to the fort by his own knowledge.

On the 20th of October we started to hunt buffalo and make meat for the winter. The party consisted of fifteen men. We travelled to the head of the Jefferson Fork of the Missouri, where we killed and dried our meat. From there we proceeded over the mountains through Camas prairie to the forks of the Snake River, where most of the party concluded to spend the winter. Four of us, however, who were the only Americans in the party, returned to Fort Hall on the 10th of December. We encamped near the fort and turned our horses among the springs and timber to hunt their living during the winter, whilst ourselves were snugly arranged in our skin lodge, which was pitched among the large Cottonwood trees, and in it provisions to serve us till the month of April. There were four of us in the mess. One was from Missouri, one from Massachusetts, one from Vermont, and myself from Maine.

We passed an agreeable winter. We had nothing to do but to eat, attend to the horses and procure firewood. We had some few books to read, such as Byron, Shakespeare and Scott's works, the Bible and Clark's Commentary on it, and other small works on geology, chemistry and philosophy. The winter was very mild and the ground was bare in the valley until the 15th of January, when the snow fell about eight inches deep, but disappeared again in a few days. This was the deepest snow and of the longest duration of any we had during the winter.

CHAPTER 27

Supply Train Reaches Fort Hall on June 14, 1840

On the 10th of March I started again with my old companion Elbridge. We travelled from the fort on the Blackfoot near the foot of the mountain, where we set some traps for beaver, the ice being broken up. On the 15th we tried to cross the mountain to Gray's valley, but were compelled to turn back for the snow. On the 20th made another trial and succeeded and encamped at the forks of Gray's Creek. Here the ground was bare along the stream and on the south sides of the hills, but very deep on the high plains. I killed two bulls, which came in good time, after living on dried meat all winter.

March 19th—We travelled up Gray's Creek about ten miles. There we found the snow very deep and hard enough to bear our horses in the morning. On the 22nd we travelled on the snow up this stream about five miles and encamped on a bare spot of ground, where we staid three days, then started on the snow, as usual, and went about eight miles to the valley about Gray's marsh, where we found a bare spot about forty rods square on the south side of a ridge, and encamped. The snow in the valley was about three feet deep on a level. March 28th we started on foot in the morning on the snow to hunt buffalo. After going about two miles we found eleven bulls, approached and killed ten of them on the spot.

We then butchered some of them and took out the tongues of the others, buried the meat about three feet deep in a snow drift, laid some stones on the snow over it and burned gun powder upon them to keep away the wolves. We then took meat enough for our suppers and started for the camp. By this time the snow was thawed so much that we broke through nearly every step.

Early next morning, the snow being frozen, we took two horses and went for our meat, but when we reached the place where we had buried it we found the wolves had dug it up and taken the best of it, notwithstanding our precautions. The carcasses of the bulls yet remained untouched by them, and from these we loaded our horses and returned to camp. About noon the rays of the sun shining upon the snow and reflecting upward began to affect our eyes, insomuch that toward night we could scarcely look abroad. We lay down to sleep, but it was useless, for our eyes felt as if they were filled with coarse sand. After four days of severe suffering with what the trappers call snow blindness, we began to recover our eyesight by degrees, although we had not been at any time totally blind, yet we had been the whole time very near it.

We staid here until the 10th of April when, finding the snow did not abate, we returned to the forks of Gray's Creek, where we remained until the 20th. We then travelled to the fork which sinks in the plain, on Lewis Fork, where we set our traps and staid until the 1st of May. On the 2nd we arrived again at the marsh on Gray's Creek, where we found the ground mostly bare but the streams overflowing their banks. On the 5th we crossed the mountain in an easterly direction, fell on to a stream running into Lewis Fork ten miles below the mouth of Salt River. We travelled down this stream, which runs through a narrow cut in the mountains for about fifteen miles and then forms a small valley, where we stopped and set our traps and staid until the 20th, when Elbridge observed he thought we had better leave our traps setting, turn and go to Salt River valley, spend a few days killing buffalo, and then return. I remonstrated against the proposal, as our horses were very poor, the streams high and the ground very muddy, but I told him if he wished to go to take his traps with him and not be at the trouble of coming back after them.

The next morning he packed his horses and left me. My two horses were now my only companions, with the exception of some books which I had brought from the fort. I staid here trapping until the 28th. Then travelled up a branch about fifteen miles, crossed the mountain in a northwest direction, fell on to the head of muddy creek, where I killed a bull and stopped for the night. The next day I stopped at this place and dried some meat.

30th—Went on the right fork of Muddy and set some traps. Here I staid six days and then went to Gray's marsh, intending to kill and dry some meat and go to the fort, but finding no buffalo here, I crossed on to Salt River, and finding no buffalo there I ascended Gardner's Fork, crossed the mountain and fell on to Blackfoot Creek, where I killed a fat bull, dried the meat and started for Fort Hall, where I arrived on the 10th of June. June 14th Mr. Ermatinger arrived at the fort with eighty horse loads of goods to supply the post the ensuing year. On the 15th Elbridge arrived, having fallen in with a party of hunters soon after leaving me in the mountains, after having lost his traps in crossing Gray's River. A few days after he arrived he expressed a wish that I would go with him and two others to make a hunt in the Yellowstone mountains. I replied I had seen enough of the Yellowstone mountains, and, moreover, I intended to trap in the future with a party who would not leave me in a pinch.

On the 22nd of June I started with two horses, six traps and some few books, intending to hunt on the waters of Snake River in the vicinity of Fort Hall. I went to Gray's Hole, set my traps and staid five days. From there I went on to Milk Fork, where I staid until the 15th of July. From there I took a northerly direction through the mountains and fell on to a stream running into Lewis Fork near the mouth of Salt River, where I staid twelve days and then returned to Gray's marsh and staid until the 3rd of August. I then travelled through the mountains, southeast, on to the head stream of Gardner's Fork, where I spent the time hunting the small branches until the 15th. From there I started toward the fort, hunting the streams which were on the route, and arrived on the 22nd.

After stopping here a few days I started, in company with three trappers, one of whom was Major Meek, and travelled to the forks of Snake River. From there we ascended Henry's Fork about fifteen miles and then took up a stream in a southwest direction into the mountains, but finding no beaver, we crossed the mountain and struck Lewis Fork in the canyon, where, after trapping some days, we went on to Gray's Creek, where, after staying seven days, we killed a fat grizzly bear and some antelope, loaded the meat on our horses and started to the fort, where we arrived on the 22nd of September.

CHAPTER 28

Christmas Dinner à l'Indian

On the 1st of October I again left the fort with a Frenchman who had an Indian wife and two children, and was going on to Green River to pass the winter with them. We travelled up Portneuf about fifteen miles, where we stopped the next day and hunted antelope, and the day following we travelled up the stream about twenty miles, when, after staying ten days, we went to the Soda Springs on Bear River. Here we concluded to spend a month on Bear River, travelling slowly, hunting beaver and antelope, as the latter is the only game in this part of the country. Beaver also were getting very scarce. On the 15th of November the snow began to fall and my comrade started, with his family, across the mountains to Green River and I returned towards the fort.

On my way down Bear River I met thousands of antelope travelling towards their winter quarters, which is generally Green River valley. I followed Bear River down to Cache valley, where I found twenty lodges of Snake Indians and staid with them several days. They had a considerable number of beaver skins, but I had nothing to trade for them. They told me if I would go to the fort and get some goods, return and spend the winter with them, they would trade their furs with me. I started for the fort with one of them whom I engaged to assist me with my horses.

I arrived at the fort on the 23rd of November, when, after getting such articles for trade as I wished, and my personal supplies for the winter, I returned to Cache valley, accompanied by a half-breed. On arriving at the village I found several Frenchmen and half-breed trappers encamped with the Snakes. One Frenchman, having an Indian wife and child, invited me to pass the winter in his lodge, and as he had a small family and large lodge, I accepted the invitation and had my baggage taken into his lodge and neatly arranged by his wife, who was a Flathead. The neat manner in which her lodge and furniture was kept would have done honour to a large portion of the "pale-faced" fair sex in the civilized world.

We staid in this valley until the 15th of December, when it was unanimously agreed to go to the Salt Lake and there spend the remainder of the winter. The next day we travelled across the valley in a southwest direction, then took into a narrow defile which led us through the mountain into the valley on the eastern borders of the lake. The day following we moved along the valley in a southerly direction and encamped on small branch close to the foot of the mountain. The ground was still bare and the autumnal growth of grass was the best I ever saw at this season of the year.

18th—I arose about an hour before daylight, took my rifle and ascended the mountain on foot to hunt sheep. The weather was clear and cold but the mountain being steep and rugged and my rifle heavy, the exercise soon put me in a perspiration. After climbing about half a mile I sat down on a rock to wait for daylight, and when it came I discovered a band of about 100 rams within about eighty yards of me. I shot and killed one. The others ran about fifty yards further and stopped. While I was reloading my rifle one of them ascended a high pinnacle of rock which jutted over a precipice. There were others nearer me, but I wished to fetch this proud animal from his elevated position. I brought my rifle to my face, the ball whistled through his heart, and he fell headlong over the precipice. I followed the band at some distance among the crags and killed two more, butchered them, then returned and butchered the two I had first killed, and returned to camp and sent some men with horses to get the meat.

Dec. 20th—We moved along the borders of the lake about ten miles and encamped on a considerable stream running into it called Weaver's River. At this place the valley is about ten miles wide, intersected with numerous springs of salt and fresh hot and cold water, which rise at the foot of the mountain and run through the valley into the river and lake. Weaver's River is well timbered along its banks, principally with Cottonwood and box elder. There are also large groves of sugar maple, pine and some oak growing in the ravines about the mountains. We also found large numbers of elk which had left the mountains to winter among the thickets of wood and brush along the river.

Christmas

December 25th—It was agreed on by the party to prepare a Christmas dinner, but I shall first endeavour to describe the party and then the dinner. I have already said the man who was the proprietor of the lodge in which I staid was a Frenchman with a Flathead wife and one child. The inmates of the next lodge were a half-breed Iowa, a Nez Perce wife and two children, his wife's brother and another half-breed; next lodge was a half-breed Cree, his wife (a Nez Perce) two children and a Snake Indian. The inmates of the third lodge was a half-breed Snake, his wife (a Nez Perce) and two children. The remainder were fifteen lodges of Snake Indians. Three of the party spoke English but very broken, therefore that language was made but little use of, as I was familiar with the Canadian French and Indian tongue.

About ten o'clock we sat down to dinner in the lodge where I staid, which was the most spacious, being about thirty-six feet in circumference at the base, with a fire built in the centre. Around this sat on clean *epishemores* all who claimed kin to the white man (or to use their own expression, all who were *gens d'esprit*), with their legs crossed in true Turkish style, and now for the dinner.

The first dish that came on was a large tin pan eighteen inches in diameter, rounding full of stewed elk meat. The next dish was similar to the first, heaped up with boiled deer meat (or as the whites would call it, venison, a term not used in the mountains). The third and fourth dishes were equal in size to the first, containing a boiled flour pudding, prepared with dried fruit, accompanied by four quarts of sauce made of the juice of sour berries and sugar. Then came the cakes, followed by about six gallons of strong coffee ready sweetened, with tin cups and pans to drink out of, large chips or pieces of bark supplying the places of plates.

On being ready, the butcher knives were drawn and the eating commenced at the word given by the landlady. As all dinners are accompanied by conversation, this was not deficient in that respect. The principal topic which was discussed was the political affairs of the Rocky Mountains, the state of governments among the different tribes, the personal characters of the most distinguished warrior chiefs, etc. One remarked that the Snake chief, Pahda-hewakunda, was becoming very unpopular and it was the opinion of the Snakes in general that Moh-woom-hah, his brother, would be at the head of affairs before twelve months, as his village already amounted to more than three hundred lodges, and, moreover, he was supported by the bravest men in the nation, among whom were Ink-a-tosh-a-pop, Fibe-bo-un-to-wat-see and Who-sha-kik, who were the pillars of the nation and at whose names the Blackfeet quaked with fear.

In like manner were the characters of the principal chiefs of the Bannock, Nez Perce, Flathead and Crow nations and the policy of their respective nations commented upon by the descendants of Shem and Japhet with as much affected dignity as if they could have read their own names when written, or distinguish the letter B from bull's foot.

Dinner being over, the tobacco pipes were filled and lighted, while the squaws and children cleared away the remains of the feast to one side of the lodge, where they held a sociable *tête-à-tête* over the fragments. After the pipes were extinguished all agreed to have a frolic shooting at a mark, which occupied the remainder of the day.

CHAPTER 29

Solitary Hunting Bouts in the Early Spring of 1841

January 1st—The ground was still bare but the weather cold and the fresh water streams shut up with ice. On the 3rd we moved camp up the stream to the foot of the mountain, where the stream forked. The right was called Weaver's Fork and the left Ogden's, both coming through the mountain in a deep narrow cut. The mountain was very high, steep and rugged. Rising abruptly from the plain about the foot of it were small rolling hills abounding with springs of fresh water. The land bordering on the river and along the stream was a rich, black, alluvial deposit, but the high land was gravelly and covered with wild sage, with here and there a growth of scrubby oaks and red cedars.

On the 10th I started to hunt elk by myself, intending to stop out two or three nights. I travelled up Weaver's Fork in a south-easterly direction through the mountains. The route was very difficult and in many places hard travelling over high points of rocks and around huge precipices, on a trail just wide enough for a single horse to walk. In about ten miles I came into a small plain five or six miles in circumference, just as the sun was setting. Here I stopped for the night. The snow being about five inches deep and the weather cold I made a large fire. As I had not killed any game during the day, I had no supper at night, but I had a blanket, horse to ride and a good rifle with plenty of ammunition and I was not in much danger of suffering by hunger, cold or fatigue, so I wrapped myself in my blanket and laid down on some dry grass I had collected before the fire. About an hour after dark it clouded up and began to snow, but as I was under some large trees it did not trouble me much and I soon fell asleep.

At daylight it was still snowing very fast and about eight inches had fallen during the night. I saddled my horse and started in a northerly direction over high, rolling hills covered with scrubby oaks, quaking asps and maples, for about ten miles, where I came into a smooth valley about twenty miles in circumference, called "Ogden's Hole," with the fork of the same name running through it. Here the snow was about fifteen inches deep on the level.

Towards night the weather cleared up and I discovered a band of about 100 elk on the hill among the shrubbery. I approached and killed a very fat old doe, which I butchered and packed the meat and skin on my horse to an open spring about a quarter of a mile distant, where I found plenty of dry wood and where I stopped for the night. I had now a good appetite for supper. After eating I scraped away the snow on one side of the fire, spread down the raw elk hide and laid down, covering myself with my blanket. In the morning when I awoke it was still snowing, and after eating breakfast I packed the meat on my horse and started on foot, leading him by the bridle.

Knowing it was impossible to follow down this stream to the plains with a horse, I kept along the foot of the mountain in a northerly direction for about two miles, then turning to the left into a steep ravine began to ascend, winding my way up through the snow, which grew deeper as I ascended. I reached the summit in about three hours. In many places I was obliged to break a trail for my horse. I descended the mountain west to the plains with comparative ease and reached the camp about dark. On arriving at the lodge I entered and sat down before a large, blazing fire. My landlady soon unloaded my horse and turned him loose and then prepared supper, with a good dish of coffee, whilst I, as a matter of course, related the particulars of the hunt. We staid at this place during the remainder of January. The weather was very cold and the snow about twelve inches deep, but I passed the time agreeably hunting elk among the timber in fair weather and amusing myself with books in foul.

The 2nd day of February I took a trip up the mountain to hunt sheep. I ascended a spur with my horse, sometimes riding and then walking, until near the top, where I found a level bench where the wind had blown the snow off. I fastened my horse with a long cord and took along the side of the mountain among the broken crags to see what the chances were for supper. I had not rambled far when, just as the sun was sinking below the dark green waters of the Salt Lake, I discovered three rams about 300 feet perpendicular below me. I shot and killed one of them, but it being so late and the precipice so bad, I concluded to sleep without supper rather than to go after it.

I returned to my horse and built a large fire with fragments of dry sugar maple which I found scattered about on the mountain, having for shelter from the wind a huge piece of coarse sand stone of which the mountain was composed. The air was calm, serene and cold, and the stars shone with an uncommon brightness. After sleeping till midnight I arose and renewed the fire. My horse was continually walking backward and forward to keep from freezing. I was upwards of 6000 feet above the level of the lake. Below me was a dark abyss, silent as the night of death.

I sat and smoked my pipe for about an hour and then laid down and slept until near daylight. My chief object in sleeping at this place was to take a view of the lake when the sun rose in the morning. This range of mountains laid nearly north and south and approached the lake irregularly within from three to ten miles. About eight miles from the southeast shore stood an island about twenty-five miles long and six wide, having the appearance of a low mountain extending north and south and arising 300 or 400 feet above the water. To the north of this about eight miles arose another island, apparently half the size of the first. North of these about six miles and about half way between rose another about six miles in circumference, which appeared to be a mass of basaltic rock with a few scrubby cedars standing about in the cliffs. The others appeared to be clothed with grass and wild sage, but no wood except a few bushes. Near the western horizon arose a small white peak just appearing above the water, which I supposed to be the mountain near the west shore.

On the north side a high promontory about six miles wide and ten miles long projected into the lake, covered with grass and scattered cedars. On the south shore rose a vast pile of huge, rough mountains, which I could faintly discern through the dense atmosphere. The water of the lake was too much impregnated with salt to freeze any, even about the shores. About sun an hour high I commenced hunting among the rocks in search of sheep, but did not get a chance to shoot at any till the middle of the afternoon, when crawling cautiously over some shelving cliffs, I discovered ten or twelve ewes feeding some distance below me. I shot and wounded one, reloaded my rifle and crept down to the place I last saw her, when I discovered two standing on; the side of a precipice. I shot one through the head and she fell dead on the cliff where she had been standing. I then went above and fastened a cord (which I carried for the purpose) to some bushes which overhung the rock.

By this means I descended and rolled her off the cliff where she had caught, and her body fell upwards of 100 feet. I then pulled myself up by the cord and went around the rock down to where she fell, butchered her, hung the meat on a tree, then pursued and killed the other. After butchering the last I took some of the meat for my supper and started up the mountain and arrived at the place where; I had slept about an hour after dark. I soon had a fire blazing and a side of ribs roasting, and procured water by heating stones and melting snow in a piece of skin. By the time supper was over it was late in the night, and I lay down and slept till morning. At sunrise I started on foot to get my meat and left my rifle about half way down the mountain.

When I came to where the first sheep had been hung in a tree I discovered a large wolverine sitting at the foot of it. I then regretted leaving my rifle, but it was too late, he saw me and took to his heels, as well he might, for he had left nothing behind worth stopping for. All the traces of the sheep I could find were some tufts of hair scattered about the snow. I hunted around for some time, but to no purpose. In the meantime the curious thief was sitting on the snow at some distance, watching my movements as if he was confident I had no gun and could not find his meat, and wished to aggravate me by his antics. He had made roads in every direction from the foot of the tree, dug holes in the snow in a hundred places apparently to deceive me. I soon got over my ill humour and gave up that a wolverine had fooled a Yankee.

I went to the other sheep and found all safe; carried the meat to my horse, mounted and went to camp.

February 15th—The weather began to moderate and rain and on the 23rd the ground was bare about the mountain.

CHAPTER 30

A Visit to the Eutaw Indian Village

February 24th—I left the camp with a determination to go to the Eutaw village at the southeast extremity of the lake to trade furs. I travelled along the foot of the mountain about ten miles, when I stopped and deposited in the ground such articles as I did not wish to take with me. The next day I travelled along the foot of the mountain south, about thirty miles, and encamped on a small spring branch which ran a distance of four miles from the mountain to the lake. This was a beautiful and fertile valley, intersected by large numbers of fine springs which flowed from the mountain to the lake and could, with little labour and expense, be made to irrigate the whole valley. The following day I travelled about fifteen miles along the lake, where a valley opened to my view, stretching to the southeast about forty miles and upward of fifteen miles wide.

At the further extremity of this valley laid Trinpannah or Eutaw Lake, composed of fresh water, about sixty miles in circumference. The outlet of it was a stream about thirty yards wide, which, after cutting this valley through the middle, emptied into the Salt Lake. I left the lake and travelled up this valley over smooth ground which the snow had long since deserted and the green grass and herbage were fast supplying its place. After crossing several small streams which intersected this vale, I arrived at the village, rode up to a lodge, and asked of a young Indian who met me where Want-a-Sheep's lodge was; but before he could reply a tall Indian, very dark complexion, with a thin visage and a keen, piercing eye, having his buffalo robe thrown carelessly over his left shoulder, gathered in folds around his waist and loosely held by his left hand, stepped forth and answered in the Snake tongue, "I am Want-a-Sheep, follow me," at the same time turning round and directing his course to a large, white lodge.

I rode to the door, dismounted and followed him in. He immediately ordered my horses to be unsaddled and turned loose to feed, whilst their loads were carefully arranged in the lodge. After the big pipe had gone around several times in silence, he began the conversation. I was asked the news, where travelling, for what, whom and how. I replied to these general inquiries in the Snake tongue, which was understood by all in the lodge. He then gave me an extract of all he had seen, heard and done for ten years past. He had two sons and one daughter grown to man and womanhood and the same number of less size. His oldest son was married to a Snake squaw and his daughter to a man of the same nation. The others yet remained single. After supper was over the females retired from the lodge and the principal men assembled to smoke and hear the news, which occupied the time till near midnight, when the assembly broke up, the men retiring to their respective lodges, and the women returned. I passed the time as pleasantly at this place as I ever did among the Indians.

In the daytime I rode about the valley hunting wild fowl, which, at this season of the year, rend the air with their cries during the night. The old chief would amuse me with traditional tales, mixed with the grossest superstition, some of which were not unlike the manners of ancient Israelites. There seems to be happiness in ignorance which knowledge and science destroys. Here was a nation of people contented and happy. They had fine horses and lodges and were very partial to the rifles of the white man. If a Eutaw had eight or ten good horses, a rifle and ammunition, he was contented. If he brought a deer at night from the hunt, joy beamed in the faces of his wife and children and if he returned empty a frown was not seen on the faces of his companions. The buffalo I had long since left the shores of these lakes and the hostile Blackfeet had not left a footprint here for many years.

During my stay with these Indians I tried to gain some information respecting the southern extremity of the Salt Lake, but all that I could learn was that it was a sterile, barren, mountainous country, inhabited by a race of depraved and hostile savages who poisoned their arrows and hindered the exploring of the country.

The chief's son informed me he had come from the largest island in the lake a few days previous, having passed the winter upon it with his family, which he had conveyed back and forth on a raft of bulrushes about twelve feet square. He said there were large numbers of antelope on the island, and as there was no wood, he had used wild sage for fuel. The old chief told me he could recollect the time when the buffalo passed from the mainland to the island without swimming, and that the depth of the waters was yearly increasing. After obtaining all the furs I could from the Eutaws, I started toward Fort Hall on the 27th of March and travelled along the borders of the lake about twenty-five miles. The fire had run over this part of the country the previous autumn and consumed the dry grass. The new had sprung up to the height of six inches, intermingled with various kinds of flowers in full bloom. The shores of the lake were swarming with water fowl of every species that inhabit inland lakes.

CHAPTER 31

Old Partners Reunite

The next day I went on to Weaver's River. April 1st I left Weaver's River and travelled along to the northeast extremity of the lake, about twenty-five miles. The next day I went on to Bear River and struck it about fifteen miles below Cache valley and twelve miles from the mouth. There I found my winter comrades and staid one night and then pursued my journey toward Fort Hall, where I arrived on the 7th of April.

I hunted beaver around the country near the fort until the 15th of June, when the party arrived from the Columbia River, accompanied by a Presbyterian missionary with his wife and one child, on their way to the States. I left the fort with them and conducted them to Green River, where we arrived on the 5th of July. On learning that no party was going to the States, they concluded to return to the Columbia River, and we retraced our steps to Fort Hall, where we arrived on the 8th day of August.

I remained at the fort until the 15th of September, and then started with Elbridge and my old comrade from Vermont to hunt a few more beaver. We went to the headwaters of Blackfoot, where we staid ten days and then crossed the mountain in a southwest direction on to Bear River, which we struck about twenty-five miles below the Snake Lake. We continued hunting beaver and antelope between this place and the Soda Springs until the 10th of October. We then travelled down Bear River to Cache valley, where we stopped until the 21st, then we followed down the river near where it empties into the Salt Lake. Along the bank of this stream for about ten miles from the lake extends a barren, clay flat, destitute of vegetation excepting a few willows along the bank of the river and scattering spots of salt grass and sage. In one place there was about four or five acres covered about four inches deep with the most beautiful salt I have ever seen. Two crusts had formed, one at the bottom and the other on the top, which has protected it from being the least bit soiled. Between those crusts the salt was completely dry, loose and composed of very small grains of a snowy whiteness.

We stopped about this place until the 5th of November and then returned to Fort Hall, where, after remaining a few days, we concluded to go on to the head streams of Portneuf and stop until the waters froze up. We travelled up about forty miles and arranged an encampment in a beautiful valley, as the weather began to grow cold.

In the year 1836 large bands of buffalo could be seen in almost every little valley on the small branches of this stream. At this time the only traces of them which could be seen were the scattered bones of those which had been killed. Their deeply indented trails which had been made in former years were overgrown with grass and weeds. The trappers often remarked to each other as they rode over these lonely plains that it was time for the white man to leave the mountains, as beaver and game had nearly disappeared. On the 15th of November I started up a high mountain in search of sheep. After hunting and scrambling over the rocks for half a day without seeing any traces of sheep I sat down upon a rock which overlooked the country below me. At length, casting a glance along the south side of the mountain, I discovered a large grizzly bear sitting at the mouth of his den. I approached within about 180 paces, shot and missed him. He looked around and crept slowly into his den.

I reloaded my rifle, went up to the hole and threw down a stone weighing five or six pounds, which soon rattled to the bottom and I heard no more. I then rolled a stone weighing 300 or 400 pounds into the den, stepped back two or three steps and prepared myself for the outcome. The stone had scarcely reached the bottom when the bear came rushing out, with his mouth wide open, and was on the point of making a spring at me when I pulled trigger and shot him through the left shoulder, which sent him rolling down the mountain. It being near night, I butchered him and left the meat lying and returned to camp. The next day I took the meat to camp, where we salted and smoked it, ready for winter's use.

We stopped about on these streams until the 15th of December, then returned to Fort Hall, where we staid until the 24th of March. The winter was unusually severe. The snow was fifteen inches deep over the valley after settling and becoming hard. We had no thawing weather until the 18th of March, when it began to rain and continued for four days and nights, which drove the snow nearly all from the plains.

CHAPTER 32

Closing Incidents of an Interesting Experience

March 25th—I started, in company with Alfred Shutes, my old comrade from Vermont, to go to the Salt Lake and pass the spring hunting water fowl, eggs and beaver. We left the fort and travelled in a southerly direction to the mountain, about thirty miles. The next day we travelled south about fifteen miles through a low defile and the day following we crossed the divide and fell on to a stream called "*Malade*" or Sick River, which empties into Bear River about ten miles from the mouth. This stream takes its name from the beaver which inhabit it living on poison roots. Those who eat their meat become sick at the stomach in a few hours and the whole system is filled with cramps and severe pains, but I have never known or heard of a person dying with the disease. We arrived at the mouth of Bear River on the 2nd of April.

Here we found the ground dry, the grass green and myriads of swans, geese, brants and ducks, which kept up a continual hum day and night, assisted by the uncouth notes of the sand hill cranes. The geese, ducks and swans are very fat at this season of the year. We caught some few beaver and feasted on fowls and eggs until the 20th of May and returned to the fort, where we stopped until the 20th of June, when a small party arrived from the mouth of the Columbia River on their way to the United States, and my comrade made up his mind once more to visit his native Green Mountains, after an absence of sixteen years, while I determined on going to the mouth of the Columbia and settle myself in the Willamette or Multnomah valley.

I accompanied my comrade up Ross Fork about twenty-five miles on his journey and the next morning, after taking an affectionate leave of each other, I started to the mountains for the purpose of killing elk and drying meat for my journey to the Willamette valley. I ascended to the top of Ross mountain (on which the snows remain till the latter part of August), sat down under a pine and took a last farewell view of a country over which I had travelled so often under such a variety of circumstances. The recollections of the past, connected with the scenery now spread out before me, put me somewhat in a poetical humour, and for the first time I attempted to frame my thoughts into rhyme, but if poets will forgive me for this intrusion I shall be cautious about trespassing on their grounds in future.

In the evening I killed an elk and on the following day cured the meat for packing. From thence I returned to the fort, where I staid till the 22nd of August.

In the meantime there arrived at the fort a party of emigrants from the States, on their way to the Oregon country, among whom was Dr. E. White, United States sub-agent for the Oregon Indians.

23rd—I started with them and arrived at the falls of the Willamette river on the 26th day of September, 1842.

It would be natural for me to suppose that after escaping all the dangers attendant upon nearly nine years' residence in a wild, inhospitable region like the Rocky Mountains, where I was daily, and a great part of the time, hourly, anticipating danger from hostile savages and other sources, I should, on arriving in a civilized and an enlightened community, live in comparative security, free from the harassing intrigues of Dame Fortune's eldest daughter, but I found it was all a delusion, for danger is not always the greatest when most apparent, as will appear in the sequel.

On arriving at the Falls of the Willamette, I found a number of Methodist missionaries and American farmers had formed themselves into a company for the purpose of erecting mills and a sawmill was then building on an island standing on the brink of the falls, which went into operation about two months after I arrived. In the meantime, Dr. John McLoughlin, a chief factor of the Hudson Bay Company, who contemplated leaving the service of the company and permanently settling with his family and fortune in the Willamette valley, laid off a town (the present Oregon City) on the east side of the falls and began erecting a sawmill on a site he had prepared some years previous by cutting a race through the rock to let the water on to his works when they should be constructed.

The following spring the American company commenced building a flour mill and I was employed to assist in its construction. On the 6th day of June I was engaged with the contractor in blasting some points of rock in order to sink the water sill to its proper place, when a blast exploded accidentally by the concussion of small particles of rock near the powder, a piece of rock weighing about sixty pounds struck me on the right side of the face and knocked me, senseless, six feet backward.

I recovered my senses in a few minutes and was assisted to walk to my lodgings. Nine particles of rock of the size of wild goose shot each had penetrated my right eye and destroyed it forever. The contractor escaped with the loss of two fingers of his left hand.

The Hunter's Farewell

Adieu, ye hoary, icy-mantled towers, .
That oft-times pierce the onward fleeting mists,
Whose feet are washed by gentle summer showers.
While Phoebus' rays play on your sparkling crests;
The smooth, green vales you seem prepared to guard,
Beset with groves of ever-verdant pine.
Would furnish themes for Albion's noble bards,
Far 'bove a hunter's rude, unvarnish'd rhyme.

Adieu, ye flocks that skirt the mountain's brow
And sport on banks of everlasting snow.
Ye timid lambs and simple, harmless ewes.
Who fearless view the dread abyss below;
Oft have I watched your seeming mad career
While lightly tripping o'er those dismal heights,
Or cliffs o'erhanging yawning caverns drear.
Where none else tread save fowls of airy flight.

Oft have I climbed these rough, stupendous rocks
In search of food 'mongst Nature's well-fed herds.
Until I've gained the rugged mountain's top.
Where Boreas reigned or feathered monarch soar'd;
On some rude crag projecting from the ground
I've sat a while my wearied limbs to rest.
And scanned the unsuspecting flocks around
With anxious care selecting out the best.

The prize obtained, with slow and heavy step
Pac'd down the steep and narrow winding path.

To some smooth vale where crystal streamlets met,
And skilful hands prepared a rich repast;
Then hunters' jokes and merry humour'd sport
Beguiled the time, enlivened every face.
The hours flew fast and seemed like moments, short,
'Til twinkling planets told of midnight's pace.
But now those scenes of cheerful mirth are done,
The antlered herds are dwindling very fast,
The numerous trails so deep by bison worn,
Now teem with weeds or overgrown with grass;
A few gaunt wolves now scattered o'er the place
Where herds, since time unknown to man, have fed.
With lonely howls and sluggish, onward pace,
Tell their sad fate and where their bones are laid.
Ye rugged mounts, ye vales, ye streams and trees.
To you a hunter bids his last farewell,
I'm bound for shores of distant western seas.
To view far-famed Multnomah's fertile vale;
I'll leave these regions, once famed hunting grounds.
Which I, perhaps, again shall see no more.
And follow down, led by the setting sun.
Or distant sound of proud Columbia's roar.
June 22, 1842.   —Osborne Russell.

Appendix

It has been my design whilst keeping a journal to note down the principal circumstances which came under my immediate observation as I passed along, and I have mostly deferred giving a general description of Indians and animals that inhabit the Rocky Mountains until the last end in order that I might be able to put the information I have collected in a more compact form. I have been very careful in gathering information from the most intelligent Indians and experienced white hunters, but have excluded from this journal such parts (with few exceptions) as I have not proved true by experience. I am fully aware of the numerous statements which have been given to travelers in a jocular manner by the hunters and traders among the Rocky Mountains, merely to hear themselves talk, or according to the mountaineers' expression, give them a long yarn or "fish story" to put in their journals, and I have frequently seen those "fish stories" published with the original very much enlarged which had not at first the slightest ground for truth to rest upon. It is utterly impossible for a person who is merely travelling through or even residing one or two years in the Rocky Mountains to give an accurate description of the country or its inhabitants.

I have never known but one Rocky Mountaineer to keep a regular journal, and he could not have visited the northern part of them, as I am confident his compiler (Mr. Flint) would not knowingly be led into such errors as occur in James O'Pattie's *Journal*, both in regard to the location of the country and Indians inhabiting the northern section of it. He says, "The Flathead nation of Indians flatten their heads and live between the Platte and Yellowstone Rivers," which is not nor ever was the case in either instance. He also says that Lewis River and the Arkansas head near each other in Long's Peak. I never was at Long's Peak or the head of the Arkansas River, but am fully confident can be within 300 miles of the source of Lewis River. These are among the numerous errors which I discovered in reading James O'Pattie's *Journal*, embellished by Mr. Flint of Cincinnati. These are among the reasons for which I offer this to public view, hoping that it not only may be of interest to myself but the means of correcting some erroneous statements which have gone forth to the world, unintentionally perhaps by their authors.

The Wolverine, Carcajou or Glutton

This species of animal is very numerous in the Rocky Mountains and very mischievous and annoying to the hunters. They often get into the traps setting for beaver or search out the deposits of meat which the weary hunter has made during a toilsome day's hunt among mountains too rugged and remote for him to bear the reward of his labours to the place of encampment, and when finding these deposits the *carcajou* carries off all or as much of the contents as he is able, secreting it in different places among the snow, rock or bushes in such a manner that it is very difficult for man or beast to find it. The avaricious disposition of this animal has given rise to the name of glutton by naturalists, who suppose that it devours so much at a time as to render it stupid and incapable of moving or running about, but I have never seen an instance of this kind; on the contrary I have seen them quite expert and nimble immediately after having carried away four to five times their weight in meat. I have good reason to believe that, the *carcajou's* appetite is easily satisfied upon meat freshly killed, but after it becomes putrid it may become more voracious, but I never saw one myself or a person who had seen one in a stupid, dormant state caused by glutting, although I have often wished it were the case.

The body is thick and long, the legs short, the feet and claws are longer in proportion than those of the black bear, which it very much resembles, with the exception of its tail, which is twelve inches long and bushy. Its body is about three feet long and stands fifteen inches high; its colour is black excepting the sides, which are of a dirty white or light brown.

Its movements are somewhat quicker than those of the bear and it climbs trees with ease. I have never known, either by experience or information, the *carcajou* to prey upon animals of its own killing larger than very young fawns or lambs, although it has been described by naturalists and generally believed that it climbs trees and leaps down upon elk, deer and other large animals and clings to their back till it kills them in spite of their efforts to get rid of it by speed or resistance, but we need go no further than the formation of the animal to prove those statements erroneous. Its body, legs, feet and mouth are shaped similarly to the black bear, as has been already stated, but its claws are somewhat longer and stronger in proportion, and like the bear, its claws are somewhat blunted at the points, which would render it impossible for them to cling to the back of an elk or deer while running. I do not pretend to say, however, what may be its habits in other countries, I only write from experience. They do not den up like the bear in winter, but ramble about the streams among the high mountains, where they find springs open. Its hair is three inches long and in the summer is coarse like the bear, but winter it is near as fine as that of the red fox. The female brings forth its young in April and generally brings two at a birth.

The Wolf

Of this species of animal there are several kinds, as the buffalo wolf, the big prairie wolf and the small prairie or medicine wolf. The buffalo wolf is from two to three feet high and from four to five feet long from the tip of his nose to the insertion of the tail. Its hair is long, coarse and shaggy. Its colour varies from a dark grey to a snowy whiteness. They are not ferocious toward man and will run at the sight of him. The big prairie wolf is two feet high and three and a half feet long; its hair is long and shaggy, its colour is a dirty grey, often inclining to a brown or brindle. The least known is little prairie or medicine wolf. Its size is somewhat larger than the red fox; its colour is brownish grey and its species something between the big wolf and the fox. The Indians are very superstitious about this animal. When it comes near a village and barks they say there is people near. Some pretend to distinguish between its warning the approach of friends or enemies and in the latter case I have often seen them secure their horses and prepare themselves to fight. I have often seen this prophecy tolerably accurately fulfilled and again I have as often seen it fail, but a superstitious Indian will always account for the failure.

The habits of these three kinds of wolves are similar. Their rutting season is in March. The female brings forth from two to six at a birth.

The Panther

This animal is rarely seen in the plains, but confines itself to the more woody and mountainous districts. Its colour is light brown on the back and the belly is a sort of ash colour; its length is five feet from the tip of the nose to the insertion of the tail, which is about one-half the length of the body. It is very destructive on sheep and other animals that live in the high mountains, but will run at the sight of a man and has a great antipathy to fire.

The Marmot

This animal inhabits the rocks and precipices of the highest mountains. Its colour is a dark brown, its size less than the smallest rabbit; its ears and paws are shaped like those of the rat, and its cry resembles that of the bleating of the young lambs. During the summer it collects large quantities of hay and mud with which it secures its habitation from the cold during the winter. On my first acquaintance with this animal I was led to suppose that the hay which they accumulate in summer was calculated to supply them with food during the winter, but this I found to be erroneous by visiting their habitation in the early part of spring and finding their stock in nowise diminished. I have good reason to suppose that they lie dormant during the winter.

The Porcupine

This species of animal is too well known to need a minute description in this place. They are, however, very numerous and their flesh is much esteemed by some of the Indian tribes for food, and their quills are held in the highest estimation by all for embroidering their dresses, and other functions, which is done with peculiar elegance and uncommon skill. It subsists chiefly on the bark of trees and other vegetables.

The Badger

This species of animal are numerous in the Rocky Mountains. Their skins are much used by the Snake and Bannock Indians for clothing, as well as their flesh for food. They make their habitation in the ground in the most extensive plains and are found ten miles from water.

The Ground Hog

These animals are also very numerous and their skins much used by the Indians for clothing in sections of country where deer and buffalo are not to be found. They are not so large as the ground hog of the United States, but are in all respects the same species. They live among the rocks near streams and feed upon grass and other vegetables. The shrill cry with which their sentinels give warning of danger resembles that of the United States species.

THE GRIZZLY BEAR

Much has been said by travellers in regard to this animal, yet while giving a description of animals that inhabit the Rocky Mountains, I do not feel justified in simply passing over in silence the most ferocious species without undertaking to contribute some little information respecting it which, although it may not be important, I hope some of it at least will be new. It lives chiefly upon roots and berries, being of too slow a nature to live much upon game of its own killing, and from May to September it never tastes flesh. The rutting season is in November and the female brings forth from one to three at a birth. I have not been able to ascertain the precise time that the female goes with young, but I suppose from experience and inquiry it is about fourteen weeks. The young are untameable and manifest a savage ferocity when scarcely old enough to crawl. Several experiments have been tried in the Rocky Mountains for taming them, but to no effect. They are possessed of great muscular strength. I have seen a female, which was wounded by a rifle ball in the loins so as to disable her, kill her young with one stroke of her forepaws as fast as they approached her.

If a young cub is wounded and commences making a noise, the mother invariably springs upon it and kills it. When grown they never make a noise except a fearful growl. They get to be fatter than any other animals in the Rocky Mountains during the season when wild fruit is abundant. The flesh of the grizzly bear is preferable to pork. It lives in winter in caves in the rocks or holes dug in the ground on high ridges. It loses no flesh while confined to its den during the winter, but is equally as fat in the spring when it leaves the den as when it enters it at the beginning of the winter. There is seldom to be found more than one in a den excepting the female and her young. I have seen them measure seven feet from the tip of the nose to the insertion of the tail. It will generally run from the scent of a man, but when it does not get the scent it will often let him approach close enough to spring on him and when wounded it is a dangerous animal to trifle with. Its speed is comparatively slow down hill but much greater in ascending. It never climbs trees, as its claws are too straight for that purpose.

The Black Bear

The black bear of the mountains are much the same species as those of the States. In comparison with the grizzly it is entirely harmless. It is seldom found in the plains, but inhabits the timbered and mountainous districts. They are not very numerous and their habits are too well known to need a detailed description here.

The Mountain Sheep or Big Horn

These animals answer somewhat to the description given by naturalists of the musmon or wild sheep which are natives of Greece, Corsica and Tartary. The male and female very much resemble the domestic ram and ewe, but are much larger. The horns of the male are much larger in proportion to the body than the domestic rams, but those of the females are almost in the same proportion to the domestic ewe. In the month of May, after they have shed their old coat and the new one appears, their colour is dark blue or mouse colour, except the extremity of the rump and hinder parts of the thighs, which are white. As the season advances and the hair grows long it gradually turns or fades to a dirty brown.

In the month of December the hair is about three inches long, thickly matted together, rendering it impenetrable to the cold. Its hair is similar in texture to that of the deer, and like the latter it is short and smooth upon its forehead and legs. They inhabit the highest and most craggy mountains and never descend to the plains unless compelled by necessity. In the winter season the snow drives them down to the low craggy mountains facing the south, but in the spring as the snow begins to recede they follow it, keeping close to where the grass is short and tender. Its speed on the smooth ground is slower than the deer, but in climbing steep rocks or precipices it is almost incredible, insomuch that the wolf, lynx and panther give up the chase whenever the sheep reach the rugged crags.

The fearful height from which it jumps and the small points on which it alights without slipping or missing its footing is astonishing to its pursuers, whether man or beast. Its hoofs are very hard and pointed and it reposes upon the most bleak points of rock both in summer and winter. The male is a noble looking animal as he stands upon an elevated point with his large horns curling around his ears like the coil of a serpent, and his head held proudly erect, disdaining the lower regions and its inhabitants. Its flesh has a similar taste to mutton, but its flavour is more agreeable and the meat more juicy.

Their rutting season is in November, when the rams have furious battles with each other in the same manner as the domestic rams. The victor often knocks his opponent over a high precipice when he is dashed to pieces in the fall. The sound of their heads coming in contact is often heard a mile distant.

The female produces from one to three at a birth. The lambs are of a whitish colour, very innocent and playful. Hunting sheep is often attended with great danger, especially in the winter season, when the rocks and precipices are covered with snow and ice, but the excitement created by hunting them often enables the hunter to surmount obstacles which at other times would seem impossible. The skins, when dressed are finer, softer and far superior to those of the deer for clothing. It is of them that the squaws make their dresses which they embroider with beads and porcupine quills dyed with various colours, which are wrought into figures displaying a tolerable degree of taste and ingenuity.

The Gazelle or Mountain Antelope

This animal, for beauty and fleetness, surpasses all the ruminating animals of the Rocky Mountains. Its body is rather smaller than the common deer; its colour on the back and upper part of the sides is light brown, the hinder part of the thighs and belly are white, the latter having a yellowish cast. The under part of the neck is white with several black stripes running across the throat down to the breast. Its legs are very slim, neat and small. Its ears are black on the inside and around the edges with the remainder brown. Its horns are also black and flattened; the horns of the males are much longer than those of the females, but formed in the same manner; they project up about eight inches on the males and then divide into two branches, the one inclining backward and the other forward with sometimes an additional branch coming out near the head inclining inward.

The two upper branches are six inches long, the hindermost forming a sort of hook. The nose is black and a strip of the same colour runs round under the eyes and terminates under the ears. It runs remarkably smooth and in the summer season the fleetest horses but rarely overtake it. Its natural walk is stately and elegant, but it is very timid and fearful and can see to a great distance, but with all its timidity and swiftness of foot its curiosity often leads it to destruction. If it discovers anything of a strange appearance (particularly anything red) it goes direct to it and will often approach within thirty paces. They are very numerous in the plains, but seldom found among timber. Their flesh is similar to venison. The female produces two at a birth and the young are suckled until a month old. They are easily domesticated.

The Black-Tailed Deer

This animal is somewhat larger than the common deer of the United States. Its ears are very long, from which it has derived the appellation of mule deer. Its colour in summer is red, but in the latter part of August its hair turns to a deep blue ground with about half an inch of white on each hair one-fourth inch from the outer ends, which presents a beautiful grey colour. It lives among the mountains and seldom descends among the plains. Its flesh is similar in every respect to the common deer. The tail is about six inches long and the hair upon it smooth except upon the end, where there is a small tuft of black. The female goes six months with young and generally produces two at a birth. The young is brought forth in April and remains in an almost helpless state for one month. During its state of inability the mother secretes it in some secure place in the long grass and weeds, where it remains contented while she often wanders half a mile from it in search of food.

The colour of the fawn is red intermingled with white spots, and it is generally believed by Indians that so long as those spots remain (which is about two and one-half months) that no beast of prey can scent them. This I am inclined to believe, as I have often seen wolves pass very near the place where fawns were lying without stopping or altering their course, and were it not for some secret provision of nature, the total annihilation of this species of animal would be inevitable in those countries infested by wolves and other beasts of prey as in the Rocky Mountains. This safeguard is given by the Great Founder of Nature, not only to the black tailed deer but all of the species, including elk and antelope, whose young are so spotted at their birth. I do not consider that the mere white spots are a remedy against their scent of wild beasts, but they mark the period of inability, for when these disappear the little animals are capable of eluding their pursuers by flight. The male, like the common deer, drops its horns in February. It then cannot be distinguished from the former except by its larger size.

The Rabbit

This species of animal is very numerous and various in their sizes and colours. The large hares of the plains are very numerous, the common sized rabbits are equally or more numerous than the others, and there is also the small brown rabbit which does not change its colour during the winter season as do the others, but the most singular kind is the black rabbit. It is a native of mountainous forests. Its colour is coal black excepting two small white spots which are on the throat and lower part of the belly. In winter its colour is milk white. Its body is about the size of the common rabbit with the exception of its ears, which are much longer. Another kind is the black-tailed rabbit of the plains. It is rather larger than the common rabbit and derives its name from the colour of its tail, which never changes its colour.

The Elk

This animal is eight feet long from the tip of the nose to the insertion of the tail, and stands four and one-half feet high. Its proportions are similar to those of the deer, except the tail, which is four inches long and composed of a black gummy substance intermingled with fibers around the bone, the whole being clothed with skin and covered with hair like the body. Its colour in summer is red but in winter is a brownish grey except the throat and belly, the former being dark brown and the latter white inclining to yellow, extending to the hind part of the thighs as far as the insertion of the tail. They are very timid and harmless even when so disabled as to render escape impossible. Its speed is very swift when running single, but when running in large bands they soon become wearied by continual collision with each other, and if they are closely pressed by the hunter on horseback they soon commence dropping down flat on the ground to elude their pursuers and will suffer themselves to be killed with a knife in this position.

When the band is first located the hunters keep at some distance behind to avoid dispersing them, and to frighten them the more a continual noise is kept up by halloing and shooting over them, which causes immediate confusion and collision of the band and the weakest elk soon begin to fall to the ground exhausted. Their rutting time is in September, when they collect in immense bands among the timber along the streams and among the mountains. It has been stated by naturalists that the male is a very formidable and dangerous animal when pursued, but I never saw it act on the offensive, neither have I ever known one to offer resistance in defence of itself against man otherwise than by involuntary motions of its head or feet when too much disabled to rise from the ground. I have often seen the female come about the hunter who has found where her young is secreted uttering the most pitiful and persuasive moans and pleading in the most earnest manner that a dumb brute is capable of for the life of her young. This mode of persuasion would, I think, excite sympathy in the breast of any human that was not entirely destitute of the passion. The fawn has a peculiar cry after it is able to run which resembles the first scream of a child, by which it answers the dam, who calls it by a note similar to the scream of a woman in distress.

In the month of September the males have a peculiar shrill call which commences in a piercing whistle and ends in a coarse gurgling in the throat. By this they call the females to assemble and each other to the combat, in which by their long antlers they are rendered formidable to each other. The hair stands erect and the head is lowered to give or receive the attack, but the victor seldom pursues the vanquished.

The Buffalo or Bison

This animal has been so minutely described by travellers that I have considered it of little importance to enter into the details of its shape and size, and shall therefore omit those descriptions with which I suppose the public to be already acquainted, and try to convey some idea of its peculiarities which probably are not so well known. The vast numbers of these animals which once traversed such an extensive region on North America are diminishing. The continued increasing demand for robes in the civilized world has already and is still contributing in no small degree to their destruction, whilst on the other hand the continued increase of wolves and other four-footed enemies far exceeds that of the buffaloes. When these combined efforts for their destruction are taken into consideration, it will not be doubted for a moment that this noble race of animals, so useful in supplying the wants of man, will at no far distant period become extinct in North America.

The buffalo is already a stranger, although so numerous ten years ago, (as at 1921), in that part of the country which is drained by the sources of the Colorado, Bear and Snake Rivers, and occupied by the Snake and Bannock Indians. The flesh of the buffalo cow is considered far superior to that of the domestic beef and it is so much impregnated with salt that it requires but little seasoning when cooked. All the time, trouble and care bestowed by man upon improving the breed and food of meat cattle seems to be entirely thrown away when we compare those animals in their original state which are reared upon the food supplied them by nature with the same species when domesticated and fed on cultivated grasses and grains, and the fact seems /to justify the opinion that nature will not allow herself to be outdone by art, for it is fairly proven in this enlightened age that the rude and untaught savage feasts on better beef and mutton than the most learned and experienced agriculturists. Now if every effect is produced by a cause, perhaps I may stumble upon the cause which produces the effect in this instance. At any rate I shall attempt it:

In the first place, the rutting season of the buffaloes is regular, commencing about the 15th of July when the males and females are fat, and ends about the 15th of August. Consequently the females bring forth their young in the latter part of April and the first of May, when the grass is most luxuriant and thereby enables the cow to afford the most nourishment for her calf and enables the young to quit the natural nourishment of its dam and feed upon the tender herbage sooner than it would at any other season of the year. Another proof is the fact that when the rutting season commences the strongest, healthiest and most vigorous bulls drive the weaker ones from the cows, hence the calves are from the best breed, which is thereby kept upon a regular basis. In the summer season they generally go to water and drink once in twenty-four hours, but in the winter they seldom get water at all.

The cows are fattest in October and the bulls in July. The cows retain their flesh in a great measure throughout the winter until the spring opens and they get at water, from whence they become poor in a short time. So much for the regularity of their habits, and the next point is the food on which they subsist. The grass on which the buffaloes generally feed is short, firm and of the most nutritious kind. The salts with which the mountain regions are impregnated are imbibed in a great degree by the vegetation and as there is very little rain in summer, autumn or winter, the grass arrives at maturity and dries in the sun without being cut it is made like hay; in this state it remains throughout the winter and while the spring rains are divesting the old growth of its nutritive qualities they are in the meantime pushing forward the new. The buffaloes are very particular in their choice of grass, always preferring the short of the uplands to that of the luxuriant growth of the fertile alluvial bottoms.

Thus they are taught by nature to choose such food as is most palatable and she has also provided that such as is most palatable is the best suited to their condition and that condition the best calculated to supply the wants and necessities of her rude, untutored children for whom they were prepared. Thus nature looks with a smile of derision upon the magnified efforts of art to excel her works by a continual breach of her laws. The most general mode practiced by Indians for killing buffalo is running upon horseback and shooting them with arrows, but it requires a degree of experience for both man and horse to kill them in this manner with any degree of safety, particularly in places where the ground is rocky and uneven.

The horse that is well trained for this purpose not only watches the ground over which he is running and avoids the holes, ditches and rocks by shortening or extending his leaps, but also the animal which he is pursuing in order to prevent being "homed" when 'tis brought suddenly to bay, which is done instantaneously, and if the buffalo wheel to the right the horse passes as quick as thought to the left behind it and thereby avoids its horns; but if the horse in close pursuit wheels on the same side with the buffalo he comes directly in contact with its horns and with one stroke the horse's entrails are often torn out and his rider thrown headlong to the ground. After the buffalo is brought to bay the trained horse will immediately commence describing a circle about ten paces from the animal in which he moves continuously in a slow gallop or trot which prevents the raging animal from making a direct bound at him by keeping it continuously turning around until it is killed by the rider with arrows or bullets.

If a hunter discovers a band of buffalo in a place too rough and broken for his horse to run with safety and there is smooth ground near by, he secretly rides on the leeward side as near as he can without being discovered. He then starts up suddenly without apparently noticing the buffalo and gallops in the direction he wishes the band to run. The buffalo, on seeing him run to the plain, start in the same direction in order to prevent themselves from being headed and kept from the smooth ground. The same course would be pursued if he wished to take them to any particular place in the mountains. One of the hunters' first instructions to an inexperienced hand is "run toward the place where you wish the buffalo to run but do not close on them behind until they get to that place."

For instance, if the hunter is to the right, the leading buffaloes keep inclining to the right and if he should fall in behind and crowd upon the rear they would separate in different directions and it would be a mere chance if any took the direction he wished them. When he gets to the plain he gives his horse the rein and darts through the band, selects his victim, reins his horse alongside and shoots, and if he considers the wound mortal, he pulls up the rein, the horse, knowing his business, keeps along galloping with the band until the rider has reloaded when he darts forward upon another buffalo as at first.

A cow seldom stops at bay after she is wounded, and therefore is not so dangerous as a bull, who wheels soon after he is pushed from the band and becomes fatigued, whether he is wounded or not. When running over ground where there is rocks, holes or gullies, the horse must be reined up gradually if he is reined at all. There is more accidents happen in running buffalo by the riders getting frightened and suddenly checking their horses than any other way. If they come upon a *coulee* which the horse can leap by an extra exertion the best plan is to give him the rein and the whip or spur at the same time and fear not, for any ditch that a buffalo can leap can be cleared with safety by a horse and one too wide for a buffalo to clear an experienced rider will generally see in time to check his horse gradually before he gets to it. And now, as I have finished my description of the buffaloes and the manner of killing them, I wish put a simple question for the reader's solution:

If kings, princes, nobles and gentlemen can derive so much sport and pleasure as they boast of in chasing a fox or simple hare all day, which when they have caught is of no use to them, what pleasure can the Rocky Mountain hunter be expected to derive in running with a well trained horse such a noble and stately animal as the bison, which when killed is of some service to him? There are men of noble birth, noble estates and noble minds who have attained to a tolerable degree of perfection in fox hunting in Europe and buffalo hunting in the Rocky Mountains, and I have heard some of them decide that the points would not bear a comparison if the word "fashion" could be stricken from the English language.

It also requires a considerable degree of practice to approach on foot and kill buffalo with a rifle. A person must be well acquainted with the shape and make of the animal and the manner in which it is standing in order to direct his aim with certainty. And it also requires experience to enable him to choose a fat animal. The best looking buffalo is not always the fattest and a hunter by constant practice may lay down rules for selecting the fattest when on foot which would be no guide to him when running upon horseback, for he is then placed in a different position and one which requires different rules for choosing.

The Beaver

The beaver, as almost everyone knows, is an amphibious animal, but the instinct with which it is possessed surpasses the reason of a no small portion of the human race. Its average size is about two and one-half feet long from the point of the nose to the insertion of the tail, which is from ten to fifteen inches long and from five to nine broad, flat in the shape of a spade rounded at the corners and covered with a thick, rough skin resembling scales. The tail serves the double purpose of steering and assisting it through the water by a quick up and down motion. The hind feet are webbed and the toe next the outside on each has a double nail which serves the purpose of a toothpick to extract the splinters of wood from their teeth. As they are the only animals that cut large trees for subsistence, they are also the only animals known to be furnished with nails so peculiarly adapted to the purpose for which they are used.

Its colour is of a light brown generally, but I have seen them of a jet black frequently, and in one instance I saw one of a light cream colour having the feet and tail white. The hair is of two sorts, the one longer and coarser, the other fine, short and silky. The teeth are like those of the rat but are longer and stronger in proportion to the size of the animals. To a superficial observer they have but one vent for their excrements and urine, but upon a closer examination without dissection separate openings will be seen, likewise four gland openings forward of the arms, two containing oil with which they oil their coats, the others containing the *castorium*, a collection of gummy substance of a yellow colour which is extracted from the food of the animal and conveyed through small vessels into the glands. It is this deposit which causes the destruction of the beaver by the hunters.

When a beaver, male or female, leaves the lodge to swim about their pond, they go to the bottom and fetch up some mud between their forepaws and breast, carry it on the bank and emit upon it a small quantity of *castorium*. Another beaver passing the place does the same, and should a hundred beaver pass within the scent of the place, they would each throw up mud covering up the old *castorium* and emit new upon that which they had thrown up. The trapper extracts this substance from the gland and carries it in a wooden box. He sets his trap in the water near the bank about six inches below the surface, throws a handful of mud upon the bank about one foot from it and puts a small portion of the *castorium* thereon.

After night the beaver comes out of his lodge, smells the fatal bait

200 or 300 yards distant and steers his course directly for it. He hastens to ascend the bank, but the trap grasps his foot and soon drowns him in the struggle to escape, for the beaver, though termed an amphibious animal, cannot respire beneath the water.

The female brings forth her young in April and produces from two to six at a birth, but what is most singular, she seldom raises but two, a male and a female. This peculiarity of the beaver has often been a matter of discussion among the most experienced of hunters, whether the dam or father kills the young, but I have come to the conclusion that it is the mother for the following reasons:

First, the male is seldom found about the lodge for ten or fifteen days after the female brings forth; second, there is always a male and female saved alive; third, I have seen the dead kittens floating in the ponds freshly killed and at the same time have caught the male when he was living more than one-half mile from the lodge. I have found, where beaver are confined to a limited space, they kill nearly all the kittens, which is supposed to be done to keep them from becoming too numerous and destroying the timber and undergrowth too fast. I have caught fifty full grown beaver in a valley surrounded by mountains and cascades where they had not been disturbed for four years and with this number there were but five or six kittens and yearlings.

The young ones pair off generally at three years of age to set up for themselves and proceed up or down a stream as instinct may suggest until they find the best place for wood and undergrowth connected with the most convenient place for building a dam, which is constructed by cutting small trees and brush, dragging them into the water on both sides of the stream, and attaching one end to each bank, while the other extends into the stream inclining upward against the current. Then mud, small stones and rubbish are dragged or pushed onto it to sink it to the bottom. They proceed in this manner till the two ends meet in the middle of the stream, the whole forming a sort of curved line across, but the water raising often forces the dam down the stream until it becomes nearly straight.

In the meantime they have selected a spot for the lodge either upon the bank or upon a small island formed by the rising water, but it is generally constructed on an island in the middle of the pond with sticks and mud in such a manner that when the water is raised sufficiently high, which generally is from four to seven feet, it has the appearance of a potash kettle turned on the surface bottom upwards, standing from four to six feet above the water. There is no opening above the water, but generally two below. The floor on which they sleep and have their beds of straw or grass, is about twelve inches above the water level. The room is arched over and kept neat and clean. When the leaves begin to fall, the beavers commence laying in their winter store. They often cut down trees from twelve to eighteen inches in diameter and cut off the branches covered with smooth bark into pieces from two to six feet long. These they drag into the water, float them to the lodge, sink them to the bottom of the pond, and there fasten them. In this manner they proceed until they have procured about half a cord of wood, solid measure, for each beaver's winter supply.

By this time the dam freezes over and all is shut up with ice. The beaver has nothing to do but leap into the water through the subterranean passage and bring up a stick of wood which is to furnish him his meal. This he drags up by one end into the lodge, eats off the bark to a certain distance, then cuts off the part he has stripped and throws it into the water through another passage, and so proceeds until he has finished his meal. When the ice and snow disappears in the spring, they clear their pond of the stripped wood and stop the leaks which the frosts have occasioned in their dam. Their manner of enlarging their lodge is by cutting out the inside and adding more to the out. The covering of the lodge is generally about eighteen inches thick, formed by sticks and mud intermingled in such a manner that it is very difficult for man, beast or cold to penetrate through it.

The Snake Indians

The appellation by which this nation is distinguished is derived from the Crows, but from what reason I have never been able to determine. They call themselves Sho-sho-nies, but during an acquaintance of nine years, during which time I made further progress in their language than any white man had done before me, I never saw one of the nation who could give me either the derivation or definition of the word "Sho-sho-nie." Their country comprises all the regions drained by the head branches of Green and Bear Rivers and the east and southern head branches of the Snake River. They are kind and hospitable to whites, thankful for favours, indignant at injuries and but little addicted to theft in their large villages. I have seldom heard them accused of inhospitality; on the contrary I have found it to be a general feature of their character to divide the last morsel of food with the hungry stranger, let their means be what it might for obtaining the next meal.

The Snakes, and in fact most of the Rocky Mountain Indians, believe in a Supreme Deity who resides in the sun and in infernal deities residing in the moon and stars, but all subject to the supreme control of the one residing in the sun. They believe that the spirits of the departed are permitted to watch over the actions of the living and every warrior is protected by a guiding angel in all his actions so long as he obeys his rules, a violation of which subjects the offender to misfortunes and disasters during the displeasure of the offended deity. Their prophets, judges or medicine men are supposed to be guided by deities differing from the others, insomuch as he is continually attendant upon the devotee from birth, gradually instituting into his mind the mysteries of his profession, which cannot be transmitted from one mortal to another.

The prophet or juggler converses freely with his supernatural director, who guides him up from childhood in his manner of eating, drinking and smoking, particularly the latter, for every prophet has a different mode of handling, filling, lighting and smoking the big pipe—such as profound silence in the circle while the piper is lighting the pipe, turned around three times in the direction of the sun by the next person on the right previous to giving it to him, or smoking with the feet uncovered. Some cannot smoke in the presence of a female or a dog, and a hundred other movements equally vague and superstitious which would be too tedious to mention here. A plurality of wives is very common among the Snakes and the marriage contract is dissolved only by the consent of the husband, after which the wife is at liberty to marry again. Prostitution among the women is very rare and fornication whilst living with the husband is punished with the utmost severity. The women perform all the labor about the lodge except the care of the horses. They are cheerful and affectionate to their husbands and remarkably fond and careful of their children.

The government is a democracy. Deeds of valour promote the chief to the highest points attained, from which he is at any time liable to fall for misdemeanour in office. Their population amounts to between 5,000 and 6,000, about half of which live in large villages and range among the buffaloes; the remainder live in small detached companies comprised of from two to ten families, who subsist upon roots, fish, seeds and berries. They have but few horses and are much addicted to thieving. From their manner of living they have received the appellation of "Root Diggers." They rove about in the mountains in order to seclude themselves from their warlike enemies, the Blackfeet. Their arrows are pointed with quartz or obsidian, which they dip in poison extracted from the fangs of the rattlesnake and prepared with antelope liver. These they use in hunting and war, and however slight the wound may be that is inflicted by one of them, death is almost inevitable, but the flesh of animals killed by these arrows is not injured for eating. The Snakes who live upon buffalo and live in large villages seldom use poison upon their arrows, either in hunting or war.

They are well armed with fusees and well supplied with horses. They seldom stop more than eight or ten days in one place, which prevents the accumulation of filth which is so common among Indians that are stationary. Their lodges are spacious, made of dressed buffalo skins sewed together and set upon eleven or thirteen long smooth poles to each lodge, which are dragged along for that purpose. In the winter of 1842 the principal chief of the Snakes died in an apoplectic fit and on the following year his brother died, but from what disease I could not learn. These being the two principal pillars that upheld the nation, the loss of them was and is to this day, (1921), deeply deplored. Immediately after the death of the latter the tribe scattered in smaller villages over the country in consequence of having no chief who could control and keep them together. Their ancient warlike spirit seems to be buried with their leaders and they are fast falling into degradation. Without a head the body is of little use.

The Crow Indians

This once formidable tribe once lived on the north side of the Missouri, east of the mouth of the Yellowstone. About the year 1790 they crossed the Missouri and took the region of country which they now inhabit by conquest from the Snakes. It is bounded on the east and south by a low range of mountains called the "Black Hills," on the west by the Wind River mountains, and on the north by the Yellowstone River. The face of the country presents a diversity of rolling hills and valleys and includes several plains admirably adapted for grazing. The whole country abounds with coal and iron in great abundance and signs of lead and copper are not infrequently found, and gypsiun exists in immense quarries. Timber is scarce except along the streams and on the mountains. Wild fruit such as cherries, service berries, currants, gooseberries and plums resembling the pomegranate are abundant. The latter grow on small trees generally six or eight feet high, ranging in colour and flavour from the most acute acid to the mildest sweetness. Hops grow spontaneously and in great abundance along the streams.

When the Crows first conquered this country their numbers amounted to about 8,000 persons, but the ravages of war and small-pox combined have reduced their numbers to about 2,000, of which 1,200 are females. They are proud, treacherous, thievish, insolent and brave when they are possessed with a superior advantage, but when placed in the opposite situation they are equally humble, submissive and cowardly. Like the other tribes of Indians residing in the Rocky Mountains, they believe in a Supreme Deity who resides in the sun and lesser deities residing in the moon and stars. Their government is a kind of democracy. The chief who can enumerate the greatest number of valiant exploits is unanimously considered the supreme ruler.

All the greatest warriors below him and above a certain grade are councillors and take their seats in the council according to their respective ranks—the voice of the lowest rank having but little weight in deciding matters of importance. When a measure is adopted by the council and approved by the head chief it is immediately put in force by the order of the military commander, who is appointed by the council to serve for an indefinite period. A standing company of soldiers is kept up continually for the purpose of maintaining order in the village. The captain can order any young man in the village to serve as a soldier in turn and the council only can increase or diminish the number of soldiers at pleasure. The greatest chiefs cannot violate the orders which the captain receives from the council. No office or station is hereditary, neither does wealth constitute dignity. The greatest chief may fall below the meanest citizen for misdemeanour in office and the lowest citizen may arise to the most exalted station by the performance of valiant deeds. The Crows, both male and female, are tall, well proportioned, handsome featured, with very light copper coloured skins. Prostitution of their wives is very common but sexual intercourse between near relatives is strictly prohibited.

When a young man is married he never after speaks to his mother-in-law nor the wife to the father-in-law, although they may all live in the same lodge. If the husband wishes to say anything to the mother-in-law, he speaks to the wife, who conveys it to the mother, and in the same way communication is conveyed between the wife and father-in-law. This custom is peculiar to the Crows. They never intermarry with other nations, but a stranger if he wishes can always be accommodated with a wife while he stops with the village but cannot take her from it when he leaves. Their laws for killing buffalo are rigidly enforced. No person is allowed to hunt buffalo in the vicinity where the village is stationed without first obtaining leave of the council. For the first offense the offender's hunting apparatus are broken and destroyed, for the second his horses are killed and his property destroyed and he beaten with rods, the third is punished by death by shooting.

When a decree is given by the council it is published by the head chief, who rides to and fro through the village like a herald and proclaims it aloud to all. They generally kill their meat by surrounding a band of buffaloes, and when once enclosed but few escape. The first person who arrives at a dead buffalo is entitled to one-third of the meat and if the person who killed it is the fourth one on the spot, he only gets the hide and tongue, but in no case can he get more than one-third of the meat if a second and third person appear before it is placed on the horses for packing. A person, whether male or female, poor or rich, gets the second or third division according to the time of arrival, each one knowing what parts they are allowed. This is also a custom peculiar to the Crows which has been handed down from time immemorial.

Their language is clear, distinct and not intermingled with guttural sounds, which renders it remarkably easy for a stranger to learn. It is a high crime for a mother or father to inflict corporal punishment on their male children, and if a warrior is struck by a stranger he is irretrievably disgraced unless he can kill the offender immediately.

Taking prisoners of war is never practiced with the exception of subjugating them to servile employment. Adult males are never returned as prisoners but generally killed on the spot, but young males are taken to the village and trained up in their mode of warfare until they imbibe the Crow customs and language, when they are eligible to the high station their deeds of valour permit. The Crows are remarkably fond of gaudy and glittering ornaments. The eye teeth of the elk are used as a circulating medium and are valued according to their size.

There exists among them many customs similar to those of the ancient Israelites. A woman after being delivered of a male child, cannot approach the lodge of her husband under forty days and for a female fifty is required, and seven days' separation for every natural menses. The distinction between clean and unclean animals bears a great degree of similarity to the Jewish law. They are remarkable for their cleanliness and variety of cooking, which exceeds that of any other tribe in the Rocky Mountains. They seldom use salt, but often season their cooking with herbs of various kinds and flavours.

Sickness is seldom found among them and they naturally live to a great age. There is no possibility of ascertaining the precise age of any mountain Indians, but an inference may be drawn with tolerable correctness from their outward appearance and such indefinite information from their own faint recollection of dates as may be collected by an intimate acquaintance with their habits, customs, traditions and manner of living. I have never known a mountain Indian to be troubled with the toothache or decayed teeth, neither have I ever known a case of insanity except from known and direct causes.

I was upon one particular occasion invited to smoke in a circle comprising thirteen aged Crow warriors, the youngest of whom appeared to have seen upwards of 100 winters, and yet they were all in good health and fine spirits. They had long since left the battle ground and council room to younger aspirants of sixty and under. It is really diverting to hear those hoary headed veterans when they are collected together conversing upon the good old times of their forefathers and condemning the fashions of the present age. They have a tradition among them that their most powerful chief who died sometime since, commanded the sun and moon to stand still two days and nights in the valley of Wind River whilst they conquered the Snakes and that they obeyed him. They point out the place where the same chief changed the wild sage of the prairie into a band of antelope when the village was in a starving condition. I have also been shown a spring on the west side of the Big Horn River, below the upper mountain, which they say was once bitter, but through the medicine of this great chief the waters were made sweet.

They have a great aversion to distilled spirits of any kind, terming it the "white man's fool water," and say if a Crow drinks it he ceases to be a Crow and becomes a foolish animal so long as the senses are absorbed by its influence.

Journal of Captain Nathaniel J. Wyeth's
Expeditions to the Oregon Country

Contents

1st Journal	185
2nd Journal (with Pencil)	261
Copy of a Letter and a Statement of Facts Pertaining to a Claim Based upon Operations Involved in the Two Expeditions	298

1st Journal

(The book containing the Journal has been mutilated. There are traces of the removal of four leaves just preceding the page that has the first of the narrative preserved. According to Wyeth's Oregon Expedition the Wyeth party on his first expedition left Independence, Mo., May 3rd., 1832. June 6th would thus have been the thirty-fifth day on the route.)

June 6th, 1832.
. . . .gray and my face like a plumb pudding the skin is entirely bare of skin is entirely off one of my ears. On the bluffs the ghnats are equally troublesome but they do not annoy us much except in the day. Geese appear here mated and I have seen some broods of gooselings. Some rain last night, still barren and grass bad. Our horses about the same, our men troubled with the relax. Toward night found buffaloe killed one which made a scanty meal for all hands for supper. Made 25 miles

7th Started out hunting killed two antelope. About 10 saw a herd of buffaloe crossing the river waited til they rose the bank and commenced slaughter, killed 3 and wounded many more, these afforded a timely supply to the party and we ate heartily. Saw today the first appearance of muskrat since leaving the settlements also pelicans. Last night in cutting a tree for fuel caught two young grey epagles one of which we ate and found it tender and good also a badger saw some rattlesnakes and some other kinds not known to me. The men appear a little better the men about the same. Ther. 90 deg. wind S. E. My face so swelled from the musquitoes and ghnats that I can scarce see out of my eyes and aches like the toothache

9th I date this the same[1] on ace of a mistake of a day heretofore.

---
1. "Same" here seems to mean "as I do".

Made 30 miles and yesterday 25. Arrived at the Chimney or Elk Brick the Indian name this singular object looks like a monument about 200 feet high and is composed of layers of sand and lime stone in layers the sand blowing out lets the lime rock fall down and this action has in time reduced what was once a hill to a spire of nearly the same dimensions at top and bottom. it looks like a work of art and the layers like the ranges of stone

It is scituated about 3 miles from the river. Rain and thunder at night wind strong S. E. River as muddy as ever the bluffs for the last 20 miles have occasionally a few stinted trees apparently pitch pine and cedar.

The small streams that here empty into the Platte are frequently dry near the river during the day while above they are running free while at night there is running water entirely to the river. Party in better order horses about the same. We now judge ourselves within 4 days march of the Black Hills

10th. 28 miles, 2 buffaloe

11th 30 miles, 6 buffaloe

12th Nothing remarkeable crossed Wild Horse Creek coming in from the S.

13th Came in sight of the Black hills and crossed Larrimee fork of the Platte. In getting over one of my rafts broke the tow line the raft went down stream lodged on a snag and upset wetting most of the goods on it and loosing two horse loads as it lodged in the middle of the river and the stream being very rapid the goods were with difficulty passed ashore. Here an alarm was occasioned by the appearance of 4 men on the bluffs behind us and an attack was expected every moment which would have been bad as our party was much scattered in crossing.

They however proved to be apart of a party of 19 men in the employ of Gant & Blackwell. They last winter lost all but 3 of their animals and in going to Sante Fee got enclosed by snow in the mountains and nearly starved to death, and at first they were hard to tell from Indians or devils, they are now in good health having felt well for some time. All of them joined Mr. Fitzpatricks party and proceeded on foot with us to the mountains. Killed an antelope.

14th Started late and left the river at which we had encamped and proceeded 16 miles. Killed one antelope and one elk

15th Went out for game killed one antelope, 2 deer 2 buffaloe. Made this day 20 miles and passed the first of the Black hills. The country is now thinly wooded with box elder, ash, pitch pine, cedar and cotton wood and a variety of small shrubs among which are the cherry, currant and thorn. Wild sage here almost covers the country and is a plant of many years' growth.

Arrived at camp found the company had killed plenty of buffaloe and were encamped on a small stream coming in from the S. 20 miles.

16th Warm in morning cold and rainy in the afternoon a little hard snow on the peak of the Black hills. A white bear was seen this day black ones for some days past. The lime rock still continues primitive pebbles in the streams and on the knols the hills pointed up very sharp from the same cause as the Chimney. The country appears desolate and dreary in the extreme no one can conceive of the utter desolation of this region. Nevertheless the earth is decorated with a variety of beautiful flowers and all unknown to me hard travelling disenables our botanist to examine them.

We have on the whole meat enough but the supply is too unsteady. There are here two kinds of rabbits the largest weighing about 15 lbs ears 6 inches long. Plover and other marsh birds are common and some 2 or 3 kinds of gulls. Struck the Platte River again here about 100 yds wide the water high and rapid. We here find a small kind of parsnip the blossom yellow root about 5 inches long ½ inch thick of more than one year's growth. The men appear better horses about the same. Made this day 20 miles

17th Wind high N.W. Ther. 40 deg. A drear and cheerless day made 25 miles. Killed 3 buffaloe 1 antelope 1 deer. Crossed 2 small streams from the Black hills running into the Platte. Saw some rabbits and white bears, hops.

18th Reached the place for fording the Platte

19th Passed over my goods during a severe wind without accident.

20th Mr Subblettee passed over his goods and at night moved on about 3 miles

21st Made a long march of 30 miles during which one of my horses gave out. Killed this day 3 buffaloe and fired at a white bear arrived at camp at 11 o'clock at night. I have ommitted one day on the other side of the Platte I date this right. We arrived at Rock Independence at noon after a march of 15 miles

23[2] Yesterday we left the Platte and struck the Sweetwater on which this rock stands. It is scituated in a gorge within 30 feet of the stream and is granite. Today is warm last night frost and the two last days cold and disagreable, from this time to 2nd July frost each night and snow once. Our course lay in various directions from S. W. to N. W. following the Sweetwater and leaving the first snowy mountains on the right hand. On the 29th we crossed on to the head waters of the Colorado. During all this time we found abundance of buffaloe. The travelling good but the grass poor the streams all fordable but rapid. Five streams have been crossed to this time and we are now encamped on the 6th all running into the Colorado. Trout are found here also some beaver.

Some of my men talk of turning back and I give them all free liberty. Many of my horses have given out and the rest are failing fast and unless we soon come to better grass they will all die and leave me on foot. The waters running into Lewis River are not more than 8 miles distant. On the creek where we are there are pine trees in shape like a balsam tree, leaves like a pitch pine, bark rough yellowish and scaly. The mountains in this region are not conspicuous are isolated and admitting free passage between them in any direction the creeks are sufficiently numerous for watering but feed is poor. The 1st July we rested all the afternoon a respite quite acceptable to our weary legs. Our average during these days about 20 miles but in some cases quite circuitous. White bears are seen but none have been killed. Wolves and antelopes plenty, kingfishers.

Our hunters have just brought part of 4 buffaloe. At night encamped on the same creek that we passed this morning and soon after were visited by 6 men from Dripps & Fontenelles concern who with 13 others are encamped 5 miles from this place. This night at about 12 o'clock. we were attacked by Indians probably the Blackfoot. They approached within 50 yds. and fired about 40 shots into the camp and some arrows they wounded three animals got 5 from Mr. Subblette, one from an independent hunter and 4 which I left out of camp for better feed. Mine were all poor and sore backed and useless

---

2. The "23" is placed a little above and to the left of the word "left". From the 21st on the journal was evidently not written up until the evening of July 2nd.

3rd Decamped and in company with the men above mentioned proceeded to their camp and passed on to our route which lay W. This night encamped on the waters of the Colorado 25 miles

4th Decamped and at noon crossed the divide and drank to my friends with mingled feelings from the waters of the Columbia mixed with alcohol and eat of a buffaloe cow. Made this day 30 miles and 25 yesterday. The snow clad mountains now entirely surround us the streams this side increase rapidly. One bear seen this day. The grass much better and some fertile land. Here the earth in some places was frozen snow yesterday and today. Three of my men are sick and I have no spare animals for them.

5th We passed along a wooded river and through a very difficult road by its side so steep that one of my horses loosing his foothold in the path was rooled down about 100 feet into the river. He was recovered but so much injured as we had to leave him shortly after. Made this day 20 miles

6th We marched early and at 2 o'clock stopped on Lewis River and within 20 miles of the Trois Tetons three very conspicuous snow covered mountains visible in all this region. This river here runs nearly S. and is divided over a bottom about 2 miles and into 8 streams very rapid and difficult. These we forded which consumed the time until night and encamped after making 18 miles on the W. bank with no grass. In the morning of the 7th we proceeded up a small brook coming from a gap of the mountains due south of the Trois Tetons and passed the range of mountains of this range without much difficulty it is a good pass for such a range and fresh animals would have no difficulty in passing through it.

On the highest point we had snow accompanied with heavy thunder and being out of meat fed upon the inner bark of the balsam trees a tree similar if not the same with the eastern balsam. At night we encamped at the foot of the pass on the western side and at the commencement of a large valley with several streams running through it into Lewis River surrounded with high and snow-clad mountains. The weather is here warm in the day time but frost every night, the grass is good the land ordinary. On the 8th we proceeded into the plain and after a march of 10 miles arrived at the rendesvous of the hunters of this region.

Here we found about 120 lodges of the Nez Perces and about 80 of the Flatheads a company of trappers of about 90 under Mr. Dripps of the firm of Dripps & Fontenelle connected with the American Fur Co. Many independent hunters and about 100 men of the Rocky Mountain Fur Co under Mess Milton Sublette and Mr Frapp. I remained at this encampment until the 17th during which time all my men but 11 left me to these I gave such articles as I could spare from the necessities of my own party and let them go. While here I obtained 18 horses in exchange for those which were worn out and for a few toys such as beads, bells, red and blue cloth, powder and balls fish hooks, vermillion old blankets. We also supplied ourselves with buffaloe robes we have now a good outfit and here we found plenty of meat which can be had of the Indians for a trifle.

On the 17th we put out and steered S. E. in direction to a pass through the same mountains by which we entered the valley these mountains. run E. & W. and the pass I refer to is the next E. of the one referred to and through it the waters of this valley reach Lewis River which is on the S. side of this range. At night we encamped within about 8 miles of the commencement of the pass. On the 18th we did not leave camp when near starting we observed 2 partys of Indians coming out of the pass about 200 in number with but few horses. After securing our camp our riders went out to meet them and soon found them to be Blackfeet a little skirmish ensued one of the Blackfeet was killed and his blankett and robe brought into camp. On this the Indians made for the timber the women and children were seen flying to the mountains. At this time only 42 men being the party of Mess Milton Sublette & Frapp mine and a few independent hunters were in sight and the Indians were disposed to give us their usual treatment when they meet us in small bodies. But while the Indians were making their preparations we sent an express to camp which soon brought out a smart force of Nez Perces Flatheads and whites the Indians finding they were caught fortified themselves in a masterly manner in the wood.

We attacked them and continued the attack all day there were probably about 20 of them killed and 32 horses were found dead. They decamped during the night leaving most of their utensials lodges &c and many of the dead. We have lost 3 whites killed 8 badly wounded among which is Mr Wm. Sublette who was extremely active in the battle about 10 of the Indians were killed or mortally wounded of the Nez Perces and Flatheads. In the morning we visited their deserted fort they had dug into the ground to reach water and to secure themselves from our shot.

It was a sickening scene of confusion and bloodshead one of our men who was killed inside[3] their fort we found mutilated in a shocking manner. On the 19th we removed back to our former ground to be near our whole force and to recruit the wounded and bury the dead. We think that 400 lodges or about 600 warriors of the Blackfeet are on the other side of the pass and if they come they must be met with our whole force in which case the contest will be a doubtful one.

We have made horse pens and secured our camp in as good a manner as we can and wait the result this affair will detain us some days. On 24th we again moved out of the valley in the same direction as at first *viz* about S. E. and encamped at night in the gorge of it. During the march I visited the scene of our conflict for the first time since the battle the din of arms was now changed into the noise of the vulture and the howling of masterless dogs the stench was extreme most of the men in the fort must have perished. I soon retired from this scene of disgusting butchery.

On the 25th we proceeded through the pass which is tolerably good and in a direction of about S. W. by S. and encamped 15 miles on Lewis River (here concentrated into one rapid stream) and about 30 miles S. of where we crossed it in going into the valley. We are now employed in making bull boats in order to cross it. One buffaloe and some antelope killed today. 26 crossed the river in a bull boat without accident in 4 hours and moved on in a westerly direction about 4 miles when we struck into a deep ravine with a little water in it. This ravine is bordered by high presipices on each side and is small. 3 miles up this we encamped for the night. This stream is called Muddy as there is several of this name it is requisite to distinguish this by the cognomen of Muddy that falls into the "Lewis."

26th We moved up the Muddy until we found the forks of it then followed the right hand say 3 miles then took a south direction and struck another stream (small) and running in the opposite direction this we followed about 5 miles making 15 this day and encamped

27th. We moved down the stream until its junction with another called Grays Creek which we crossed and assended a high bluff and travelled an average course of S. W. and encamped on a small creek making 15 miles this day. 2 days since I first this side the mountain met

---

3. The word "inside" is crossed out with pencil and "near" written above it with pencil.

with the prickly pear and since leaving the valley of the rendesvous the fruit that was green one day is ripe the next. The nights are still frosty but the days are very warm as in N. E. at this time. Fruits we have 3 kinds of currants one of gooseberry all different from those of the U. S. and service berry's, all the first are sour the latter sweet. The country through which we have travelled for these two days past has a strong volcanic appearance the streams occupy what appear to be but the cracks of an over heated surface the rocks are blown up in blubbers like a smiths cinders some rocks ten feet through are but a shell being hollow.

A substance abounds like bottle glass of about the same weight not so transparent about as brittle the fracture is smooth and glossy with the exception of the cracks as above the country is tolerably level for a mountainous country but excessively dry. During our first days march from Lewis River beside the ravine above mentioned we passed three craters of small volcanoes (as I suppose) and I am told there is a boiling spring near the same place. We here find buffaloe plenty and fat and entirely different from those met with in the spring on the Platte it is preferable to the best beef. Our party have taken lice from the Indians they are a great trouble as well as the musquitoes these last trouble us in the day but the frost seals their wings at night when the first relieve them until morning

On the 28th we moved in a direction about S. W. and during the march took the bearing of the Trois Tetons which was N. E. by E. and I think 75 miles. We made 7 miles and encamped on a little stream meandering through a valley of about 100 acres of fine black land with the grass as good as the buffaloe and the cold weather could admit of. Here we found plenty of cows and more bulls 13 of the first were killed they were fat and we stopped to make meat these cows were killed by running them down which is a dangerous method, expensive in horses and requiring much skill in riding. We of course were obliged to employ help for none could be got by approaching while they were running them.

29th We remained all day making meat with a hot sun. This morning sent 3 men down the creek fishing they caught 21 salmon trout and returned at 10. This afternoon it rained hard and during the storm the squaw of one of the party was delivered of a boy in the bushes whither she had retired for the purpose. Its head was thickly covered with black hair it was, as white as is usual with the whites. In less than an hour afterwards the squaw made her appearance in camp as well and able for a day's travel as usual. It continued raining all night and until 8 of the 30 on which account our march was deferred for the day which was afterward fine and our meat dried well. 4 beavers were caught from about 12 traps last night. During this day one of the party saw an Indian which must have been a Blackfoot as otherwise he would have come to camp. Yesterday and today we had thunder and hail as well as rain.

1st. Augt I date this the 1st. on account of having missed a day in the time past. This day we made about 15 miles in a S. W. direction and most of the way in a deep valley and encamped on a small creek running into one called Blackfoot. This latter is the second stream we have passed which empties into S. fork of Lewis River the first was called Grays River and is also small (this since crossing Lewis River). Here we stopped until the 4th to make meat of which I made enough to eat and no more while the other two parties who had good buffaloe riders and horses made considerable. While here. we lost one horse while attempting to run buffaloe by throwing his rider and running among the buffaloe and going off with them. I sent out a party to get fish of two men they returned with about a peck of craw fish and a dozen of trout these average about 1lb and are fine eating. We have here the sandhill cranes in plenty.

On the 4th we moved due south and crossed Blackfoot and struck over to a stream emtying into the same as Blackfoot called Portneuf from a man killed near it 18 miles here we found buffaloe in the bottom and the hunters are now out running them. Here we remained this day and the 5th when the men I had sent out to hunt the horse returned as I had expected them on the 4th I was much alarmed for their safety being in a dangerous country. While here we made 7 bales meat. On the 5th. we moved S. down the valley 3 miles and encamped on a creek running into the valley. On the 7th we made 21 miles first down the N. side of the valley and taking the first creek running out of the valley then in a S.W. direction and encamped on it. From the valley above mentioned rises Bear River running into the Big Salt Lake distant about S. E. 50 miles. Currants and service berrys are now ripe.

I have been sick from indigestion for some days more so than I ever was before. We have here the sandhill crane, turtle dove, robbin, blackbirds, (crow & cow) kingfishers, black and mallard ducks, geese.

We find meat making a tedious buisness. On the 8th we moved S.W. 15 miles following the main Portneuf out of the valley for about 12 miles then took one of its tributaries for about 3 miles and encamped on the S.W. side of the valley in which this branch runs. Here we *cached* 6 horse loads of goods and remained on the 9th, 10th and 11th moved on in a S.W. direction not following any stream but passing the ridge bordering the valley in a low place near where a small run puts into the valley from a very rugged pass. We made this day 15 miles and encamped on a small run going into the Portneuf.

12th We made in a S.W. direction about 6 miles not following any stream but encamped on a very small run with poor grass.

13th We made 24 miles in a west and by N. direction and met no water for this distance and encamped on a very small run issuing from a spring a few miles from Lewis River. We are here in sight of the river running through an extensive valley in a S.W. direction. Here are the American falls, the place may be known by several high and detached hills arising from the plain. The falls at one place are 22 feet and the rapids extend a considerable distance down the river. We found here plenty of buffaloe sign and the Pawnacks come here to winter often on account of the buffaloe, we now find no buffaloe. There are here abundance of service berrys now ripe. During a short walk from camp this morning I saw a buff coloured fox with a white tip on his tail. Wolves here serenade us every night making more noise than 50 village dogs and better music for they keep in chord and display more science. Yesterday we parted from 16 men bound out trapping. We are now in a country which affords no small game and a precarious chance for buffaloe

14th We made 30 miles in a S.W. direction and encamped on a creek called Casu[4] River it joins the main river below the American falls. This day's ride was through an excessively barren country with no water. Between the two last camps on the N. side of the Lewis River and about 50 miles distant from it is a range of snowy mounts. There are also two or three points in the chain of this side with snow on them.

15th We made along the banks of the Ocassia about 25 miles and encamped on the west bank of it. The valley of the Ocassia is about 4 miles wide and of a rich soil but the excessive cold and drouth of

---

4. The name is thus written above "Ocassia" crossed out.

this country prevents vegetation from assuming a fertile character. The air is so dry that percussion caps explode without striking and I am obliged to put the caps on and fire immediately except in the night when we consider it safe to keep the caps on the guns. We have in this country a large kind of black crickett 2 inches long said to be used as food by the Indians they are in great numbers and roost on the sage at noonday. There are also in the streams abundance of craw-fish. We see antelope and old buffaloe sign

16th We made 25 miles up the same side of the Ocassia then crossed it and followed S.W. 3 miles and encamped on a small mountain run making in all 28 miles in a W by S. direction. Yesterday's march was in a direction W by S.

17th We moved in a W. by S. direction about 15 miles to a creek putting into Lewis River on which we found no beaver of consequence having been trapped out by the H. B. Co. some years before.

18th We moved out up the creek about 8 miles and still found no beaver saw one pidgeon woodpecker. This creek runs through what are called cut rocks otherwise volcanic in this region I found one mountain of mica slate enclosing garnetts. The basaltic rock appears to be the same formerly and the remains of the garnetts are in some cases to be seen, also I have found here granite in small blocks there is also much white sandstone compact the clefts (cliffs?) on each side of this creek are high and perpendicular but the bottom affords good grass for this country. There is no timber except willow and alder in the bottom and cedar on the hills this days course about S. along the creek

19th We moved up the creek about 12 miles in a S. W. direction there was still little beaver. This afternoon I took 2 men and proceeded from camp about 8 miles about W. following the creek and slept there at sunrise. On the 20th we moved up about 12 miles in a W direction and while I was engaged in the brook setting a trap we found three Indians following us. The two men were on the bank and were seen but myself in the creek was unnoticed when they crossed to go to the men I presented my pistol to the first one who made a precipitate retreat back while I made mine to my gun having got which I beckoned them to come to me which they did. We then went to camp which we found had moved this day about 10 miles in same direction. These Indians were Snakes the first we had seen during the march. The party passed a hot spring the country still volcanic.

21st We followed the creek in a N.W. direction about 5 miles when we met a village of the snakes of about 150 persons having about 75 horses they were poorly off for food and clothing but perfectly friendly they are diminutive in person and lean. We encamped to trade with them but did nothing except getting a few skins for *moccasins* this morning caught my first beaver a large one.

22nd We followed the same creek about 2 miles and then struck into a ravine in a west direction and in about 6 miles came to a warm spring near a cold one which formed a run which we followed in a west by S. direction this we followed about 2 miles and encamped making this day 18 miles

22nd We proceeded in a S.W. direction and struck the same stream on another branch about 2 miles from the junction about 15 miles this day these two streams unite and run in a N. direction through impassable cut rocks. This night caught 2 beaver and slept out of camp.

24th Proceed up the creek in a S.W. by W. direction about 18 miles then in a W. by N. direction about 6 miles. The last half of this day's travel was through clefts of scienite rock pretty well broke to pieces by heat apparently. We have here 2 kinds of lizards the one like that of the United States as far as I could see the other shorter and more sluggish. Here we find the banks of the streams lined with diggers' camps and trails but they are shy and can seldom be spoken and then there is no one who could understand them and they appear to know little about the signs which afford other Indians a mode of intelligence. From this region specimens No. 1 are obtained.

25th We made in a W. direction along the same creek 20 miles.

26th In a W by N. direction about 20 miles

27th In a S W direction toward a snowy mountain and leaving the last creek 24 miles and struck one here running S. E. Country desolate in the extreme most of the creeks which have water in them on the mountains dry up in the plains of this region.

28th Did not move more than 2 miles up.

29th About 5 miles in a S. W. direction to cross a range of high hills until we struck a creek running in a N. W. direction which we followed 12 miles and encamped where the creek goes into the cut rocks. This day we parted from Mr. Sublette's party with feeling of regrett for this party have treated us with great kindness which I shall long remember.

30th We followed the creek in a N. W. direction about 12 miles through tremenduous cut rocks. I went ahead to look the route I passed the smoking fires of Indians who had just left 4 of whom I saw running up the mountain endeavoured by signs to induce them to come to me but could not. Soon after I came to another camp I happened to find their plunder this induced them to come to me, 3 men, one boy, 4 women. From these Indians I procured fresh salmon spawn which was very encouraging as we are nearly out of provisions and the country would afford us a scanty subsistence. I gave these Indians a few small presents to convince them of our friendly disposition. This day for the first time in this country saw raspberrys. These Indians gave me a cake made of service berrys quite good. They had about a dozen of spotted fish of a kind I had never seen resembling a tom-cod. These Indians are small about 120 of a good countenance they are Snakes or Sosshonees.

30th [5] We followed the same creek and made about 15 miles in a N. N. W. direction through a continued defile in many places admitting just room for the water through which in many places we were obliged to make our way The mountains on each side are about 1000 feet above the creek which has a rapid decent here are a small fish about 14 lb. similar to a trout but with large dark spots. We meet here plenty of cherrys, currants and gooseberrys the latter sour. The last of yesterdays and the first of today's route lay through porphritic granite rocks in their natural state. The latter part of today's was through a stratified blue sandstone untouched by fire for a short distance then assumed a volcanic appearance.

This day we assended the highest mountain in sight and found the exhibit an indescribable chaos the tops of the hills exhibit the same *strata* as far as the eye can reach and appear to have once formed the level of the country and the valley to be formed by the sinking of the earth rather than the rising of the hills through the deep cracks and chasms thus formed the rivers and creeks of this country creep which renders them of the most difficult character to follow. In the brooks we have fresh water clams on which we look with some feeling, for

---

5 The author seems to have lost his bearings with his dates. His uncertainty first appears on the 17th and continues patently through to the 4th *prox.*

the small quantity of buffaloe meat now remaining admonishes us look for some other means. Of living game there is little and being obliged to travel prevents our hunting much. From this place the specimen in Bag No. 1 of vitrified quartz was taken.

31st We followed the same creek about 4 miles in a N. direction then took a dry ravine 2 miles in a S. E. then in a N. direction and then followed down another dry ravine about 1 mile, when the rocks on each side closed over the top and formed a natural bridge elevated about 50 feet, while the sides approached to within 20 feet of each other and the bottom decended perpendicularly about 60 feet. We of course returned on our trail and then steered a N. E. direction about 4 miles and encamped on a little ravine in which there was only a little water standing in deep places and barely enough for us and our horses. The first half mile of our route lay through the bed of the creek and among rocks from 1 foot to 3 or 4 in diameter, this was a very difficult task and several of our horses fell in the water this day. We lost two horses which gave out. The country still bears the same appearance as for several days past.

2nd Sept. We left our camp in the ravine assended to the height of land which we found to be a high level plain over which we marched in a N. N. W. direction and found during a 10 hours march 2 springs which as the day was warm were acceptable. At the end of 30 miles we reached the creek which we left on the 31st. We found rabbits plenty on the plain, our camp was made surrounded by high and perpendicular clifts say 800 feet bearing every mark of fire. Here we found little grass for our horses.

3rd We lay at the same camp and got fish from the brook enough for breakfast, after which I took a horse and followed the creek down about 1 mile and found another larger joining it a little. Below which there is a warm spring issuing from the bank about 40 feet above the stream it gives out smoke when it meets the air and discharges a large quantity of water. About 2 miles farther down I found a small party of Indians from whom I obtained 8 fish weight about 4 lbs each and looking like a salmon, for these I gave 4 hooks. They were friendly they advise me to follow the right hand trail but I have determined to take the left and shall perhaps repent it. The left leads N. W. which I think is my direction. I returned to camp and three of the Indians with me. One of these Indians had a bad wound on the side of his head and from his signs and appearance was made with a poisoned arrow.

3rd We moved camp in the proposed direction *viz* N. W. 16 miles. During which distance we found stagnant water once and encamped near about 15 Indians diggers. 3 of our men we left at the last camp to set their traps at some signs there seen. These Indians are very poor and timid, when I approached them alone on a gallop they all began to run but by moderating my pace and making signs they suffered me to come to them. They gave me some sweet root to eat for which I gave them 3 hooks. They had a young yellow-legged eagle with them and most of the diggers we have met had a small kind of hawk at their camps these they feed and tame.

This party also had a young bird tame resembling a king bird. This day's travel was on a high plain and good going on an old trail, these Indians had with them staves for fish spears so we presume they are going to the river for fish and so think ourselves on the right trail. For three nights passed there has been no frost, a thing which has not before happened for three nights in all since leaving rock Independence. Snow spit we had the 28th Aug. Today a slight sprinkle of rain being the 2nd time since leaving the rendesvous.

4th We left the camp early and proceeded over a high and pretty level plain gradually decending to the N. W. in a N. N. W. direction and after 20 miles travel without water came to ravines running E. and dry having gravelly and sandstone (untouched by fire) bluffs. And in 5 miles more came to the creek we had left on morning of the 3rd. On the banks of which we found every 20 steps or thereabouts warm or hot springs and the creek tho large and discharging a great quantity of water too warm to be palatable. Here we found an Indian and family of whom for 2 fish hooks we bought 7 salmon of about 4 lbs weight each when green, they were split and dried. The two men left behind not having yet come up we intend halting here for them. The creek is here lined with volcanic rock. Today we saw the first fish hawk in this country.

4th Lay at camp and repacked our goods and held a smoke with some Indians one of whom we engaged as a guide down the river and to beaver. Smoked too much and made myself sick.

5th Moved on about 5 miles N. N. W. and again struck the creek and good grass found beaver sign very plenty and for the first time set all our traps at good sign. Had a mess of fresh clams for dinner after which 2 Indians came to us with 4 salmon which we bought for 2 hooks. This day heard what we all took for a cannon at about 10 miles distance, time will determine whether we were mistaken. In this creek there are a great number of snakes about 3 feet long with a large head and of a brownish grey colour, almost the proportion of the striped snake of N. E. They inhabit the water and I saw one catch a small fish within two feet of me while bathing at a warm spring which put into the main stream. The bathing at these warm springs is delicious there are hundreds of them and some large enough to dive in. Some gush out of the rocks at an elevation of 40 feet above the stream and discharge enough water for a mill I can perceive no unusal taste in the water.

6th Remained at same camp and were visited at 10 o'clock in the morning by two Indians with whom we held a smoke. We can learn nothing of any white post by these Indians. Caught 7 beaver.

7th Remained at same camp and exchanged two horses with some Pawnack Indians three of whom visited us, also about 10 Sohonees with salmon of which they have plenty. Here we caught a N. England sucker also a fish a little resembling a pike of about 3 lbs weight but without teeth. Caught 3 beaver. Ravens are here very plenty and tame they light on the perpendicular sides of the creek waiting for fish on which they live. Geese and ducks are also plenty as well as grouse. Some of the Indians have guns but most of them go unarmed The creek here for about 10 miles runs W. N. W.

8th Moved camp down the creek about 12 miles and came to the village under the escort of about 20 Indians on horseback, one of whom by the direction of the chief shewed us the place for our camp where grass and water could be had. Here the chief harangued his people telling them not to come into our lines nor steal from the white people. He sent his squaws with wood for us and also sent salmon for us to eat. I gave him a present of tobacco, awls, hooks, powder, vermillion, knives *ect*. Here I traded a beaver skin robe for two knives and six skins with many muskrat which are plenty here. I found these Indians great thieves in the small line knives *ect*. Missing mine I went to one of the sub chiefs and told him of it he made enquiry and pointed out the thief who refusing to open his robe I gently did it for him. But instead of finding the knife found a coat of one of the men, which he held upon until I drew a pistol, on which he gave it up and caught up what he supposed to be one of our guns but it happened to be my covered fishing rod. He was then held by the other Indians and sent to the village and I saw him no more.

9th In the morning went to see the Indians catch salmon which is done by entangling them in their passage up the creek among dams which they erect and spearing them. They catch an immense quanity, the operation commences in the morning at a signal given by their chief. This chief is a good sized man and very intelligent and the president would do well if he could preserve the respect of his subjects as well or maintain as much dignity.

10th Moved down the main river in a S. W. direction which here runs through moderate banks in a moderate current. We are told that the next creek has beaver by the chief and that it is 4 days march. The main river is here full of salmon which continually jump above the surface like sturgeon.

10th Moved camp along the bank of the river 3 miles there the river diverging to the northward we left it and followed the main trail. The river here goes through cut rocks about 30 miles. We made this day 20 miles in all in a W. N. W. direction and encamped in poor grass on a small creek 1 mile from the main river. During the march we crossed a small creek up which about 2 miles is a fine camp.

11th Moved at 3 a. m. and followed the trail 24 miles in a W. N. W. direction and encamped on the bank of the main river which is here a fine stream about a 1/3 mile or over. I swam across it and found it over my head all the way. Here we found Indians and bought beaver, 3 skins for 1 shoe knife and 4 charges powder and lead we also got salmon of them. The basalt here occurs resting on sand and gravel in some places the rock is not more than 4 feet thick and appears to have suffered from intense heat. The country is barren in the extreme there is usually a difference of 40 deg. between the day and night the heat at noonday about 75 to 85 deg. The Indians here have large nets made in the European manner of the hemp of the country. The trail on the river so far is fine and much used.

12th Moved camp 15 miles on the trail in a W. N. W. direction and following the bank of the river which is here a gentle stream of about 4 miles and ½ mile wide. Gnats here trouble us much and the days are extremely hot about 85 deg. and the nights warm enough for comfort. The river is full of salmon and a plenty of them are to be had of the Indians whom we meet every few miles fishing on the banks of the stream. Some of the grass is here so salty that it can be washed in a pot of water and enough seasoning for boiling, obtained grass is generally poor. The banks are here generally sand. Many kinds of water fowl frequent the river here. Today we bought a fish of the Indians dried excessively fat and when alive a large fish, sturgeon probably.

13th Moved camp along the bank of the river and following the trail 24 miles only deviating from the river about 3 miles of the last of the travel. The first 6 miles the river is W. the next 3 N. W. then S. W. 3 then taking a circular sweep round to N. by E. which was 9 miles. Then left the river and in 3 miles struck a creek about as large as Charles River at Watertown, where we found grass, salmon and Indians and the first timber we have seen since leaving. The mountains. in sight on what appears to be a river coming in from the N. side. This I mean to ascertain tomorrow and the next day I shall start to explore the creek for beaver. This forenoon and yesterday forenoon were cloudy and the first cloudy weather for 2 months except as mentioned before. Weather still as warm as 80 deg. in daytime. Buy salmon for a hook apiece.

14th moved camp in a N. N. W. direction 5 miles and encamped on the main river. Being out of provisions I sent a man on a mule to buy some salmon he went up the river about 3 miles and called to some Indians on one of the islands to bring some, these he bought. Afterward another Indian came over with some, the man thinking he had got nearly enough offered him a less price, this displeased the Indian who slapped him in the face and at the same time hit the mule, a kick which set him out on the run and the Indian ran quick enough to avoid vengeance. The man came to camp much displeased having had to walk most of the way and carry his fish. This day also visited by Indians from below with salmon

15th Sent 3 men and 4 animals to examine the small river for beaver. This day a N. W. wind much like the N. E. of the Atlantic with some little rain (at the same camp) this day took a ride down the river to examine for a camp.

16th N. W. wind still, took a ride up the river to find a camp where timber, fit for a raft which we propose to build to carry some of the loose baggage and some men who are on foot can be found, found none saw some beaver sign. In trading for some salmon an Indian attempted to snatch a paper of fish hooks from me but he did not make out. Returned to camp and sent two men to trap for the beaver they left their horses and went into the willows to look for the sign during which time the Indians none of whom were in sight stole a cloak from Mr. Ball. They found the beaver had lately been trapped out say within 3 weeks next morning they returned to camp

17th moved camp N. by W. 16 miles and encamped on a creek about as large as the last near a few lodges of Indians the main river about two miles to N. E. This creek appears to run S. W. The Indians say there is beaver on it the main river here makes a considerable detour to the N. Yesterday had hail and rain and snow and today the mountains. to the northward are white with it.

18th With 2 men I went up the creek this I followed about 50 miles and found its general course about W by N. the first 15 miles S. W. then W. 20 then N. N. W. 15 where the cut rocks begin. This is a large stream when the waters are high in the spring but now is sluggish. Here we got a few beaver it had been trapped by the H. B. 2 years before. We saw no Indians on it during the 9 days I was up. On the 10th day I returned to where I left the party and feeling in the mood of banter I told the Indians at the mouth of the creek (the party having left) that I had eaten nothing for two days this to see if they would give me anything for charity sake. One of them went and looked at my saddle and pointed to me the fresh blood of a beaver I had that morning caught and left with the two men. I then bought 2 salmon for one awl. Afterward I told him I had three children at home he brought forward three tawny brats and his squaw who was big I backed out of story telling with Indians.

I then proceeded on until the moon went down, when seeing a light I made for it, after traveling 5 miles I found it to be an Indian camp on the other side of the river. I then unsaddled my horse and slept until 4 o'clock when I mounted and at 9 o'clock found where my party had camped the same night and a notice in the trail of their motions at 11 o'clock. I overtook them with my horse lame and jaded. I found an Indian with the party who seems to know the route to Wallah Wallah and he intends going with us.

During my absence the three men sent up the creek above the one I went up returned without accident, and during the same time Mr. Sublette with Mr. Frapp and party joined our camp and crossed by fording to the other side of the river intending to divide into 3 parties and trap up three streams coming in opposite the upper one of which we thought to be Salmon River. It proves to be called Big Woody on account of the timber on it. They attempted to come down on the creek above the one I asscended but after toiling long and wearing down their horses in a cruel manner they crossed to the one that we decended and arrived at the Indian village the day after we left it. He left before I returned I regretted much not seeing this party, from information gained here we suppose that we shall meet no Indians between this and the fort have threfore provided as much salmon as we could get and put ourselves on allowance.

Subblette who went to 2 creeks further than I did saw a large stream running S. W. this must either turn and be some large river coming into Lewis below here or be the head water of some river going to the Gulph of California. After joining camp we proceeded on to a creek coming from the N. W. which is our route the river here being impracticable and taking a great bend to the N. and shall wait here until the two men who went up with me come to camp. The river from where I left camp runs about N. 20 miles then west 10 miles then N. again into cut rocks found the party all well and the horses much recruited.

29th We lay at same camp.

30th moved about 5 miles the creek running about W.

1 Oct moved camp along same creek about 5 miles still W.

2nd At same camp at this place the bears' dung was plenty but we saw but one.

3rd Moved camp about 15 miles creek still west and trail good.

4th With an Indian and 4 men I left camp in order to explore this creek the N. W. trail here leaving it after leaving camp I proceeded over bad hills about 18 miles and encamped among cut rocks on the same creek it here being W. by S. during the march we observed a range of high snowy mountains to the N. of us but whether on our side of the river or not could not determine.

5th Made about 5 miles through intolerable cut rocks. Some beaver.

6th At same camp.

7th 5 miles on same creek which bears W. by S here left it. Having sent a messenger to camp with orders to proceed on the route to Wallah Wallah and steering north passed some snow clad mounts, which we walked up with bare feet and after 25 miles struck a small run going into the next creek. During this day we passed through an immense forest of pine of different kinds and unknown to us altho very similar to some of ours. On these mountains we found unripe service berrys, cherrys and thorn apple all of which are gone. On the rivers it snowed and rained most of the day many of the pines were 4 feet through.

8th Moved 4 miles to the main creek and laid down cold and hungry and supperless hoping that our traps would give us beaver in the morning

9th Got 7 beaver and went to eating like good fellows. Moored this day 6 miles down creek here running about N.

10th Moved N. and down creek about 15 miles and found the rest of the party who had come on the mail trail in an average N.W. direction about 45 miles This day rain this creek from where we struck it to this place runs in an extensive plain of fertile soile equal to the best I ever saw of about 5 miles average width here we raised a great smoke and am told by our Indian that the Nez Percys will see it and come to smoke with us

11th To the S.W. of us is a range of snow clad mountains. The Indian says it is 7 days to Wallah Wallah. This creek runs about N. E. by E.

11th Started at 8 o'clock and moved about N. N.W. 30 miles over high ground of good soil.

12th Left the party after killing a horse of the poorest kind for food in order to go ahead to find Indians or whites or food. The party here remained one day in a valley of about 20 miles long and 15 wide of a very fertile soil. In this valley saw extensive camps of Indians about one month old. Here they find salmon in a creek running through it and dig the Kamas root but not an Indian was here at this time we put out in a N.W. direction and assended the hills which soon became wooded with good timber, our course this day was about N. N.W. and 40 miles. I had with me an Indian and three men and a little horse meat we camped this night in the woods without water.

13th Arose early and continued our route until 9 o'clock and stopped for breakfast of bad horse meat on a creek of some size where we found the red thorn apple and a few cherries. After 3 hours stop we moved across the creek which runs west and is called Ottillah. On ascending the opposite bluff we saw a smoke about 20 miles down on it to which we went and found some poor horses in charge of a squaw and some children, the men were all out hunting. They had no food but rose berrys of which we made our supper they were much frightened at our approach there having been some Indians of this tribe *viz* Walla Walla killed by the Snakes above, and this family was murdered the night after we left them

In the morning of the 14th we put out about N. and arrived at fort Walla Walla about 5 o'clock in the evening distance 30 miles. Near the fort the River Walla Walla was crossed which is about 75 feet wide and about 2 feet deep current moderate the size of the last creek passed. I was received in the most hospitable and gentlemanly manner by Peanbron (Pambrun) the agent for this post. The fort is of no strength merely sufficient to frighten Indians, mounting 2 small cannon having two bastions at the opposite corners of a square enclosure there were 6 whites here. My party arrived on the 18th having fared for food in the same manner as myself but for a longer time. They met a Nez Perce village on the 16th and got a supply of food. They passed my trail and went N. of it and struck the main river above the fort they brought in all the horses. At the post we saw a bull and cow and calf, hen and cock, punkins, potatoes, corn, all of which looked strange and unnatural and like a dream. They gave me a decent change of clothes which was very acceptable. I took a ride up the river 9 miles to the junction of Lewis River which comes in from the S. E. and soon takes a S. course the Columbia comes here from the N. W.

On the 19th I took leave of my hospitable entertainer in one of the Cos. barges with my party leaving my horses in his charge at the fort and proceeded down the river about 4 miles and stopped to tighten our boat. The river forms fine eddies to work up with and about 3 mile current down the 2nd run of fish failed this year in the river and the Indians are picking up the most nauseous dead fish for food the course of the river is about S. W.

20th Left the beach at sunrise the river still S. W. and kept on until about noon when a furious wind arose from the S. W. and stopped our further progress the sand flew so as to obscure the air. Here we traded a few fish from the natives for hooks, awls, powder &c. Made 10 miles during which we passed some rapids of a bad character at which in times of high water portage is necessary. The geese are numerous seated on the banks of the river. River W. by S. a large snowy mountain S. W. by W. ahead which the river leaves to the left called by the French "*Montagne de Neige*" made 10 miles.

21st Wind same but more moderate. Put down the river still W by S. passed a large island at the lower end of which we stopped for the night. Ther. 22 deg. Made 16 miles during the day. Our boatman bought a colt which we found fine eating. Shagg and geese plenty.

22nd Made 30 miles wind moderate and no rapids of much difficulty stopped at night at a village where was a chief sick to whom our conductor administered some medicine and bled him, his eyes were exceeding yellow and his blood after standing a short time was covered with a scum of yellowish green. He gave us a horse to eat of which he had 260 in fine order and of good breed we found the meat equal to any beaf and quite different from the poor and sick old ones we had eaten. They here sell horses for 100 loads ammunition, 1 blankett and ¼ lb tobacco.

23rd The chief much better and we left him. Yesterday our people in search of wood of which there is none but drift here, found a pile which they brought to our fire but were soon told by the natives that they had robbed the dead. We will avoid the like mistake in the future. We made this day 28 miles during which distance we passed one bad rapid and the river John Day from a trader of that name. This river is large but obstructed by rapids and enters from the S. is 79 miles below Walla Walla. No rain as yet but we are informed that the rain is now constant below the falls. We see Indians every few miles who come off to trade what little articles they have sometimes with nothing to beg a chew of tobacco sometimes with a little wood for fuel sometimes with two 3, one or ½ a fish, a few berrys. Our conductor appears to have a wife at each stopping place, 4 already and how many more sable beauties god only knows these Indians are tolerably honest but will steal a little.

24th Started about 9 and after about 6 miles[6] passed the grand falls of the Columbia just above which a small river puts into the Columbia about the size of the small rivers above the Wallah Wallah, for instance these falls now the water is low are about 25 feet. When the water is high these falls are covered, the water not having a sufficient vent below the water here rises about 40 feet, just before arriving at the falls are considerable rapids. The falls are easily passed in boats, at high water we hired the Indians about 50 for a quid of tobacco each

---

6. So written but crossed out.

to carry our boat about 1 mile round the falls, the goods we carried ourselves. Shortly after passing the falls we passed what are called the dalles (small) or where the river is dammed up. Between banks steep and high of not more than 100 feet apart, through which the whole waters of the mighty Columbia are forced with much noise and uproar, I passed through with some Indians, while my men went round they not being good boatmen enough to trust and frightened withall.

We are now camped at the Great Dalles which are still narrower and more formidable than the small, having stopped after making 20 miles the wind being high and unfavourable for passing. At the gorge of this pass the water rises by the mark on the rock at least 50 feet forming a complete lock to the falls above the back water, covering them entirely. The Indians are thieves but not dangerous. Before us and apparently in the river rises the most formidable mountain we have seen, the country ahead is clothed with forest to the river side which has not been the case before and the western horizon is covered by a dense cloud denoting the region of constant rain during the winter.

25th Made this day 6 miles and passed the Great Dalles similar to the small ones which we passed yesterday but still narrower being 75 feet about in width. Through this pass we went with an unloaded boat at an immense speed, the goods and baggage were carried past on the backs of my men and some Indians hired for that purpose. My men not being good boatmen and timorous I hired Indians to work ours through going with them myself to learn the way. During part of this day we had a fair wind the river still W. by S. Here we saw plenty of grey headed seals. We bought some bear meat from the Indians which we found very fine.

We encamped for the first time on the river among timber among which I saw a kind of oak and ash. Indians plenty, one chief at whose lodge we stopped a short time gave me some molasses obtained from the fort below to eat. He had a large stock of dried fish for the winter, 4 tons I should thin, roots &c. He was dressed in the English stile; blue frock coat, pants, & vest comported himself with much dignity enquired my name particularly and repeated it over many times to impress it on his memory. His sister was the squaw of an American of the name of Bache who established a post on the river below the Great Dalles three years ago last fall and who was drowned in them with 11 others the following spring.

The remains of the fort I saw as also the grave of the woman who died this fall and was buried in great state with sundry articles such as *capeau* vest, pantaloons, shirts &c. A pole with a knob at the top is erected over her remains at the foot of the dalles is an island called the Isle of the Dead on which there are many sepulchres. These Indians usually inter their dead on the islands in the most romantic scituations where the souls of the dead can feast themselves with the roar of the mighty and eternal waters which in life time afforded them sustenance and will to all eternity to their posterity.

26th After 30 miles of beautiful navigation with little current and fair strong wind and no rapids we arrived at the Cascade or lower obstruction of the river. Here it is necessary to carry the boat and the Indians are all dead. Only two women are left a sad remnant of a large number, their houses stripped to their frames are in view and their half buried dead this portage will be a hard job. During this day I went ashore to a small lake near the river I killed at one discharge of my double barrelled gun 5 (*missing word in journal*), of them which gave 5 of us a hearty supper. No rain as yet but constant appearance of it ahead. At these rapids are a great many seal it is a mystery to me how they assend them. The direction of the river is here about W. by S. and a little snow on some of the highest of the hills this day we passed the high mountain covered with snow heretofore mentioned it is on the left of the river and is a more stupendous pile than any of the Rocky Mountains. Always covered with snow and is called the Snowy Mountain.

27th In the morning commenced carrying the boat and goods which we finished at 1 o'clock. and making 9 miles in all stopped to repair the boat which was leaky from damage sustained in carrying. Rained all this day and saw but two Indians.

28th With a fair wind and a little rain we decended the river at a great rate. On the route we killed a goose which dropped in the water. A white headed eagle from a distance seeing this took occasion to come, he seized it and lifted it into the air a few feet but our near approach frightened him away. Made this day 26 miles and stopped at a saw mill belonging to the H. B. Co. under charge of a Mr. Cawning(?) a gentleman who came here 22 years since with a Mr Hunt he is in the service of the Co. We were treated by him with the greatest kindness he gave us *moccasins* and food in plenty.

29th Started at 10 o'clock and arrived at the fort of Vancouver at 12, 4 miles. Here I was received with the utmost kindness and hospitality by Doct. McLauchland (McLoughlin) the acting gov. of the place Mr McDonald, Mr Allen and Mr Mckay gentlemen resident here. Our people were supplied with food and shelter from the rain which is constant. They raise at this fort 6000 bush of wheat, 3 of barley, 1500 potatoes, 3000 peas, a large quantity of punkins. They have coming on apple trees, peach trees, and grapes. Sheep, hogs, horses, cows, 600 goats, grist 2, sawmill 2. 24 lb guns powder magazine of stone. The fort is of wood and square they are building a sch. of 70 tons. There are about 8 settlers on the Multnomah they are the old engages of the Co. who have done trapping. I find Doct. McLauchland a fine old gentleman truly philanthropic in his ideas he is doing much good by introducing fruits into this country, which will much facilitate the progress of its settlement (Indian corn 3000 bush).

The gentlemen of this Co. do much credit to their country and concern by their education deportment and talents. I find myself involved in much difficulty on account of my men some of whom wish to leave me and whom the Co. do not wish to engage nor to have them in the country without being attached to some Co. able to protect them, alledging that if any of them are killed they will be obliged to avenge it at an expense of money and amicable relations with the Indians. And it is disagreeable for me to have men who wish to leave me. The Co. seem disposed to render me all the assistance they can they live well at these posts they have 200 acres of land under cultivation the land is of the finest quality.

30th to 5th. Nov Remained at Vancouver and except the last day rain.

6th started down the river to look with a view to the salmon business. We decended the river at about 4 miles per hour and accomplished the journey in parts of 4 days. The river is full of islands but they are all too low for cultivation being occasionally overflowed as also the praries (what few there are) on the main land with the exception of these small levells the country is so rough that a great part of the earth must be inhabited before this. But the soil is good and the timber is heavy and thick and almost impenetrable from underbrush and fallen trees the description of Mess. Lewis & Clark and others is fully borne out as to size and more also the river is so well known at this part of it that I will not insert any observations of my own.

There are a great number of fowl on this river at this time and there will be more as they say soon there are large swan, white geese, a goose with a motled breast and yellow bill a trifle smaller than the goose of N. E. A white goose almost exactly like the domestic goose of N. E. yellow feet and legs as also the former. There is another goose like that of N. E. but I think smaller, there is the tame duck of N. E. with 19 tail feathers and a fine duck to eat. There is the grey duck of N. E. green winged teel, buffle heads, cape races, dippers of the sea, loons, seal, deer, I killed one swimming the river, I saw no elk but only tracks.

Fort George now occupied as a trading post by the H. B. Co. is well scituated on a sloping bank of the river about 2 miles outside of Tongue point and 6 miles inside of Clatsop point. Chinnook point is opposite the latter and inside Chinnook is a river of small size is also inside Tongue point. Above Tongue point about 6 miles are the Cathlametts they are an archipelago of reedy islands overflown at high water. Here are ducks innumerable. The Indians in this part of the river are of late much reduced they appear good and hosptable as far as an Indian ever is that is they are willing to sell provisions for all they can get for them they appear to live well and I believe anyone may with plenty of powder and lead on this river either as a purchase or to shoot there are no beaver here. We arrived at the Fort of V. on the 15th Nov having had no rain during this time.

I must here mention the very kind gentlemanly conduct of Mr. Jas. Bernie suprintendent of Ft. G. who assisted me to a boat and pilot for the outer harbour and acted the part of host to perfection. I had much pleasure with a little liquor and a pipe in his company he has seen much of this country and is of the old N. W. Concern, I derived much information from him. On my return to the fort my men came forward and unanimously desired to be released from their engagement with a view of returning home as soon as possible and for that end to remain here and work for a maintenance until an opportunity should occur. I could not refuse they had already suffered much and our number was so small that the prospect of remuneration to them was very small. I have therefore now no men these last were Mr. Ball Woodman Sinclair, Breck, Abbot, Tibbits.

They were good men and persevered as long as perseverance would do good. I am now afloat on the great sea of life without stay or support but in good hands *i. e.* myself and providence and a few of the H. B. Co. who are perfect gentlemen. During my absence Guy

Trumbul died on the 7th of Nov. of the cholic an attack of which he had on the Platte of which he nearly died. In this case he was taken in the evening and died early in the morning His funeral was attended by all the gentlemen at the place and prayers were said according to the form of the Church of England, for this attention to my affairs in my absense was considerate to my feelings and I hope will be duly appreciated. Service is here performed on Sunday and on the days prescribed by the church of Eng. Our excursion down the river was performed in an Indian canoe which we hired for a 3 ½ point blanket. We found it very kittish but withall a good craft for sailing and easy to paddle but the men were exceedingly awkward.

19th From this to the 29th I remained at Fort Vancouver eating and drinking the good things to be had there and enjoying much the gentlemanly society of the place.

On the 29th. with Abbot and Woodman in an Indian canoe I started for a journey up the Wallamet or Multonomah River this river which is highest in the winter was so at this time but is not rapid until near the falls the subjoined scetch will shew its course as I made it distance by the river by my estimate 27 ½ miles to the falls which are perpendicular about 20 feet past these we carried our canoe about ¼ mile and launched above the falls the water though generally more rapid above would admit of the running of a steamboat. In this river at this time there is more water than in the Missouri and not of a more difficult character to navigate the tide flows to within 8 miles of the falls below the full the banks of the river are not suitable for cultivation being overflowed as far as the bottom extends which is not far and beyond these the country rises into rocky hills unfit for tillage but producing very large timber mostly if not all of the pines. On the bottoms there is considerable oak of a kind not found in the States but of excellent quality for ship building and is the only kind of oak found in the country of the Columbia.

I noticed but two streams coming into the river below the falls. The river to within 6 miles of its junction with the Columbia runs along the N. E. side of a range of hills or as they would be called in N. E. mountains at the falls it passes through this range. This river has two mouths the East one is the one I assended, the West one follows the range of hills above, described to their falling on the Columbia about 3 miles below the eastern entrance, the mouth of this river is in latt 45 deg. 36 min. 51 sec. long. 122 deg. 48 min. Above the falls for 22

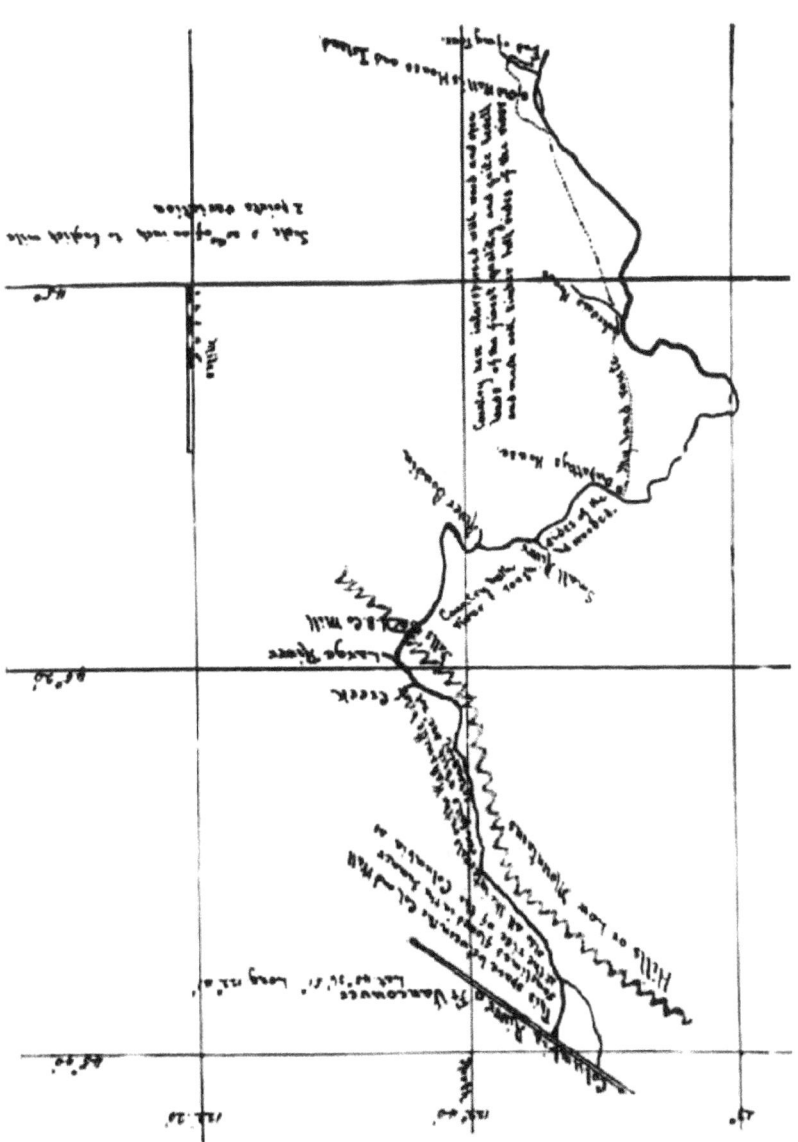

miles by estimate the banks of the river are high enough to prevent overflowing but timbered and not fertile and rough and the country apparently not valuable except for timber, which is here mostly of the pines, except a small quantity of cotton wood and alder. The latter is here a tree of sometimes a foot and an half through at the falls the H. B. Co. are erecting a sawmill to which they contemplate adding a grist mill. The scituation for mill priviledges is beyond anything I have ever seen. 22 miles from the falls are 3 or 4 Canadians settled as farmers they have now been there one year have hogs, horses, cows, have built barns, houses, and raised wheat, barely, potatoes, turnips, cabbages, corn, punkins, melons.

The country here becomes open, but still wood enough and a much greater proportion of oak prairies of from 1 to 30 miles in extent bound by a skirting of timber. This country seems a valley between the mountains to the East and West of about 50 miles wide including both sides of the river and is very level of nearly uniform soil extremely rich equal to the best of the Missouri lands. Accounts vary much as to its southerly extent I have seen it at least 75 miles in a southwardly direction and from all I can learn I think it extends with but little interruption as far south as the valley of the Buneventura, which is also of the same description of country, and I have never seen country of equal beauty except the Kanzas country and I doubt not will one day sustain a large population. 10 miles by land above the first settlement and 30 by the river is another by a Mr Jervie which was a very fine beginning of one year's standing of the same character and product as the one below. In all about 9 settlers are on this river if this country is ever colonised this is the point to commence the river is navigable for canoes to its very sources but as I understand very circuitous. Deer abounds in this district and wolves one of which a large devil I shot. These settlers I found exceeding attentive to my comforts especially Mr Jervie at whose house I slept 2 nights. I was absent from the fort this time 10 days.

To the 4th Jany. the weather was little better than a continual rain not however a hard rain often but a drizzling uncomfortable air. During December there fell 9½ inches rain by a pluviometer on the 4th the wind came strong to N. N. E. with fair and cool weather, ther. averaging about 19 deg. This continued to the 8th when there is much floating ice in the river and those here think that with two days more of this weather the river will close. The readiness with which the river freezes must arise from the water getting intensely cold in the upper country. During this month Mr. McKay gave our room a treat of buffaloe meat salted and smoked and this being the first opportunity of comparing good buffaloe meat with other good meat was highly acceptable. I think it equal to the best meat ever eaten. Up to the 4th there was no frost in the ground and ploughing is commonly done all the winter.

During the latter part of January the river rose about 4 feet which must have arisen from the rains as there could be no melting of snow on the mountains at this season. These rains must have I think extended farther back than is described to be their range *viz* the falls at which the timbered country terminates. Carrots are here finer and larger than I have ever before seen, one I think was 3 inches through and of fine flavour. There appears much sickness among the people here especially among the common people which I think arises from low diet and moist weather for as far as I can observe the gentlemen who live well are not much subject to disorders. The main disorder is an intermittent fever which has carried off all or nearly all the Indians who live even worse than the engages. The *Lima* which sailed a month since had not to the 1st Jany. got out of the river. I have been informed by Mr Douglas and Mr. Finlesson that vessels have laid off the bar 7 weeks before they could enter.

11th Jany. The river closed with ice and I am detained here until it opens. Last winter the river remained frozen 5 weeks there is yet no snow. Today heard by Mr Hermatinger of the death of Mr Vanderburg killed by the Blackfeet. Up to this time the weather continued clear and cold for this country, the ther. varying from 12 deg. to 20 deg.

On the 18th at 2 o'clock it commenced hailing and at daylight the hail was about 2 inches on the ground, the river closed on the 10th and so remains at present. On the 14th I walked across the Columbia and found the ice about 6 inches thick where it lay smooth but it was much turned up edge wise. Afternoon of the 18th commenced raining and on the 19th rains still. The hail was at one time from 1½ to 2 inches deep on the 18th.

19th After raining hard all night there is no snow left it is warm and showery today ther. 54 deg.

20th Raining still and ther. 52 deg. River not yet cleared ice stationary.

21st, 22nd warm and rainy.

23rd The river broke up still warm ther. 51 deg. I am informed by Mr Dav. Douglas that a Mr Woodard whom he saw in Calafornia was intending to come to the Columbia for salmon, he is a brother-in-law to Capt. Ebbets and is from New York Mr. Douglass saw him in Calafornia in July 1832. I am informed by Doct J. McGlaucland that he has seen strawberry's ripe here in Dec. and in blossom in Jany. The weather warm up to the 28th with occasional rains there is now little ice on the river. On the banks the wreck and rubbish of the breaking up of the river. The H. B. Co. are now making a fort at Nass. to counteract the Am. vessells on the coast.

28th Warm still and fair the Co. are about sending a party under Mr. Manson to make a fort at Milbank Sound.

30th Today a party sent to enquire after another reported to be cut off beyond the Umquoi or near the Clammat River under a man by the name of Michelle returned having ascertained that one white and two Indians only of said party had been killed. This party I am informed was under a man by the name of Duportt I requested to accompany him but the gov. would not consent alledging they would conceive that I came to avenge the death of Mr. Smith's party who was cut off by the Umquoi Indians, all which I interpreted into a jealousy of my motives. This party brought back 200 skins which they had traded they did not go beyond the Umquoi, they were gone 2 months lost no men and but 2 horses which died of fatigue.

31st to the 3rd. Feb. We had warm and wet weather. On the 3rd at 10 o'clock. we started for Wallah Walla I had with me two men and am in company with Mr Ermatinger of the H. B. Co. who has in charge 3 boats with 120 pieces of goods and 21 men. I parted with feelings of sorrow from the gentlemen of Fort Vancouver their unremitted kindness to me while there much endeared them to me more so than it would seem possible during so short a time. Doct. McGlaucland the gov. of the place is a man distinguished as much for his kindness and humanity as his good sense and information and to whom I am so much indebted as that he will never be forgotten by me. This day we came to the Prarie Du Lis 15 miles. Raining most of the day.

4th Left the Prairie Du Lis on the lower end of it this prairie is about 3 miles long and through it the River Du Lis a small creek enters the Columbia. We made but 2 miles when one of our boats ran foul of a rock and was stove. It landed its cargo without wetting much this accident detained us till ¼ before 12 o'clock when we started and kept on till 2 o'clock and stopped 20 minutes to dine, then kept on till ½ past 5 o'clock making 17 miles this day. This river is at medium water the rivers banks high precipitous and rocky from the Lea prairie in one place the bank on the N. side rises to 200 feet perpendicular. I saw a hawk light on a projecting crag about halfway up which gave me a good idea of the height of the rock. From this rock a small stream casts itself into the Com. whether a permanent one or not cannot say but should think not. There are here many white headed eagles, one skunk we saw today, the timber appears much smaller than below, no rain but cloudy this day wind West and ther. about 40 deg. now at 8 o'clock at night the full moon is looking down calmly upon us apparently thinking that the cares of us humble individuals concern her little.

5th We left camp at 7 o'clock and made 4 miles to breakfast and in 7 miles more the foot of the cascades. Our breakfast was made on a small island abreast of a rock rising perpendicular from the bed of the river as I should think 400 feet high Lewis & Clark call it I think 700 feet, this rock is nearly surrounded by the waters of the river

The cascades occasion a portage of 100 rods our goods were carried across this day, the river is here compressed into a very small place and the bed is full of rocks I should think the fall to be about 8 feet in the space of the 60 rods. There are here two fishing villages both now deserted as the people here say from the inmates being all dead of the fever, but I suspect some are dead and the rest and much larger part frightened away. We made the portage by the North side on which is one of the above villages it is near the river on a little clear spot with a little lake in the rear.

Here the Indians were once hostile and great caution was once used in passing,- now but little is requisite. It rained all the latter part of the day and night and morning of the 6th. Finished the portage but our boats were so bruised that the rest of the day was taken to gum them. Took a look about me the rest of the day found that the *tripe de roche* grew on the rocks here but small. Here there are many petrifactions of wood in a bank of gravell some of which are perfectly petrified and will not burn in the fire but others appear only half so and burn and cut freely they are found bedded in stone composed of rubble of some former world the gravel is cemented together by finer gravell the whole being volcanic and water worn.

7th At 1½ mile above the cascade is a small river from the N. and 4½ above this a creek from the N. Rained all the 6th and rains a little today. Came in all 27 miles passed many Indian habitations on the river and canoes. 15 miles above the cascades is a torrent that precipitates itself into the river from about 60 feet 17 miles from same. On same side *viz* south is a creek both small one between them. On the N. side timber growing gradually thinner.

8th We found that a *capeau* and 2 blanketts had been stolen by some Indians from one of our men and went to the village just below our camp to recover them, they acknowledged the theft but the thieves had run off. We took two canoes to our camp and breakfasted immediately. After breakfast the man who had lost the articles took an axe and broke the worst canoe for which he was reprimanded by Mr Ermatinger, the other he left and a little after we left I saw the Indians come and take it. We made 29 miles to the dalles which are one mile or thereabouts long and encamped having passed two of the boats the other owing to some mistake had sheered out and forced the line from those who were towing and forced one Indian into the stream and was drowned.

He was on a bank about 15 feet high he swam until he got into a whirlpool and went down. Just below the dalles the timber ceases. There are here many Indians, Tilky and Casineau are here the chiefs and very clever ones. All this day we saw Indians on the banks. The water passes even now at a furious rate and at high water it is impassible and boats are carried as much as two miles and all the goods. For assisting through this place a little tobacco is given the Indians we gave the usual quantity and saw a personal struggle for the division of it.

9th Left the Great Dalles and in three miles came to the little dalles which we passed by towing in, which we were delayed by reason of having only two lines, one having been lost at the time the Indian was drowned. In three miles more I arrived at the shutes or falls of the Columbia which are not in this stage of the water more than ten feet perpendicular, but much more than that including the rapids above and below in the immediate vicinity. These falls once during the times the whites have been here have been sailed up owing as I suppose to the dalles at such times, affording a slow outlet to the accumulated waters, and their being raised by this circumstance to above the level of the falls. This day got our baggage and goods over at the G. Dalles. I traded one horse which I sent on by Abbot. At the shutes we found about 150 to 200 Indians who were very troublesome having to pay for very trifling services however they stole nothing.

10th Passed over and gummed the boats and at ½ past 12 started up the river having traded another horse and sent it on by Woodman. One mile above the River Aux Rapide comes from the south. The size of the stream I cannot tell as I only saw the mouth of it here on the N. side of the river. Abbot came to me having lost the horse entrusted to him I took Mr. Woodman's and gave Abbot with orders to wait until 10 o'clock tomorrow and then to come on whether he got the horse or not. We came today 9 miles and 6 yesterday. Here we have to give a piece of tobacco for every stick of wood we get. Last night was the first frost I have seen since the river broke the grass is somewhat green. This part of the river affords trout in small quantity.

11th Started at an early hour and made the mouth of a considerable stream coming from the S. called John Day's River from a hunter of that name formerly in this country. Distant from our last camp 7½ miles we camped 22½ miles from this on the North side of the river having had a strong and fair wind all day. One thing I observed in this part of the river is that the savages are civil and as much as one in ten has lost an eye as I suppose from the effects of the fine sand of the river being blown about or the violent wind for which this part of the river is noted. We found some few roots and little game with the natives. The night was windy and uncomfortable but no frost but a little rain.

12th At ½ past 6 we started and made 2 miles to breakfast on the N. side fair wind and clear. One boat stove and must stop to repair and gum. Found two small logs of drift wood. At 10 o'clock recommenced our journey with a fair light wind and made in all this day 17 miles. During the day had the satisfaction of seeing Abbot come up but without finding the lost horse.

13th Calm in morning but after breakfast had a fair and middling strong wind. At 1 o'clock passed the upper end of Grand Island. An Indian today brought me a pouch and horn stolen from one of my men going down, but the balls and powder used up, which I redeemed for a little tobacco. Last night a frost not severe. Made this day 25 miles found wood enough for use on the banks but it is a custom of the Indians to run along the beach and take possession of the wood there may be and sell it to you for tobacco which appears to be their greatest luxury a quid is pay for almost anything.

14th We started at 6 o'clock and in one mile passed the River Ottillah one mile above which rapids commence these we passed one mile long making 3 to breakfast and started at ½ past 10 with a fair and strong wind and reached Wallah Walla at 5 p. m. Just before reaching this place the cut rocks close into the river in such a manner that there appears but a small perpendicular sided gap to look through. Past these and at W. W. both banks fall down to a nearly levell plain. We were again hospitably received by Mr. P. C. Pambrun we remained at this post until the 19th. of Feb. The weather mild and clear but high S. W. winds, W. W. is a place noted for high winds. A little frost during the nights only grass just getting green. My horses in tolerable good order and all found, eat horse meat all the time at this post.

On Sunday took a ride up the River W. W. found its bottoms good but not extensive and no wood. The corn for this post, 150 bushells last year, was raised at least 3 miles from the fort, none was stolen by the Indians a good test of their honesty as they are all most always starving. This place is kept by about 5 men, Indians are freely admitted inside of it. About 1200 skins traded here it is kept up mostly for trading horses and the safety of the communication. The course of the Wallah Wallah River is E. by N. near the fort when I saw it.

19th Just as we were leaving the fort an Indian brought in the horse which Abbot lost at the dalles and a short time after leaving the fort an Indian sent by Mr. P. brought one other which had strayed from Abbot at this place. We made this day 17 miles to a branch of the Wallah Wallah River. Here coming from the N. the space nearly a plain and barren and sandy but good grass. This branch appears to be about half the Wallah Wallah River. Encamped a little after sundown and for 12 yards blue cloths, 1 blanket, 2½ pt 50 balls and powder, 2 knives, 1 lb. Tobacco, bunch beads, 10 fish hooks traded a good horse this appears a fair price here.

20th We made a late start and after travelling 9 hours without water arrived at the Snake River. Here running W. our course was this day N. by E. 22 ½ miles over a country which would be considered light sandy land with little sage grass good and in tufts very level except some trifling roundly swelling hills these make one think of gently swelling breasts of the ladies. Day warm and clear. We in the first of the day followed the branch of the W. W. mentioned yesterday say four miles on which I saw blackbirds which Mr. Pambrun says stay at W.

W. all winter.

21st No frost in morning Crossed the river to the mouth of a creek coming into the river from the N. for 10 miles which was the length of our march this day. This creek is through cut rocks of moderate height for this country. We followed the stream on the east bank. These banks were about 300 feet high to the levell of the plain, if that can be called a plain where the hills rise to an almost equal height and the gullies are abrupt and narrow. The soil was what would be called in N. E. a poor sandy soil producing good grass but still no wood. Traded two horses this day at the usual rates. The people who are most used to this country are so little afraid of the Indians that they either travel without guns or with them unloaded.

22nd A pretty hard frost in the morning. Followed the river one mile on the North side then crossed it and made North 3 miles and crossed a branch of it coming from the N.W. Our course this day N. by E. and encamped at a little run of water running S. E. This is inconsiderable. Saw about 20 antelope this day in one herd. At our camp this night observed about 2 inches of frost in the ground. This day's ride over very rocky country the valleys of which are very good but small otherwise more sandy than common grass good. Made 22 ½ miles,

23rd N. 17 miles over a rough and rocky country with a few small bottoms which are good land at 9 miles from last camp passed some of the best specimens of Basaltic columns which I have seen. They were 5 sided and about 50 feet high some standing independent others tumbled down to the foot of the wall like demolished towers. This days march passed many small lakes whether formed by the snow or not I cannot say but I think some of them are permanent none larger than a few acres. Camped at a stream coming from the N. and were visited by three Indians who report the road to Colville impassable for snow, a hard frost last night and frost in the ground beside the lakes mostly frozen over but not thick these made me think of the old buisness of my life.

24th 20 miles N. through timber in the first of which we encamped last night. The stream which we camped on here forks no game except two small prairie hens. Passed many little lakes one of which is as large fresh pond and one nearly so the rest smaller. Patches of snow and one third of the trees prostrated last year by southerly gale their trunks much obstructed the path before us. On the right are snow covered and moderately high mountains. Found good wood at our camp by the light of which I now write, the scene reminds me of my ice men at work by torch light. Not frost enough in the ground to prevent driving tent stakes the little rain and snow made streams which are running southerly.

25th In a N. direction 15 miles to Spokan River a stream now about half as large as the Snake River it is now high from the melting of the snow its sources are not distant and in a range of mountains. in sight this range runs about N. W. which is here the general course of the stream but how far I cannot say as it is visible but a short distance. At this place are the remains of the old Spokan House one bastion of which only is now standing which is left by the Indians from respect to the dead, one clerk of the Co. being buried in it. The banks of this river are here rocky and precipitous I observed among the rocks of its bed granite, green stone, quartz, sandstone, lava or basalt. The country on approaching this river from the South resembles the pine plains of N. Hampshire. Near Concord we passed the divide between the waters of this and the last river about 5 miles from our last night's camp striking hen after passing the isolated wood in which we had camped and a large plain devoid of wood a deep valley running N. Crossed the most of our baggage today.

26th Arrived. After perusing the enclosed loose papers I proceed.[7]

27th March [8] due N. E. by N 24 miles we made this day This line cuts the Spokan River This point we turned but I call the course direct for convenience this course is through a tolerable fertile prairie the grass good and flowers plenty on the W. side are low range of rocky hills which are granite and a better development of the broken rock named yesterday I find it to be volcanic by its being (*missing word*) blending with porous rock on our left and about half way of the days march passed a mile distant a little lake ½ mile across to the E. by N. of this is a lake 3 miles across from which the Spokan flows neither of

---

7. The loose papers referred to were probably pinned to the preceding leaf of the journal, but have been lost. They no doubt were the journal notes made by Mr. Wyeth while taking a trip from the "Spokan House" to Fort Colville and back. That Mr. Wyeth took such a trip is evident from the fact that one of the letters bearing the date of March 12th 1833 was written from Fort Colville. The journal of March 28th refers to such a trip and the return to the "Spokan house".

8. The word "March" is to be read as part of the date. The trip referred to above seems to have consumed exactly a calendar month.

these I have seen but take this from hearsay arrived at our camp and all well and in better order I have forgot to mention that the stream that comes into the Spokan near the house brings down pebbles of volcanic rock also that the streams near our present camp come from the hills enter the prairie of the Spokan River and disappear in the ground.

28th Made 18 miles N. through a level and wooded country and camped with only snow water and poor grass, the rocks seen today are holders of granite and observed that the compass in one place would not traverse. This happened while going to Colville from Spokan and coming from there back also observed. Today and yesterday the effects of some former gale in prostrated trees direction here S. W.

29 horses missing in morning and not found till noon. Went N. 9 miles and struck Flat Head River. Compass again refused to traverse through deep snow today and yesterday and thick young trees and fallen timber observed here the white pine and hemlock. Snow and rain all yesterday found our people at the river with the boats.

30th Remained at the same place crossed the river, I here saw an Indian who was entirely blind he seemed to be taken good care of by his relatives, made him a small present for which he thanked me parted company with Mr Ermatinger he to go on with the goods by water myself with horses by land last night the coldest for some time today warm and pleasant

31st Moved early N. 7 miles passing a point and two little streams. Excessively bad going in crossing the point from snow and brush E. two miles along the river N. N. E. 5 miles to the lake then a line to our camp cutting the lake 5 miles more N. N. E. This lake is about three miles broad and indeed the river so far resembles a long lake little or no current and ¾ miles wide plenty of partridges, geese, and duck and some deer meat of the Indians. All clay country mountainous. One horse gave out and left him. A good lodge made of branches of pine had almost made me forget that it had snowed and rained all day ourselves and goods were wet through we had no human comfort except meat enough to eat and good.

1st April E. 2, N 3, E by S. 3, and found that from this spot the place where I entered on the lake, bore S. W. N. by E. 2, E. by S. 5 N. 3 and made the traverse of a large peninsular at one mile E. by N. Struck the head of a creek which after 3 miles more led us back to the lake at the entrance into it of the River Fete Plate. This lake is a large and fine sheet of water it appears of a good depth. There looks as if a large river entered on the S. side at the east end it is widest and there are two islands it is surrounded by lofty and now snowy mountains. but their summits are timbered. Yesterday saw nothing but granite today saw slate and sandstone not the least volcanic appearance in this part of the country.

2nd Made E. S. E. 6 miles through a difficult swamp over a hill and to the main river again during which time we passed two small streams this swamp had the largest cedars apparently the same as those of the N. E. that I have ever seen I measured one at my height from the ground of 31 feet circumferance and I presume some were larger. No rocks today but sandstone and slate. Camped on account of my horses having had no feed lately.

The slate is tortuitous and I think mica slate. Here my Indian brought me in some onions and two kinds of trout, some of the trout I have bought of the Indians as large as 10 lbs. they are plenty and taken with the hook. There are plenty of ducks and geese, the ducks are as the tame ducks of N. E.

3rd 10 miles almost due E. cutting a mountain and through almost impenetrable wood and deep snow much trouble and delay to keep the trail from the mountain. 4 miles from last night's camp saw our last camp on this lake which bore W. by N. tonight we camped without grass but could not go further some of the horses strayed in the trail behind.

4th Started our Indian early to find the strayed horses and started camp ahead 9 miles E. following the river the whole way although the trail cuts off the point and encamped where the trail again strikes the river. At this place there is a considerable creek coming from the E. by N. into the river. Here for the first time since reaching Walla Walla I saw fresh beaver sign. The Indian has not yet come up with the horses and little feed for those we have with us. Today saw a small sized bear but he was off too soon for a shot.

5th 12 miles E. S. E. through deep snow and thick wood most of the way sometimes miry sometimes slippery with ice and always obstructed by the great quantity of fallen wood. Last night late the Indian brought up all the lost horses .

6th 9 miles E. S. E. trail better slate rock only. Camped on the river last night in the mountains. Yesterday two horses gave out left a man to keep them and bring them up if possible. Today one gave out which I will leave at this camp for same man.

7th Arrived at the Flathead post kept by Mr. Rivi and one man after a ride of 17 miles E. S. E. through thick wood not very good trail and a snowstorm which loaded the pines in such a manner as to bend them down to the ground frequently loading me with the snow, as passing I disturbed the branches trees loaded down in this way and frozen so as to be firm constitute much of the difficulty of the route from Flathead or Ponderay Lake to this place. Want of grass at this time of the year the residue with some mire rock, mica slate. This place is scituated on a fine prairie 2 miles long, 1 wide and seems pleasant after coming through thick woods and mountains. Counting my horses found 32 of 47 with which I started but think I shall recover all but one left on the lake having sent men and Indians in search of them.

Mr E. came in the boats in 5 days. I have now news by four Indians who came in on the 6th on foot. The Nez Perces have lost all but 4 horses of their band of about 500 stolen by the Blackfeet. The Flatheads expected in about 15 days. On the 11th started out to see if there were many beaver in the country with intention of staying 12 days but was recalled by the arrival of the buffaloe. Indians found few beaver and the country can only be trapped on foot plenty of partridges to be found in this country. Arrived again at the post on the 17th of April my route was back on the Flathead River.

18th to 20th Remained at the post having now found all my horses. Started camp 2 miles east up the river and to the upper end of the prairie on which the house is built. At this place is a large creek coming from the N.

21st Rained hard last night and from the 17th to this day have had one or more slight showers each day the plain is now good grass. We are much annoyed by the dogs of the Indian village which are numerous they eat all our cords and fur flesh they can get at in the night. This is always a great trouble while travelling with Indians until you get to buffaloe where they find better food. For three nights no frost. This valley is the most romantic place imaginable a level plain of two miles long by one wide. On the N a range of rocky and snow clad mountains. on the S. the Flathead river a rapid current and plenty of good fishing running at the immediate base of another lofty snowy and rocky range of mountains.

Above and below the valley the mountains of each range close upon the river so as apparently to afford no outlet either way. About 200 horses feeding on the green plain and perhaps 15 Indian lodges and numerous barking dogs with now and then a half-breed on horseback galloping gracefully with plenty of gingling bells attached to all parts of himself and horse. It is really a scene for a poet nought but man is wanting to complete it

22nd Moved 8 miles E. N. E. along the river. At 6 miles passed a very bad rock called le Roche Mauvais. The mountains as yet closely follow the river on both sides but seem declining in height. As we stopped early we spent the rest of the day in preparing to prevent the Blackfoot from stealing our horses they have never but once passed the bad rock and then the Flatheads gave them such a beating as keeps them since in better order they infest much the country we are now about entering.

23rd Moved 8 miles E. N. E. to horse plain thence N. E. 5 miles cutting a hill and leaving the river which we had heretofore followed decending the mountains E. N. E. 6 miles to a large open valley in the hills with little timber and much grass. Opposite to our camp is a mountain where 200 Flatheads Conterays, Ponderays and other Indians were killed by the Blackfoot Indians. During the first part of the last division of the day's march passed a small lake with many waterfowl and one sand hill crane. We are now fairly in the dangerous country through horse plain and into the River Flathead is a small brook. Today 2 Indians arrived from the main Flathead Camp at Porte D'enfer with news that the Blackfoot have made 2 hauls of horses from them. The Flathead Camp consists of men of various tribes.

24th moved E. by S. down the valley to Flathead River then 4 miles E. following the river then forded it and made 3 miles E. by N. and encamped on it at a place where last year a man by the name of La Couse was killed by the Blackfoot Indians. The river is not now high when so it is not fordable and is here a good sized stream the salts here whiten in the ground and the animals are almost crazy after it which makes them bad to drive. The morning was sultry and I travelled without my coat but in the afternoon we had a fine shower with some thunder of good quality the valley we left today abounds with the finest Kamas I have yet seen as provisions are scarce in camp the women dug much of it.

25th moved camp up the main river 12 miles E ½ N. then up a large but fordable branch 3 miles E. by S. trail fine grass good weather beautiful no frost for three nights the climate appears much as at Baltimore at this season.

26th Made E. along the creek last named 5 miles then crossed and followed it 4 miles S. E. then recrossed it and followed it E. S. E. 3 miles crossing a small branch then 2 miles recrossing the main creek again then followed 1 mile E S. E. and recrossed it and followed a small branch of it S. E. 1 mile crossed the branch and followed it 2 miles S. E. to camp. Clear except 1 shower but only comfortably warm. Country hilly but open.

E. lay a heavy pile of snowy mountains. 5 miles distant apparently running N. and S. the rocks for a few days have been sandstone mica slate. This day saw a white bear which we surrounded to kill but he broke through and escaped. Earth in some places whitened with salt which makes the horses bad to drive. Horses getting fat grass good as also the bottom lands which are tolerably extensive.

27th Remained at same camp snowed a little. This day the Indians went hunting and got one deer.

28th Abbot brought in one beaver. Started camp 2 miles S. E. 2 S.S.E.2 S.4 S. by W. thus far through woods and a defile crossing the vide between the creek which we were on and another going to that branch of the Flathead River to which we came this day. Then into open plains snowy mountains on each side 3 miles S. S. E. then 5 miles S. E. by E. crossing two slews of the Flathead River and camped on a third and larger one, which we shall be obliged to raft over, I judge it twice as large as the one we crossed some days since. The river here runs S. W. A little snow today. Quarrelled and parted with my man Woodman he appeared to think that as I had but two he might take libertys, under such circumstances I will never yield an inch, I paid him half as I conceive he had gone half the route with me. Here we met some Indians from the great camp which they say is a moderate camp distant.

29th Forgot to mention in proper place that I saw plumb trees at the place we left W. branch of the Flathead River, these are said to be good about one inch through ripe in Sept. and found nowhere else but at this place, I tried hard to get some stones but could not. Moved this day S. S. W. we crossed by fording contrary to expectation by loading high and taking high horses. At 8 miles struck another branch of same river as large as those already passed at 4 miles further a creek from opposite side ford tolerably good. At 20 miles came to main camp of no lodges, containing upward of 1000 souls with all of which I had to shake hands. The custom in meeting these Indians is for the coming party to fire their arms, then the other does the same then dismount and form single file both sides and passing each other, shake hands with men women and children a tedious job.

Buffaloe have come here and even further but they are killed at once and do not get wonted. Here the *racine amani* or *spetulum* is found. This camp is on the river good grass river direct S. S. W. Six nights since the Blackfoot stole horses from this camp. Here I found three Canadians one of whom was one who came to us the night before we were fired on on the heads of the Spanish River. This day's march between two parralled ranges of mountains now snowy but I think not always so. There is much *kamas* in this region we find little meat in the Indian camp and are therefore much shortened for food.

30th Went out to collect some flowers for friend Nuttall, afterwards to see the camp. Find 120 lodges of us today some having arrived they are collecting to go to the buffaloe in force to meet the Blackfeet. Looked at their games one is played by two men at a time a level place is made on the ground about 15 feet long by 3 feet wide with a small log of wood at each end to stop a small iron ring which one of them rools from one end of the alley to the other both following it, each having an arrow which they endeavour to throw after and under it so that when stopped it will rest on one of them. The one on whose arrow it is wins, at least this is all I understand of the game the game is kept by a third by means of placing sticks on one side or the other. Another feat much in practice from the smallest to the largest in camp is two with some arrows, throw them so as to go as near the first thrown as possible advancing continually untill all are expended then throwing them back again in same manner.

Another game is two or more opposite the one side, having some small article in their hand keep changing it from one hand to the other as swift as possible accompanied by a tune and motion of body and limbs except feet (for they sit all the time) the get is for the other party to designate the band in which it remains at the last. This is the most practised game and requires much dexterity on both sides it is kept with sticks as the first. Every morning some important Indian addresses either heaven or his countrymen or both I believe exhorting the one to good conduct to each other and to the strangers among them and the other to bestow its blessings he finishes with "I am done." The whole set up an exclamation in concord during the whole time. Sunday there is more parade of prayer as above nothing is done Sunday in the way of trade with these Indians nor in playing games and they seldom fish or kill game or raise camp while prayers are being said on weekdays.

    Everyone ceases whatever vocation he is about, if on horseback he dismounts and holds his horse on the spot until all is done. Theft is a thing almost unknown among them and is punished by flogging as I am told, but have never known an instance of theft among them the least thing even to a bead or pin is brought you if found and things that we throw away this is sometimes troublesome. I have never seen an Indian get in anger with each other or strangers. I think you would find among 20 whites as many scoundrels as among 1000 of these Indians they have a mild playful laughing disposition and their qualities are strongly portrayed in their countenances. They are polite and unobtrusive and however poor never beg except as pay for services and in this way they are moderate and faithful but not industrious, they are very brave and fight the Blackfeet who continually steal their horses and kill their straglers with great success beating hollow equal numbers.

    They wear as little clothing as the weather will permit, sometimes nothing on except a little thing to cover the privates and sometimes but rare this is ommitted at play, but not when there are women and allways at a race the women are closely covered and chaste never cohabiting promiscuously with the men. The pox is not much and perhaps never known among them it dies here of itself when brought from the coast where it is rife. The young women are good looking and with dress and cleanliness would be lovely. Today about 100 of them with their root diggers in their hands in single file went out to get roots they staid about two hours and returned in the same order each time passing the chief's lodge it was evidently a ceremony but the import I could not learn. In a lodge or other place when one speaks the rest pay strict attention.

    When he is done another assents by "yes" or dissents by "no" and then states his reasons which are heard as attentively. It is a practice when a woman has her courses to make a little lodge outside her husband's lodge and there remain until they are finished. The more peaceable dispositions of the Indians than the whites is plainly seen in the children I have never heard an angry word among them nor any quarrelling although there are here at least 500 of them together and at play the whole time at football bandy and the like, sports which give occasion to so many quarrels among white children.

May 1st. Same camp. The day reminds me of home and its customs it is a fine and almost summer day although the nights have been frosty of late but the days are warm. This morning the squaws left camp with their root diggers singing in good accord the tunes of their country. Yesterday Mr. Ermatinger traded 29 beavers. I find an Indian camp a place of much novelty the Indians appear to enjoy their amusements with more zest than the whites although they are simple they are great gamblers in proportion to their means bolder than the whites.

2nd Moved Camp 2 miles S. E. by E. 4 miles S by E. over a hilly but open country and diverging a little from the main river to the eastward and camped on a small river. Going to the same river the two parallel ranges of mountains still continue on either side of the river. It rained a little of the last night and some this morning, the day is cloudy and moderately warm. The absence of quarrels in an Indian camp more and more surprises me, when I come and see the various occasions which would give rise to them among the whites, the crowding together of from 12 to 1800 horses which have to be driven into camp at night to stake in morning to load the starting of horses and turning of loads the seizing of fuel when scarce, often the case, the plays of men and boys &c. At the camp yesterday saw the bones of a buffalo bull not old being the first sign of buffaloe yet seen.

3rd. Same camp.

4th Same camp. Today heard a sound like a heavy piece of ordonance and I suppose arising from the fall of some mighty fragment of rock from the mountains. The sound seemed to come from the N. I suppose the sound heard in the Snake country arose from the same cause although then no heavy mountains were in sight but there were cut rocks enough. Weather somewhat smokey but warm and clear. A party of hunters who proposed to go out for beaver deferred the thing on account of the water being too high to set a trap. A thunderstorm in the afternoon with high wind from the S. W. and rain.

5th. Sunday according to our reconing. There is a new great man now getting up in the camp and like the rest of the world covers his designs under the great cloak religion. His followers are now dancing to their own vocal music in the plain. Perhaps 15 of the camp follow him. When he gets enough followers he will branch off and be an independent chief he is getting up some new form of religion among the Indians more simple than himself like others of his class he works with the fools, women and children first. While he is doing this the men of sense thinking it too foolish to do harm stand by and laugh but they will soon find that women, fools and children form so large a majority that with a bad grace they will have to yield. These things make me think of the new lights and revivals of New England. Rains a little today.

6th. Bright and clear. Found all of my horses three of which had been missing. Moved 4 miles S. and encamped on a creek of the main river about 1½ miles from the latter.

7th. Same camp. Cloudy all night and today but warm.

8th. Same camp. Last night had a false alarm. Some Indians of the camp who were gambling for a gun, discharged it before laying it on the stakes. This though a common occurrence gave the horses a fright and one frightens another in those cases until all are alarmed the running of those that have got loose, the snorting stamping and rearing of those who cannot when there are at least 1500, the howling of dogs, men running with guns, the contrast of firelights with the darkness of the night, make altogether a scene of confusion to be recollected. This day hunters went out 2 only one returned sun two hours high with one antelope the other at night with 4. Today a small boy broke his arm but as I understood that the Indians reduce fractures well and as I am quite ignorant I did not meddle with it.

9th. Moved S. by E. 6 miles and camped on the main river. On the march saw two Blackfeet who ran with all the speed of their horses to the mountains. A little rain but warm high wind and somewhat dusty. The rain does not seem to lay the dust in the least. The country covered for the first time with sage and so far the same kind of minerals as near the Ponderay Lake. This afternoon came to us a Snake a Nez Perce and a Flathead on foot, they came from Salmon River and bring no news except that the Nez Perce Camp is at Salmon River and that they are mostly without horses.

10th Moved 7 miles E. by E. (?), rained a little shower but clear in the afternoon. This moment Chief Guineo is saying the usual afternoon prayers I observe that he first makes a long one which is responded to by the usual note in accord then a short one followed by the same note on horse back the whole time walking about the camp hat on in an audible voice and directed as though addressing the men below rather than "him" above. Today 11 Flatheads started on foot to steal horses from the Blackfeet.

11th Started out early hunting for the first time this trip. We are now short of provisions. The camp moved 10 miles S. by E. and camped on the river the wide bottom of which is done it is now jammed in between the hills. During this distance passed two small creeks big enough for beaver only saw four antelope killed nothing saw two olived green snakes about 2½ feet long blunt tail but slender. Afternoon clear and warm

12th Being Sunday remained at same camp the hills here are of granite with large bed of quartz. Mica slate is common Gneiss also, in some places the same rock as at Kittle falls observed in one place a black mineral like that found at Franconis (?) covering iron ore it looks like horse hair in a mass combed straight. The hills are now well covered with grass. The river is now at its highest but is fordable. This morning long prayers in form as usual at some lodges the Indians are singing as an act of devotion

13th Went out hunting killed one N. E. partridge only saw 4 cubs 4 deer. Camp moved 6 miles S. S. E. and camped on the W. side we approach the head of this river fast

14th. Remained at same camp snow and sleet all day. An Indian died in camp today but I do not think the camp was delayed on that account, it was a bad day which I think the reason his friends are now singing over him according to their custom

15th Made 6 miles S. S.E. and crossed the river and camped on a little creek crossing two on the W. side all too small at low water for beaver. Snowed last night and until 8 this morning although as much as 4 inches of snow has fallen it is at 11 o'clock all gone except the hills which are white grass. Good granite country and fertile in the bottoms and on the hills and mountain sides.

16th Made 9 miles S. E. following a creek of the main river about 1/3 the size of the same this we crossed 6 times during the day. This morning 4 inches snow which fell during the night but all gone at 9

o'clock, fair at 4 in afternoon. This day finishes all our provisions. In above distance river crooked .

17th. 2 miles S. E. 3 E and cutting a high mountain 1 mile S by E. and struck the river again in a large and fertile plain, here crossed the main branch of it and followed 2 miles a creek running S by E. At the place where we left the river it receives a small creek from the S and where we struck it again another quite small from the N. The main branch appears to run about E. from the plain. When arrived at camp finding no meat I took my traps out to catch beaver when returning saw the squaw bringing in moss and roots. When I came in found the hunters had come in with one bear one elk and several deer and 5 beaver this makes a timely supply. Indians are gone ahead to see the mountain is passiable. This mountain divides us from the heads of the Missouri.

18th 2 miles up the creek S. by E. then assending the mountain S. E. 2 more then 2 S by E down the mountain and struck a little thread of water which during 28 miles increased gradually to a little river and S. E. to another coming from the S. and both go off together N. This is one of the heads of the Missouri we crossed it and camped here. We found both bulls and cows which makes all merry. This pass is good going when there is no snow now there was about one foot in places drifted more. We took 8 hours to pass. There is a visible change in the apppearance, vegetation is not so forward, the trees appear stinted and small the land poorer and covered with sedge the other side. There is little on the W. side all is granite.

As soon as I passed the divide I saw Pudding Stone. We had showers of snow and rain this day but this I believe is constant in this region at this time of the year. The mountain. is much higher on the W. than on the E. side. This I observed also at the Trois Tetons. The grass is poor and has started but little. The prairie in some places has snow. The valley runs N and S. and is bounded E. and W. by a range of mountains. This day my horse keeper left me taking an offence at some misinterpretation about a horse. The 16th. Woodman came to camp from his hunt for beaver tired and famished having eated nothing for three days

19th Same camp snowed by fits most of the day. Being Sunday the medicine chief had devotional exercises with his followers he formed them into a ring men women and children and after an address they danced to a tune. In dancing they keep the feet in the same position the whole time merely jumping up to the tune keeping the hands in front of them. At intervals he addressed them. At night Blackfeet were seen prowling about the camp at least so the Indians say. Erected myself a lodge for the first time in the country and paid a treat of rum &c to the whites in camp and some of the principal Indians to wet the same as it is called.

20th. Snowing hard in the morning. One horse so lame that if we move camp today he will remain for the Blackfoot or wolves. Much the same. Started at half past 12 found. the horse could be drove a little got him along about four miles shall return for him tomorrow. This day 9 miles E. S. E. over a level plain of rich deep soil wet and miry in the extreme. Saw our Indians running buffaloe ahead. At 5 miles crossed a little brook running N by E and camped on a considerable creek running N. by E. and all falling in to the same as the creek we left

At about the junction it doubles round a point of mountains and apparently takes a north(?)eastwardly course rain snow and sunshine as usual today. 4 hunters left us today to hunt beaver in the Blackfoot country, Pellew, Charloi, Narbesse, Rivey.

21st. Same camp sent back and brought the lame horse into camp. Went out to the mountain to cut log poles found a Blackfoot lodge recently occupied. Snow as usual. Saw the Indians cooking a root resembling the yellow dock, but not so yellow tasted like parsnip raw, informed by them that it is bad before being cooked suppose it is more or less poisonous.

22nd Same camp. Blue Devils all day. Turned in.

23rd 6 miles S. S. E. and up the valley 3 S. E. by S. 3 S. E. This valley is all good land about four miles wide and perhaps 50 long and how much further it goes N. I cannot say. Went out to hunt buffaloe, killed one elk out of a large band. Mountains with snow each side of valley. Snowed a little as usual.

24th A double portion of the usual weather *viz*. Rain, hail, snow, wind, rain and thunder into the bargain we are so near where they make weather that they send it as if cost nothing. Course S. E. 6 miles up the creek then by N. E. 3 cutting a height of land but low and perfectly good going to the head of another river running S. E. down this two miles and camped. Hunted today killed one cow saw some hundreds.

25th. Followed the creek 5 miles S. S. E. then it turned round a point more eastwardly. We continued same course 4 miles and struck a creek going into the same about 2 miles below the point spoken of. Rain snow and hail today with sunshine. Grass better today. Had a long ride before sunrise after the lame horse which I brought to camp.

26th Same Camp. A Blackfoot trail discovered in our vicinity a numerous camp of them. Better weather than usual today Sunday according to our reconing. At night one of two Indians who started on an express to the Nez Perces Camp returned with three blankets one white shirt and some tobacco and powder, which articles they found buried with a Blackfoot Indian who was unscalped two bullets through his head and one through his body. We apprehend that there has been a battle between the Blackfoot Indians and perhaps the whites.

27th 17 miles S. crossing two small forks of the Missouri and camping on the third of small size near camp found a red blanket, hat and some small articles but no body. Soon after camp arrived one Indian with news and soon after 2 more and three squaws comprising the only survivors of the battle which happened thus, 21 Nez Perces, 18 Flathead and two Iroquois and 1 Ponderai started with intent to steal horses from the Blackfeet. Near the head of Salmon River they saw 4 and some horses these they attacked. Just at this moment a horse threw one of the Flatheads he seized on one of the horses of the Blackfeet and ran after him up a mountain he looked back and saw a large number of Blackfeet killing his companions not one survived but himself he made the best of his way to the Nez Perce Camp to tell the sad tale to the wives and children of the dead.

In this camp where the relatives of the deceased Flathead are, there is weeping and wailing. Fair all day and comfortably warm, there were 46 lodges of the Blackfeet do not know if women were with it or not if not it is a much larger camp than ours. The blanketts &c. found are accounted for in the practice that the Blackfeet have of cutting a piece of flesh from near the shoulder tying it to an article and throwing it away to propitiate the Deity, the circumstance of the flesh being tied with them I did not at first know.

28th Moved S. 8 miles following the left branch of the creek which forks at our last night's camp then S. S, W. 4 miles and camped on the same creek. A little rain. Just after we came to camp a band of buffaloe passed the camp which gave a fine chance to the Indians to run them one of them they chased into camp and then killed her a fine cow.

29th Moved S. by E. 6 miles cutting the divide of waters and struck a small creek going into Salmon River then 7 miles S by E. following the creek through high hills of lime rock on which we found plenty of sheep some of which were killed. Then 3 miles S. W. and struck Salmon River here a small creek running through a fine open plain valley about 6 miles wide and extending each way as far as the eye could reach. The river runs here about W. by N. On the S. side is a high range of snowy mountains perhaps not covered the whole year, this range is parrallel with the river. The country I should call for two days back, volcanic flints are found in abundance some of the stones have a white crust on the outside of them whether of lime or Epsom salts cannot say both abound. The lime rock is mostly slate blue but is found in layers of all shades from white to deep blue and very much contorted and forming frequent caves and holes. It is the intention of the chiefs to remain at this camp until the Nez Perces come to us and then to move together. This morning left my wounded horse.

30th. Same camp rained all last night and all day. Went up into the mountains to hunt sheep wounded one but a snowstorm coming on his trail was covered and I lost him. Saw plenty it is surprising to view the places where they go no one would imagine it possible for an animal to climb the rocks they do. Got nothing and hearing a firing hastened to the top of a hill to see if the camp was attacked but found that the Nez Perces had arrived with 9 whites a Mr. Hodgskins at their head. This party is 16 lodges and only escaped the Blackfeet by the latter falling in with 31 Indians 30 of whom they killed. It is supposed the 30 killed about 50 of the Blackfeet. They mustered about 700 all men and were sufficient to cut off all our camps if they would trade man for man.

31st Got news that 20 lodges of Blackfeet are now camped at our camp of 21st inst, and I think likely that these are the same who killed the 30 Indians and as usual 10 times overrated. This day moved 7 miles S. E. up the river and following a small creek near our camp of last night a creek comes in from the S. one which we followed coming from N. W. this one from the S. S. E. the main river S. E. went into the mountains. Saw antelope killed nothing. In the mountains heavy thunder with a snow and hail storm and high wind.

June 1st Same camp. Some snow on mountains. Got wet.

2nd 17 miles S. E. 1 E. by N. through an open plain nearly level finished the streams of Salmon River and struck one called little Goddin, it terminates near the three butes in a little lake here goes S. E. Through the valley the mountains. appear terminating on both sides. A fair day the S. range comprises much more of a stone which I will call quartz the same as is found at Kettle falls there is also lime stone Blue and without organic remains.

3rd 15 miles S.E. through the same valley. Gradually decending the stream became a rapid and pretty large, one as large as some that pass 300 miles. We camped at a narrow pass formed of low hills here is between the hills a slough of clay saturated with Epsom salts. The hills are of Basaltic rock in collumns the first I have seen in this region. Lime rock is found here in Pudding Rock. Killed plenty of buffaloe here.

4th. Moved through the valley following the river called as I am informed Little Goddin in a S. E. by E. 6 miles. During which space I found the lower hills of Basalt. The mountains. are of lime rock the same as passed heretofore. Wind high N. W. which brings warm weather here and clear. Grass very bad.

5th. Clear warm day moved S. E. by E. 8 miles. Went in search of buffaloe found none. Saw an old Blackfeet Camp of 65 fires half as large as our present camp. Saw several whirlwinds which raised the dust at a distance and appears much like smoke. Saw the three Butes come in sight one by one and then the Trois Tetons the Butes S. E. by S. 20 miles distant about. So far this river rapid and little brush and no beaver. Grass worse and worse.

6th. Same camp. Last night arrived 3 Kootenays with 25 beaver who left us on Flathead River being on foot the whole time. Last night sent out Indians to see in what direction were the most buffaloe one came back this morning reports cows to the S.

7th Moved E. N. E. 15 miles and without water the whole route the Trois Tetons bearing E. perhaps 90 miles distant over a level and dry plain without grass or extremely little. In the afternoon had a gale from the S. W. which blew down the lodges, accompanied with a little rain and enough dust to suffocate one. On our left there is a range of high hills from which come numerous streams, but they sink in the plain and are warm and muddy. Went out this evening to bring in the meat of a cow killed in the forenoon and found a horse extremely fat it is surprising how fat a horse gets by being left to himself. No grooming that I have ever seen will make a horse appear as beautiful as to be left to his own resources. The Butes bear due S.

8th 5 miles N. following the same creek up which grows larger as we assend. Had a fine rain and hail and thunder today which is Sunday. Water very muddy grass little and but a little.

9th. 10 miles N. and following the creek has some tolerable wild(?) cotton wood and willow on it. Wind N. clear and windy. Country same. Three Nez Perces arrived at camp bring news that Payette is with four Nez Perces' chiefs. Capt Serrey with 7 is detained by snow, that the Blackfeet village is camped at the spot where we met the Nez Perces. We find that Payette will meet us at the forks. Capt Serrey has got 31 horses. This day a bull was run into camp which I shot at my lodge door. Today an Indian was running bulls he turned, the horse stopped and threw him the bull gored him into his chest so that his breath was made through the apparture, by the help of the women he reached camp. When Mr. Ermatinger dressed his wound he very composedly made his will by word of mouth the Indians responding in concord at the end of each sentence. He appeared not in the least intimidated by the approach of death. I think the Indians die better than the whites perhaps they have less superstition in regard to the future and argue that as the deity makes them happy here he will also heareafter if there is existence for them.

10th. Same camp. Another Indian came to camp who had been looking out for the Blackfeet. He was ambuscaded by two of them and narrowly escaped by the goodness of his horse being wounded slightly in the nose.

11th Same camp. Fresh news of the Blackfeet. Made horse pen that my horses might be safe. I do not apprehend any serious attack but only that they will come suddenly with a great noise of voices and guns and frighten the horses. On such occasions horses become wild one frights another they run over the lodges this increases the confusion and the yelling firing and runing and snorting of 1200 Indians and 1800 horses is frightfull indeed. Sometimes a camp with as many horses as the above loose every one it is commonly whole or none. Day warm, clear fresh wind W.

12th. Same camp. Warm day. The Blackfeet camp about 15 miles from this they are very numerous.

13th. Same camp. Cloudy and cool with high wind from S. E. Blackfeet still near but have attempted nothing yet. Child died in camp yesterday remains to bury today. Find I have missed one day in my journal which has been done while laying at some camp and accordingly date tomorrow the 15th.

15th Last night some Blackfoot fired into our camp a ball passed through a lodge. Some straggler disappointed of stealing horses I suppose. Moved N. N. E. 5 miles and camped on a creek now almost dry and soon will be wholly. There is little but cotton wood on this creek.

16th. 8 miles N. E. by N. to a small creek which about a mile below this joins another larger one. Country nearly level. Day windy S. W. wind cool and cloudy. Trois Tetons bear E. S. E. Today saw the Indians carrying the man who was wounded by a buffaloe no one could receive more attention, one person to carry water he was on a good bed made on poles the front of which like shafts were carried by a horse led by his wife, the hinder part by 6 men and women on their shoulders. The camp moved slower than usual for him these things give a favorable impression of the Indians.

17th. Same camp. Rained very hard all last night and until noon of today. An alarm of Blackfeet last night but I believe little of these things in so large a camp when it is known that there are Blackfeet near, a man straying out of camp is enough to give rise to a report and a report once raised it gathers like a snow ball.

18th. Same camp. Severe hail and snow yesterday afternoon and rain most of last night and until noon today. Camp about out of provisions so we are in hopes of moving soon. Nothing but necessity and that immediate will induce an Indian to do the least thing, any excuse serves to stop buisness with them and a small party of whites who are not strong enough to move alone will find in traveling with them occasion for all the patience they may have.

19th. 1½ miles to the main river here going S. W. this we found quite deep enough to ford for horses the mules I was obliged to unload and put the loads on the horses. 3 (?) miles more passed three slews of our stream joining the last river mentioned. 3 miles more camped on another branch of it making 10½ miles N. E. by E. Day clear snow in patches in shaded places but the country green with herbage and mostly in blossom. All rocks for some days past volcanic. This stream looses itself in the plain.

20th. Moved 11 miles E. by N. and camped on Kamas River so called from the abundance of that root in some spots it is so abundant as to exclude other vegetation. This prairie is very extensive perhaps 15 miles each way and is intersected by numerous little streams which form one going to the S. and ends in a small lake on the plain between this and Lewis River. Day clear and cool.

Frost last night snow on all the high hills Trois Tetons bear E. S. E. I should think about 80 miles distant. Found buffaloe here the first for 10 days when we found the last I think at least 100 were killed in one day 42 tongues were given to Mr. E. H. and myself.

21st. Late last night arrived 5 hunters Pillew, Nasben, and Churboye and two Indians who left us on the head of the Missouri having seen plenty of recent sign of the Blackfeet but happily saw none, they killed 94 beaver. Today went out to hunt killed one bull. Forenoon showers and lowery. Kamas in bloom the Indians are taking large quantities of it. This plain is extensive but about 7 miles across of it only is rich and that is as good as any land I ever saw, the main plain is much of it bare rock the surface of which looks like a pan of milk when you push together the cream, evidently it was once a fiery and fluid plain or lake of lava, probably the whole plain between these mountains and the Trois Tetons. The rock is porous like honey comb the surface shows plainly the heads of Basaltic colums and in some places the colums stand not perpendicular but at an angle of 50 degrees about. Same camp.

22nd. Same camp. Arrived this morning an express from Bonneville this express came from the forks in three days they saw Blackfeet. By the way this afternoon Mr. Hodge left to go to Bonneville. Day clear and warm. Buffaloe were run into camp.

23rd. Sunday Indians singing and dancing as usual day warm and clear. These Indians do nothing on Sunday.

24th. Moved across the plain 3 miles N. E. Day warm and clear.

25th Yesterday at night some Indians came in from hunting buffaloe reported that they saw two Blackfeet and fired on them. At night we saw their fire in the mountains. Same camp. Fine clear warm day.

Employed in making a saddle.

26th. Same camp. Went out hunting saw a few buffaloe but killed nothing but a grouse. As I had some dispute with Mr. David Douglass about the grouse of this country I subjoin a discription; the bird had 10 pointed drab coloured, mottled with white, tail feathers the outer edge of the feathers are only mottled until you approach their end when both sides are mottled under the tail are 10 or 12 dark brown feathers 2/3 as long as the tail feathers white at the termination. The tail feathers are about 8 inches long. The wing feathers are nearly white underneath and dark drab outside. From the head of the breast bone to the tail are many black feathers.

On the body under the wings are redish grey feathers above the breast and nearly on the neck is a place devoid of feathers of a dirty olive colour each side and a little below this is a tuff of short sharp pointed dirty white feathers they look as if they had been clipped with a shears. The tail feathers look as though they had been burnt off leaving the stalk of the quill projecting. The bill is short and curved downwards above the bare spot on the neck are short mottled feathers cream, white and black. It is feathered to the toes which are three and a small one behind. The hinder part of the leg is not feathered from the knee downwards Toe nails short and obscure, its back pretty uniformly mottled with deep brown dirty white approaching dirty yellow and dun coloured weight 4 ½ lbs. length from point of tail feathers to tip of bill 25 inches from tips .of wings 3 ½ ft. We were regaled by thunder shower. On our return to camp saw Blackfeet trail and a cow recently killed by them.

27th. Same camp nothing remarkable.

28th. Same camp nothing but lice and dirt. Cool today.

29th. Same camp as yesterday went out to hunt killed one buffaloe which fell into the river and had to butcher him up to my middle in cold water. Some hunters who went out today came in with news that they had seen the Blackfeet camp on Tobacco River, one of the heads of the Missouri they say it is larger than ours.

30th Same camp Sunday Indians praying, dancing and singing.

1st July. Moved 2 miles S. and down the creek. Clear moderately warm day the first for three days. Nights have been frosty, ice made in our pots and pails. Men came from Bonneville in the evening.

2nd. Moved S. 12 miles and camped on same creek. On the way observed some fine luxuriant clover. Grass good about 9 miles down the creek which rapidly increases in size from numerous springs which are of fine cold water. We camped in a cluster of large cotton wood large for this place about 10 inches through.

3rd. Last night a bear made his way into camp among the horses and gave a considerable alarm but was off before guns could be got out. Today moved 16 miles S. S. W. and camped on same creek with Mr. Bonneville with about 40 men bound for Green River. I have heretofore forgot to mention that at our camp of 1st July we left about 40 lodges of the Flatheads country. This day's route dry and barren day warm.

4th. Same camp. At night saw a band of Blackfeet a little above camp. Clear warm day.

5th. Same camp.

6th. Same camp. Very warm weather.

7th. This morning our camp forked in three directions Mr. Hodgkin(?) for a trapping excursion with the Nez Perces, Mr. Ermatinger with the Ponderays to go to Flathead River, ourselves East 18 miles to Henrys fork. Here wooded with narrow leafed cotton wood. Our route over a very dry plain passing at about half the distance some low hills of pure sand with not the least appearance of vegetation. The party is 26 all told.

8th. Followed up the river where we were much annoyed by mosquitos about 8 miles N. N. E. there forded it about belly deep going E. by S. 5 miles to a large river which must be Lewis fork. Here we found buffaloe. These two rivers form a junction about 15 miles from this point as I believe near two butes but some say not until you get as low as Three Butes. On this river are not many mosquitoes.

9th. Made this day 22 ½ miles due East toward the Trois Tetons at 8 miles struck a small creek with cut rock banks running N.W. and to the river last crossed, which is not Lewis fork. At 20 miles cut a mountain which rises and is wooded to the S W. and diminishes to the plain to the N. E. We entered Pierre's Hole and camped on the N.W. side of it. Here we found buffaloe.

10th. Moved 12 miles S. E. crossing a difficult swamp and camped about 2 miles from the battle ground of last year with the Gros Ventres. Day warm and a great quantity of grasshoppers for several days past so much so as to discolour the ground in many places.

11th. Started early and made 3 miles E. S. E. to the foot of the mountains then 8 miles E. S. E. to the summit then 6 miles E. to Lewis fork and 1 mile E. across it at the same place we crossed last year found it very high for fording but succeeded at last. Wind strong N. W. clear and moderately warm. Horses troubled with horse flies on the mountains but not in this plain.

Found buffaloe in the bottom also mosquitoes. The river is here much choked up with islands and heaps of drift wood and a great quantity of mud. In coming over the mountains lost one mule and sent a man back for it he has not returned yet at sundown.

Got a wet jacket in the river trying to find a ford. There is the trail of about 8 men who have passed through this defile before us as I think about 14 days they marked a name on the trees and we suppose that they are men of Dripps & Pontenelle. We as yet see no appearance of the Blackfeet except very old forts and lodges. Lewis fork here runs S. E. about 9 miles then turns S.

12th. This morning my man came back having been out all night he found the mule at our last camp. Made this day 9 miles S. E. along the river then 3 miles E. S. E. to a small creek running into the river. At this place 9 men under Capt. Stevens were attacked by about 30 Blackfeet a little later than this time last year and several of them killed. Mr. Bonneville informs me that when he passed last year in August their bones were laying about the valley. I am apprehensive that More, a sick man whom I left in charge of Stevens, must be one of them. 6 miles more over a hilly broken limestone country S. E. to a considerable fork of Lewis River this stream is strongly impregnated with sulphur. This camp is almost without grass. In the first place this morning we moved 3 miles and crossed a creek putting into the river. At our camp of tonight there is a small branch joining the creek from the S. E.

13th. East 5 miles N. E. ½ mile through bad cut rocks on the N. side of the river there is also a trail on the S. side then ½ mile E. then ¼ mile S. E. then following a left hand fork of the river a few rods N. E. Crossed it and made E. 3 miles to the right hand fork again which we followed E. 2 miles then S. E. 4 miles to camp crossing it several times a good trail most of the way. One horse of the Indians killed by falling from the cut rock trail down to the river. In the first of the cut rocks there is a handsome cave rock lime and sand. A few boulders of granite seen today as also on the E. side of the mountains of Pierres hole. The river which we followed this day is rapid and too deep below the branches to ford during the last of the route several small forks from each side.

14th. Made 9 miles S. E. to the height of land between this river and Green River then 5 miles S. S. E. to a creek running into Green River. There are good trails all the way and to the divide much timber. The creek on which we camped last night just above the camp divided into three forks. We followed the most southwardly for a while then mounted the hill on the left side of it. There has been for two days a high range of mountains. on our left about 10 miles distant apparently of sand stone and limestone. These trend E. S. E. & N. N. W. and on the divide between this and Wind River. Also on our right there have been a range of mountains. of same composition about 15 miles distant. Both ranges have snow in patches. Many alarms today but still no enemys. Killed plenty of buffaloe.

15th. Made E. S. E. 12 miles to Green River and to Mr. Bonneville's fort. Day clear and fine. Found here collected Capt. Walker, Bonneville, Cerry, of one Co. Dripps & Fontenelle of the Am. Fur Co. Mr. Campbell just from St. Louis, Mess. Fitzpatric, Gervais, Milton Sublette of the Rocky Mountain Fur Co. and in all the Cos. about 300 whites and a small village of Snakes.

Here I got letters from home. During the last year among all the Cos there has been in all about 25 men killed two of my original party with them, *viz* Mr More and O'Neil. (O'Neal?)

16th. Same camp.

17th. Moved 10 miles down the river S. E. it is here a large and rapid stream and to be forded only in a few places. Here we were followed by the Snake village we encamped with the Rocky Mountain Fur Co.

18th to the 24 remained at the same camp during which time the weather was pleasant and warm for several nights we were annoyed by mad dogs or wolves which I cannot say but believe the latter as one was killed. I think one animal did the whole mischief as when men were bitten at one camp none were at the other about nine persons were bitten at Dripps & Fontenelles camp and three at ours. D. & Fs.

camp is 4 miles above us on the same side of the river we hope he was not mad as no simtons have yet appeared.

24th. Moved E. 12 miles cutting a small divide came to a wide valley parallel with Wind River Mountains in which we crossed 3 large creeks and camped on the 4th. which has much pine timber on it and is called Pine fork. They all come into one quite soon by appearance and are not near as large as the main fork on which we first found the whites and which we have now crossed. In coming here it passed to our left that is up stream. Found plenty of antelope and bulls.

25th. Crossed the stream and moved E. S. E. 3 miles to a creek the same on which I made a cash last year and crossed at a good ford just below two stony hills then on 7 ½ mile E. S. E. following a branch of the same creek and camped to noon. Buffaloe throwing the dust in the air in every direction and antelope always in sight. This day a Mr. Worthington in running a bull fell from his horse, the bull furious ran at the horse and passed him within 3 feet, then turned again and passed him, he having got up from the ground ran and escaped. He killed the bull and found he had but one eye owing to which circumstance he escaped. Afternoon made S. E. 13 miles leaving the last creek of what is called New fork to which all the waters we have passed since leaving rendesvous belong the one. We camped on last night heads in a lake about 1½ miles over and not far from where we slept. We now struck the west fork of Sandy and camped at an old camp of last year at a place where Ball left his rifle (?). Country covered with buffaloe.

26th. Made S. E. 9 miles and camped on another fork of Sandy then S. E. by E. 15 miles to Sweetwater. All the country is granite from rendezvous. So far buffaloe quite plenty also antelope. Today shot a cow with a very young calf the calf ran after our mules for a long way until it found the difference.

27th. Made down the creek 1½ miles E. S. E. then E. 8 miles to another branch of Sweet water then 6 miles E. by N. to another branch of same then down this branch S. E. 2 miles and camped. Saw one band of elk and many antelope plenty of buffaloe.

28th. Made E. 2 miles to another creek running S. by E. crossed made E. 6 miles E. by N. 4 miles at the creek a sort of slate prevailed but soon ran into a red sandstone. Passed at 11 miles a small pond to our right. Few buffaloe today. Last night Capt. Stewart had some sport with a bear near our camp in the willows which he wounded but did not kill. He represented him as large as a mule. In the afternoon made E. by N. 6 miles to Sweet water River then N. E. 3 miles up it and camped. I came ahead and found a white bear in a thickett and after firing a pistol and throwing stones into it started him out he came as though he meant to fight us but I gave him the shot of my rifle through the body. He then rushed on us and I ran as fast as I could Mr. Kamel (Campbell?) snapped at him. Mr Sublette ran also being on a mule. The bear followed us no great distance and turned and ran up creek some horsemen followed and killed him after putting 4 more balls into him.

29th. Same camp. Rained all day. Two men went out to hunt and at night one returned alone the other in the morning being still absent.

30th. Started out to hunt the man and in about 8 miles came to the place hunted the whole country over and found nothing but a white bear the largest and the whitest I have yet seen. Run him about a mile and fired one shot but could not kill him. After a long ride returned to camp, found the party had moved on followed them N. N. W. in 6 miles struck Porpoise in a small rapid thread running through sandstone banks this we followed N. W. 3 miles then N. by E. 9 miles more. Thousands of buffaloe in sight, and the red bottom of the streams deep and muddy with recent rains and found camp a little after sundown. The afternoon of the 29th we found lime rock almost entirely today, sand stone and a kind of glassy stone resembling Carnelian a coarse kind of which I think it is.

31st N. N. W. 8 miles through a muddy bottom and little grass to some large willows found a party of 4 whites who have lost their horses and one of them wounded in the head with a ball and in the body with an arrow very badly. They suppose the Snakes did it, but I think not. Little grass. In the afternoon moved N. 9 miles to the junction of Great Porpoise River which comes from the S. W. then N. by E. 4 miles to the junction of Wind Rive, which comes from the W. turning around as I supose and running along Wind River Mountains, which run N. W. Altogether they form a large and muddy river but fordable now which is after a heavy rain.

Aug. 1st. Same camp. Find Mr. Bonneville camped a few miles above us. On farther inquiry I changed my opinion expressed above in regard to the Indians who stole the horses I think they were 15 Snakes who left our camp at Green River a few days before we left that place. The case was this. Mr. Bridger sent 4 men to this river to look for us *viz* Mr. Smith, Thomson, Charboneau a half breed and Evans. Two days before it happened 15 Indians came to them (Snakes) and after smoking departed the second day after they were gone Thompson having been out hunting (hobbled?) his horse to the others and thought he would sit down by them until it was time to water them and having been on guard much of the time previous fell asleep.

He was waked by a noise among the horses, which he supposed to be his comrades come to water, them raising his head and opening his eyes the first thing that presented itself to his sight was the muzzle of a gun in the hands of an Indian. It was immediately discharged and so near his head that the front piece of his cap alone saved his eyes from being put out by the powder the ball entered the head outside of the eye and breaking the cheek bone passing downward and lodged behind the ear in the neck. This stunned him and while insensible an arrow was shot into him on the top of the shoulder downward which entered about 6 inches. The Indians got 7 horses all there were. Charboneau pursued them on foot but wet his gun in crossing a little stream and only snapped twice.

2nd. Found the river unfordable and assended to west crossing Porpoise and Wind River 5 miles up and made thence 20 miles N. E. by N. to a little creek going to Wind now on our right.

3rd. 11 miles N. N. E. to the summit of the mountains which are called little Wind River mountains. and run E. and W. then N. 5 miles to the river.

4th. 2 miles N. along the river to a clump of sweet cotton wood.

5th. 7 miles N. by W. to the river which between makes a considerable bend to the eastward camped in good grass and some large cotton wood trees this morning past beautiful camps afternoon N. by E. 12 miles. 3 horses found this day and yesterday probably left by some party of Indians who have passed this way saw the tracks of several more. We think that when the Crows stole horses of the Snakes last winter they came this route and left their animals on account of giving out for want of food, in the snow. Few buffaloe and those running indicates Indians near.

6th. N 10 miles to the river again to noon found little grass. Day cool. Afternoon 10 miles N. N. E. to the main river again. Since crossing the last mountains. we crossed a creek the second forenoon afternoon one yesterday 2 today 2 all small and I suppose sometimes dry.

7th. 12 miles N. N. W and camped on Grey Bull River. Here I found a piece of about 5 lbs of Bituminous coal which burned freely. It had in it some substance which I took to be amber also an impression of wood. It looked like and as good as Liverpool Coal. Its fracture was too perfect to have come far. 20 miles above and on the E. side comes in the river. Travelled in afternoon 6 miles N. N. W. and again struck Wind River. Shell River comes in 3 miles below Grey Bull on the E. side and from the mountains, in the direction E. by N. Grey Bull is from the S. W. and much the largest stream on this side since Wind River. For three days have found no buffaloe and from the nature of the country think it is not often found in abundance along here except in the winter no antelope a few elk and deer.

8th. W. N. W. 3 miles then 21 miles N. E. toward the right of two considerable mountains where Wind River passes. We camped west of these hills on a river larger than Grey Bull called Stinking River coming from the S. W. This day's travel was made between parrallel ridges of broken lime and sand rock some of it appeared calcined and much like fine caked salt. This day picked up some shell they are very numerous, also a round concretion which are found also on Cannon Ball River from which the name, also a concretion of much the same substance but long pointed at one end with a core in the middle a hole at big end. During this space there was no water to our right there is a range of mountains. running N. W. about 9 miles distant and the other side of Wind River.

9th. 10 miles N. striking a small stream of water. This day's travel and yesterday was over ground naked of vegetables in which the animals sank near six inches deep at every step. Perfectly dry and resembling, but of different colour, lime in the operation of slacking full of holes down which the waters at the wet season sink the rock is sand and lime stone.

10th. N. 15 miles passing near but not exactly on the river and through rocky hills of no great height. The river here looks tranquil but flows between two perpendicular banks of stone of perhaps 5 to 800 feet high the chasm even at the top of no great width the rock of lime and sand. This day's march saw Plaster of Paris. Found for first time this year ripe service berrys. Killed one mountain sheep which was all the meat killed this day for 48 men short commons. Hard rains last night.

11th. Went out hunting killed 2 cows and 4 bulls. The camp made about a N. course at six miles crossed a small creek at 5 more another probably another branch of the same at 9 more a creek separate from the others but not large. All these creeks have high perpendicular banks and are very bad to cross. In the course of the day saw 4 bears white. A fine grass country and a great many buffaloe.

12th. 4 miles N. E. to Big Horn River this day. Went out to get bull hydes for boat got enough and employed the rest of the day in making a boat. This day followed down a little stream.

13th. Remained at same camp made a bull boat day fine.

14th. Same camp. Day fine.

15th. Made a start in our bull boat found it to answer the purpose well large enough runs well leaks a little. Made 3 miles N. E stream rapid shoals at places 2 feet. Too much liquor to proceed therefore stopped.

16th. Made a start in our boat found travelling quite pleasant but requires much caution on account of some snaggs and bars. We frequently took one half of the river which dividing again gave too little water for our boat which draws 1½ feet it is quite too much the boat ought to have been flatter. We grounded about 6 times this forenoon it is surprising how hard a thump these bull boats will stand. Ours is made of three skins is 18 feet long and about 5 ½ wide, sharp at both ends round bottom. Have seen on the banks of the river this forenoon 3 grisly bears and some bulls in the river and on the banks they stare and wonder much. The direction of this march was as near as I can judge N. by E. we went from 5 to 11 as I think about 6 miles per hour the indirection I suppose to be not more than ¼. All feel badly today from a severe bout of drinking last night.

Afternoon made 4 hours at a good 6 mile rate grounded three times. Saw a few elk and much beaver sign all day there is here the best trapping that I have ever found on so large a river it is about 100 yards wide when all together but is much cut into slews which makes the navigation very difficult. The musquitoes have anoyed me much today they affect me almost as bad as a rattle snake. This afternoon's course about N. N. W. At 6 miles from our noon camp passed a place where we supposed the Little Horn River came in from the S. E. at least there is a considerable river at that place but it is difficult to tell a returning slew from a river. This afternoon a severe thunderstorm which compelled us to put ashore until it was over.

17th. This day the river made nearly a N. course and we made about 7½ hours at the rate of about 6 miles the river winding about ¼ of the distance we started at 5 o'clock. At about 9 o'clock. saw several persons ahead on the bank of the river which we at first supposed to be whites from the fort but soon found to be Crow Indians they informed us that the whole nation was behind. We were anxious to avoid them but could not as the river afforded us no hiding place they showed us that they meant us to land very soon by stepping and swimming into the river. Seeing this we chose to land without further trouble. In this way we were obliged to make the shore 6 times during the day.

We arrived at the Yellow Stone which was of clear water and did not mix with the waters of the Big Horn which was at this time dirty for some miles. About 3 miles below the mouth of the Big Horn we found Fort Cass one of the Am. F. Co. at which post we traded about 10 packs of beaver and 150 to 200 pack robes. Goods are brought up in boats of about 15 tons burthen 2 of which are now laying here and one of them preparing to descend in two days.

We were treated with little or no ceremony by Mr. Tullock, who we found in charge which I attributed to sickness on his part well knowing that a sick man is never disposed to be over civil to others. We therefore pushed on next morning. Just as we arrived we saw 31 Indians with two American flags come to the other side of the river they were Gros ventres du Baum the same we fought with last summer at the Trois Tetons. They came to make peace with the Crows they were treated civily at the fort and before night followed the river up to the Crow village where I expect their scalps will be taken, for the Crows informed us that not long since a few Blackfeet came and made peace with them. Shortly after three Crows went to the Blackfeet two of which they killed and they were determined to make no more peace with them.

18th. Started down the river made 3 hours with a hard wind about 4 miles an hour and put up to noon seeing some elk which we were in hopes to get to eat. Course about N. afternoon the river tended more eastwardly and at last came to E. N. E. We made at the rate of 5 miles an hour for 3½ hours and camped to fish and hunt having no meat on hand. There is along this river pretty bottoms and great quantities of sweet cotton wood which would be fine for winter camps. We saw some large bands of elk but our hunters were more conceited than good which I have generally found to be the case with the hunters in this country they are not willing that a new hand should even try, and are far from good shots themselves and commonly have miserable flint guns which snap continually and afford an excuse for not killing.

The river sometimes cuts blufs which are mostly of sand stone but the river brings down granite and porphry. Fort Cass is scituated on the E. bank of the Yellow Stone River is about 130 feet square made of sapling cotton wood pickets with two bastions at the extreme corners and was erected in the fall of 1832. The Yellow stone comes from the S. W. till it meets the Big Horn then the two go about N. until they bend to the eastward.

19th. Made 5½ hours in a calm fine day I should think about 6 miles the hour the river going E.N.E. stopped early to try a band of bBuffaloe that we see on the left of us. At first we were careful to see if they were really buffaloe for yesterday we were near approaching a band of Indians which I suppose were the residue of the Blackfeet which I saw at the fort as they appeared coming down from that way. Nooned in a fine cool place under the shade of a large cotton wood in a large green bottom. The musquitoes take much from the pleasure of the trip which is otherwise fine but I believe for a party like ours rather dangerous in afternoon. 2½ hours about 6 per H. River E. Stopped on hearing the bellowing of buffaloe on shore to get meat. Our hunters as usual having failed went myself and killed a cow got a good ducking from a shower and returned loaded with meat much fatigued. About 4 miles before we stopped we passed the mouth of Rose Bud a river coming from S. S. W.

20th. Started early and made this forenoon 6 hours at the rate of about 5½ miles. River about E. N. E. last night a smart rain which wet our clothes much. Caught just at dusk last night plenty of blue catfish and a small one which resembles an ale wife. Soon after starting this morning found an immense herd of buffaloe close to the river stopped and killed 2 fat cows and could have killed any number more but this was enough they keep up a continued grunting night and day now that we have fairly got into them. In the afternoon made 5½ hours current about 6 miles and E. N. E. at 5 hours found bad rapids but at this low stage of the water it is said to be better passing on account of the chanell being more visible.

We had a good joke on much as usual during the afternoon we had a good joke on the old hands as they call themselves in distinction to those who have been a short time in the country. Two bald headed eagles being perched on a tree on a point and ranged to the other side of the river, our motion made them appear moving the old one cried out. *Les Sauvages* others of them said on horseback, with white scarfs. I looked long but not supposing that they meant the eagles I said I saw nothing but the eagles they soon found out their mistake and we had a good laugh at them and a pleasant one as all the Indians we meet here we expect to fight. This day and yesterday whenever the river makes perpendicular banks we saw veins of poor bituminous coal in 5 to 7 veins horizontal from 3 it. to 6 inches thick and 10 to 15 feet above each other rock sandstone.

21st. Made 5 hours river about E. N. E. Passed the mouth of Powder River at 4 hours and half an hour below a bad and rocky rapid but without accident. The coal still continues and thousands of buffaloe. Day fine stopped to noon a little below the rapids in the afternoon made 5 hours current about 5 miles per hour in about E. N. E direction no rapids of consequence.

The blufs have ceased these blufs are a part of the Black hills as I am informed the Black Hills I am also informed make the Palls of Missouri at the Three Forks just on leaving the blufs the coal veins appeared thicker day fine. Bufialoe plenty.

22nd. Made at 5 ½ per hour 6 hours. In forenoon using a sail which we found of little advantage and but a little course of the river N. N. E. and from the junction on the E. side of first Rose Bud then Tongue and then Powder Rivers it is of about the colour of the Missouri altho the Yellow Stone above is of clear water quite so above the junction of the Big Horn. Our boat getting quite rotten, in afternoon made 5 hours same course 5 miles per hour river better not so many bars and country not mountainous. The coal appears to have given out.

23rd. Made in forenoon 4 hours at the rate of 5 miles per hour river about N. E. Day fine and hot plenty of Elks in herds. Afternoon made 4 hours N. then 2½ hours E. N. E. current about 4 miles per hour. Saw but little game only 2 elk. River broad and shoal.

24th Made N. N. E. 2 hours with a heavy head wind about 4

miles per hour. Then the river turned westwardly and when it enters the Missouri is running W. by S. this made one hour more when we found the Missouri which we assended N. W. about 5 miles to Fort Union where we arrived about noon and were met with all possible hospitality and politeness by Mr. McKensie the Am. F. Co. agent in this country.

27th. This day at ½ past 10 o'clock we took leave our hospitable entertainers and on the experience of a few days with prepossessions highly in their favour we found Mr. McKensie a most polite host. I was particularly pleased with a Mr. Hamilton and I am perhaps presumptions in saying that I felt able to appreciate his refined politeness, he is a man of superior education and an Englishman. I was here supplied with a *peroque* traded from the Blackfeet. A Mr. Patten shewed me a powder flask which he traded from the Blackfeet, I immediately knew it to be one of mine and on examination found No. 4 H.G.O.M. graven with a point on it. It was More's flask who was killed in Little Jackson Hole last year on his return home after rendesvous. Fort Union is pleasantly scituated on the N. bank of the Missouri 6 miles above the junction of Yellowstone. There is no timber on a high bank above the fort I am told that there is not enough moisture here to raise vegetables potatoes grass etc, Some corn is traded from the Indians lower down. The fort is of usual construction about 220 feet square and is better furnished inside than any British fort I have ever seen. At table we have flour bread bacon cheese butter they live well.

I here saw a small sturgeon but they are very rare, cat fish are good and plenty they have cows and bulls milk etc. I saw lime burning also coal. Here they are beginning to distil spirits from corn traded from the Indians below. This owing to some restrictions on the introduction of the article into the country. Above this we have met plumbs, grapes, cherrys, Currants, ash, elm. The river being already well laid down shall no longer give the course.

We left the fort and went 2 hours and stopped for Mr. Sublette who remained behind to finish some business he came accompanied by the gentlemen of the fort after leaving us we made 4 hours then supped and made one hour more and found Mr. Wm. L. Sublette at anchor with a large bull boat. This gentleman we had expected to have found on our arrival at the Missouri he is come to trade furs in opposition to the Am. F. Co. he treated us with much politeness. His brother preferred to remain and come to the states with him we are therefore left without anyone who has decended the Missouri but I can go downstream.

28th. Pulled one hour put by from wind and to regulate then pulled 6 hours and stopped to supper, the banks continually falling in after supper we floated through the night 11 hours. Calm.

29th While breakfast was preparing went out to hunt killed one deer and found a severe time in the thick swamp and mosquitoes. Pulled 8½ hours and drifted 11 hours through the night which exposed me to much rain and wind from two thunder showers. I had much difficulty to keep the boat from bars and snaggs ran several times on to bars. All hands being asleep had to jump over board to get her off. In the night elk keep up a continual squealing it being now the commencement of their running season.

30th Day pulled 9 hours. Saw three white bears this day and some elk and a herd of buffaloe. Night floated 8½ hours and were stopped by a gale from the S. E. not thinking it expedient to pull with a head wind and in the dark.

31st Blowing a gale. Made about 4 hours about the rate of 2 miles per hour and finding it too bad laid by at a considerable river coming from the S. entering by 2 mouths. This I look to be the little Missouri as laid down in the maps. In this vicinity we find primitive pebbles and boulders much petryfied wood, other alluvial productions stopped all night on account of wind and rain which made our scituation uncomfortable in the extreme. The weather had heretofore been very warm average as much as 90° this day cold like an eastwardly storm.

1st. At seven the weather having abated a little made a start. At 3 o'clock found some of Sublette's men cutting timber for a fort and learned from them that the upper Mandan was 9 miles ahead. We made it at 6 this day made only about 3 per hour this village was about 1½ miles from the river. Taking my Indian and a man with me I went to it and was well received by Mr. Dorherty, Mr. Sublettes clerk and the Indians. Stopped about one hour with him and then pulled 3 hours more passing 3 villages of Mandans and not seeing the fort and being afraid of passing it stopped for the night.

2nd. Pulled ½ hour arrived first on a high point at the village then immediately round the point found the fort and was well received by Mr Kipp. the Am. F. Co. agent for the Mandans. Stopped 2 hours took breakfast. They presented me some dry corn and some roasting ears. All these villages cultivate corn peas beans pumpkins etc. At ½ past 7 o'clock pulled a short distance when we had a good breeze and sailed until 5 o'clock then stopped to supper then floated from 6 until 12 o'clock then stopped owing to fog with head wind.

3rd. Floated 2 hours and stopped to breakfast. Having found no game have lived much upon the stores we have taken from the forts above. At the last place we were presented with some green corn which we are now roasting. Makes us think of Old Lang Sine. We have had for four days rainy cloudy and foggy weather, our bed clothes are wet and musty in consequence. After breakfast pulled 6 hours when I thought best to go on shore to cook. I sent a man out to hunt in the meantime, as soon as he assended the high bank he perceived horses on the other side. We afterwards counted 21 lodges and from the number of horses I have no doubt there might have been from 75 to 100. I immediately had the boat out into a little thicket and fortifved as well as I could then went to fishing and spent the afternoon, caught but two large catfish.

As soon as it was dark we proceeded forward with a high wind and a cloudy sky and no moon. All went well until we were just opposite the village when we perceived lodges and fires on our side also. On seeing this I steered the boat to the middle of the river but unluckly took ground on a sand bar. Here we worked hard for some time to get off, and had the Indians seen or heard us here we were in distance for shot from both sides and could have made little resistance but they did not and after some time we got off and glad we were. We proceeded in all 4 hours pulled, then stopped for the night these were probably the Aricarey and would have scalped us. I feared much for my Nez Perce for we could not speak to any Indian on the river and all would without explanation have made some fuss and perhaps have killed him.

4th. With almost a gale of wind from the W. pulled 6 hours and then stopped to eat having twice nearly upset in carrying sail and wet all our things. After drying and eating started on still blowing fresh and pulled 3 hours then floated through the night 11 hours. It was a beautiful still night the stillness interrupted only by the neighing of the elk, the continual low of the buffaloe which we came to soon after starting, the hooting of large owls and the screeching of small ones and occasionally the nearer noise of a beaver gnawing a tree or splashing into the water and even the gong like sound of the swan. It was really poetical but sleep at last laid in his claim and I gave the helm to a man. Oak is now plenty in the bottoms and for a few days past has been seen. The upland along the river is here pretty, good plumbs we occasionally see and have since we first took water on the Big Horn. Frequent squalls of rain yesterday.

5th. Pulled 7 hours stopped to eat pulled one more came to a deserted village on the S. bank fired two guns to see if there was anyone in it but had no answer. Pulled one hour more then floated 7 hours more then pulled 3 to breakfast. Saw in morning a band of elk playing like children in the water failed of killing any of them owing to the impatience of one of the men who fired too soon. Pulled through a dreadful rain 7 hours and camped wet and cold. Rained all night strong east wind.

6th. In the morning made 8 hours pulling. Seeing an elk on the sand bar stopped and killed him very aceptable as we have had nothing to eat since yesterday noon and saved his horns for my best of friends Mr. F. Tudor of Boston. Pulled 2 hours more and the night being dark and appearance of a storm did not run.

7th. Last night about 11 o'clock was awakened by the water making a breach over the boat got her off the shore but was obliged to make the shore again on account of some of the men who were so frightened that if I had not they would have jumped overboard. Laid the rest of the night on a lee shore thundering in a loud strain and raining at no allowance. Spent a most uncomfortable night and rose in the morning benumbed with cold and all hands as dead as logs. Started after eating at 8 o'clock and pulled until 2 o'clock when we had a fine breeze which gradually increased to a gale before which we scudded at a good rate almost despairing of seeing Fort Pierre which we began to think we had passed. At about sundown we saw people on the hills which we supposed to be Indians therefore kept on, they fired but we did not choose to hear.

About an hour after sundown we smelt the flavour of coal and landed and found people who had just burned a kiln who informed us that the fort was 3 miles ahead. We thought to go to sleep at the fort but soon found that night and a gale of wind was a poor time for travelling and also that 3 miles was in fact 3 leagues. After being near filled by the surf and running afoul of several sand bars and getting overboard to push off we concluded to stop for the night which we did. Cold and tired and wet we spent the night as we best could. One comfort plenty of elk meat stopped at 10 o'clock.

8th. Made by sailing 3 miles and found Fort Pierre pleasantly scituated on the right bank rather low but withall romantic were received with all hospitality imaginable by Mr. Laidlow who is in charge of the Am. F. Co. Post. Here was much pleased by the order and regularity apparent about the place. We stopped here for the day and visited Mr. and Mrs. Sublette who is scituated about one mile below. We here saw melons of two kinds corn, pork, cows, horses and stacks of hay.

9th. Remained at the fort until about 1 o'clock. when we made by pulling 2 hours an island 9 miles below the fort on which the Co. have about 15 acres of ground under cultivation. Here I remained all this day eating and drinking of the good things afforded by the earth and the cellars of the Co. Found cucumbers water and musk, melons, beets, carrots, potatoes, onions, corn and a good cabin and the Company of Mr. Laidlow and Doct.

10th. At 8 o'clock. began pulling. The water has within two days risen about 2 feet in consequence of the rains which so annoyed me above and the surface of the water is covered with all manner of drift rubbish and the water as muddy as possible. Wind ahead all day but current much improved stopped at 6 o'clock at the commencement of the great bend and remained all night.

11th. Commenced pulling at ½ past 6 after having sent a hunter across the foot of the bend and after 6 hours got past the bend and found our hunters who had hid themselves in the brush being alarmed by seeing Indians whom we also saw and gave some amunition to. Took them in and in two hours more came to the agency for the Sioux and Poncas. Mr. Bean agent but not at the post, we found it a miserable concern only three or four men but poorly fed and buildings out of order though new and shabbily built at best we were hospitably received by the young man in charge.

12th. Pulled against a severe head wind 9 hours in hopes of finding White River but camped without seeing it. Got plenty of good plumbs which were an object to stop for as we are about out of food and the vicinity almost destitute of game.

13th Pulled against a severe wind 3½ hours finding we did not make much headway laid by for the day.

14th. Blowing still fresh ahead we started and made 15 hours night and day continuing until 12 o'clock at night, it was dark and we were nearly upset by a snag but our fears of starvation impelled us to haste. Did not see an animal all day. During the latter part of the night it rained in torrents and wet all our things and persons.

15th. Commenced pulling at 7 o'clock. Still blowing fresh ahead and raining a little about 3 o'clock cleared off and stopped to cook. During meal time killed a fawn which was very good luck. After supper pulled 5 hours more and found a keel boat of the Am. F. Co. alongside of which we stopped for the night.

16th. Put ahead with a fine wind not having been asked on board of her and immediately passed the Ponca village but I believe not in its usual place. Saw and delivered a message to Mr. Sublettes agent here and gave the chief some tobacco. Made with a wind which as usual soon died away and pulling 13 hours when we ran on a sand bar and was unable in the dark to extricate her and slept all night on it the musquitoes almost murder us. Rained most of the night.

17th. Started at 5 o'clock. Pulled this day 10 hours. Rained some. In the course of the day saw Powquet the first since leaving the states also mulberry trees bass wood.

18th. Started early after a rainy night and pulled 10 hours. Saw wild turkeys this evening but killed none nearly out of all kinds of provisions. Saw this day a herd of elk tryed hard to get some but failed.

19th. Made with a strong and fine wind 12 hours and camped without meat supped on a little flour boiled in water. Saw during the day 3 deer looked with folly at them and fired two shots and they ran off.

20th. Stopped until ½ past 6 to hunt caught one goose which we eat for breakfast afterward put ashore the hunters for game. They were fortunate enough to kill a fat doe on which we feasted right merrily and having lost so much time we concluded to run until the moon went down. Although we were before informed that it was not safe a few hours we got along well enough but at last went over a snagg with limbs above which taking our mast and the boat swinging broadside she was taking in water at a jolly rate and in a little she would have gone with the suck under the rock. I immediately had the mast cut away just in time to save her escaped from this I determined to try more we ran a little and were driven head foremost on a large tree lying across the river. We stopped about midway and lay swinging like a pendulum with much danger and difficulty we extricated her. Not being yet discouraged we ran on but soon were driven into a large drift we narrowly escaped being carried under and half full of water and our oar broke we made the shore as soon as possible. Resolved to run no more nights, after making 10½ hours.

21st. Made 9 hours with a head wind and camped at the old post of Council Bluffs it is now grown up with high weeds a memento of much money spent to little purpose. It is a beautiful scituation the magazine and three or four chimneys only remain.

22nd. After 5 hours in a dead current we arrived at a trading post of the Am. F. Co. Mr. Josh. Pilcher agent by whom we were entertained with the utmost hospitality. I had met Mr. P. at St. Louis on my way out on this account I had much pleasure in stopping. We found a good assortment of vegetables and a supply of such things as we wanted. Dined with him and made three hours more and stopped to hunt. Killed a fat deer and camped for the night.

23rd. Made 2 hours pulling and passed an agency ½ mile farther a trading post of Mess. Dripps & Fontenelle. Made in all 13 hours and camped during the day. Killed one deer from the boat from Council Bluffs to this. Have found the hickory, shagbark, sicamore and coffee bean trees not seen above also nightshade, brier, ducks, geese and pelicans have been very numerous but shy. For about 8 days stopped at the above trading post found only an old negro at home the rest out cutting wood.

24th. Made this day 10 ½ hours. Killed one goose saw plenty of deer.

25th. Made 11 hours. Killed one turkey from the boat. Saw this day the first pawpau fruit and trees. Wounded one deer from boat and stopped to search for him but without success.

26th. Made 11 hours at 8 hours came to a trading house of the Am. F. Co. called Rubideau Fort at the Black Snake hills and on the N. bank of the river on a little rise of ground in the rear of a beautiful bottom. Today saw the black locust for the first time. The lands are here quite fine and the hills as far back as we can see clothed with timber and verdure of the most luxuriant appearance the country is one of the most pleasant I have ever seen.

27th. After 7 hours pulling arrived at the Cantonment Leavenworth. On the route we saw several Indian canoes with squaws, children etc. I had no letters of introduction at the fort and therefore could not expect any great extension of the laws of hospitality but was received with all the politeness that could be expected. Was offered all the stores which I might require by Lieut. Richardson the officer of the day. My boy Baptiste and the Indian were vacinated by Doct. Fellows. It was amusing to observe the actions of Baptiste and the Indian. When I went from the boat towards the barracks the boy followed me until I was hailed by the sentry at view of one so strangely attired and with a knife on the end of his gun he broke like a quarter Nag (?) crying. Pegoni and the Indian was only prevented from taking the run also by being assured that he would not be harmed. I took the two to Doct. Fellow's quarters to be vaccinated the doct's wife and another lady happened to be present they were really beautiful women but the eyes of the two were riveted on the white squaws. Baptiste who speaks a little English told the other boys when he returned to the boat that he had seen a white squaw white as snow and so pretty.

28th. Made about 45 miles to Liberty where I found Mr. E. M. Samuel an old acquaintance who received me with all hospitality supplyed me with money and all that I wanted.

29th. Rained all day did not start.

30th. Went to the landing after breakfast a boat arrived going to the garrison and joined her as I shall arrive at St Louisas soon by this means as any other and more comfortably.

Shall close memorandum here with boat I afterward returned to Leavenworth and was treated with great politeness by the officers of the garrison especially a Capt. Nichols who invited me to dinner.

MEMO OF DISTANCES ON THE COLUMBIA ACCORDING TO THE ESTIMATES OF THE ENGLISH TRADERS.

From boat encampment to Colville	309 miles
" Colville to Oakenagen	150 "
" Oakenagen to Walla Walla	207 "
" Walla Walla to Vancouver	203 "
"Vancouver to Cape Disappointment	80 "
	949 [with pencil]

From Ermatinger.

2nd Journal (with Pencil)

On the 5th of May having crossed the Kanzas at the agency without accident and in one half of a day and traded as many cuds and apishemas(?) as I wanted and some deer skins for which I paid bacon. We started with 3 less men 4 having deserted and one new one engaged. Made this day along the Kanzas about 16 miles on a small stream having crossed one called the Lautrelle.

6th. Moved along the Kanzas and made about 12 miles to noon and took an observation found the latt to be 39° 38' made this day about 18 miles.

7th Made about 15 miles and camped on Little Vermillion.

8th. In the morning Mr Sublette finding that his leg would not bear travelling turned back made this day about 15 miles This dav left Kanzas River.

9th. Made about 20 miles and camped on a small river. This day our hunter killed our first deer.

10th. Made 15 miles to Big Vermillion and then 5 miles more and camped in the praire with but little wood and a little stagnant water.

11th. Made 9 miles to a small run then lost the trail and crossed a sluggish muddy stream running N(?) and recrossed the same it rounding and heading North and camped at noon. This day latt. 40° 18'. Sent a man to hunt the trail.

12th. Spent the morning mending hobbles and endeavoured to get an observation for long., but it was too cloudy. In afternoon started and in about 8 miles found a camp of Sublettes for nooning and marched until dark and camped. The horses having had nothing to eat all day did not tie them up at 1 o'clock at night was awakened by a furious running and snorting of the animals who all broke from their hobbles and left camp running in their course over anything opposed to them, spent the night in looking them up and found all but two. About sun one hour high three Otoes came to us who I suppose occasioned the fright and got the two horses.

13th. Started and travelled 7 hours and camped on a fork of the Blue and found the long. to be 96° 7'.

14th. Made W. S. W. 21 miles and struck the main Blue.

15th. Made about W. 9 miles and found our lat. to be 4c° 17' then made 12 miles W. by N. over a very level prairie and again struck the main Blue and camped.

16th. Made 10 miles about W. by N. to dinner latt. 40° 23' and 12 more to the Pawnee trail to the head of the Arkanzas and found that a very large party had passed it about 10 days before and a smaller one this morning.

17th. Made 3 miles up the stream crossing a very small run course W. by N. then struck out N. W. 3 miles and crossed a little run the same as passed in the morning then same course 6 miles and took an observation for latt and found it to be 40° 22' then 5 miles more same course and got sight of the Platte then W. N. W. 5 miles to the river and camped.

18th, Raining in morning caught some cat fish found fresh track of Indians a small party.

19th. Rained hard all day moved camp 15 miles to a small grove of timber on the main land found our horses very skittish during the night.

20th. In the morning had just raised camp when we discovered two Indians who were shy of coming to us but after a while suffered us to approach them they said they were Pawnees but as we did not know the Pawnees this might be so or not perhaps Ricarees. Afterward saw several more on the blufs who did not come to us. At noon found our lat. 43° 1' after travelling 13 miles W. N. (?). In the afternoon travelled 13 miles W. and found our long. to be 98° 30'. This night doubled guard.

21st. Moved camp from the pickett and 12 miles W. to breakfast fine clear weather. Old buffaloe sign and antelope. After dinner started and soon saw a band of elk, one loose horse took fright at them and ran back on our trail there being no person mounted on a swift horse in camp I followed myself. After going to a little creek where we nooned they struck out S. 15 miles to the heads of some little streams with timber probably the Blue where I overtook three of them. My horse having failed I lost 2 fine horses. After riding about 12 miles found the Platte at our night's camp and followed it to the camp making in all a ride of about 50 miles arrived about midnight camp moved on 11 miles.

22nd. Moved about N. 10 miles Lat. 40° 33' afternoon 10 miles W. and camped. After a little 3 Pawnee Scouts came to us and slept with us in the morning 12 more came and wished to persuade me to go to their camp 1½ days travel N. over the river which they forded here they stole some small things from us.

23rd. Moved from the pickett and 15 miles W. about to latt. Just before nooning passed a little creek then West 11 miles and camped.

24th. 20 miles W. to the crossing of the South fork of the Platte about 8 miles above the forks found latt. to be 40° 41'.

25th. Crossed without difficulty and made up the N. side of the South Fork about 4 miles W. Then struck N. W. about 1 mile to the North fork which is here the largest then made about W. by N. about 15 miles and near to some cut blufs which come close to the river.

26th. W. by N. 12 miles passing another place where the blufs cut the river and here found much cedar on them and camped on the river in a wide bottom. Found no buffaloe today killed one antelope. Afternoon 10 miles W. N. W. at night found the variation of the compass 1° 30' west. At midnight our horses took fright but being strongly picketed and hobbled but few got out of camp.

26th. I date this the 26th having over noted one day heretofore. In afternoon 12 miles W. N. W. passing some steep cut blufs which cut the river. Afternoon made 12 miles and camped still no buffaloe latt. 40° 22' at night.

27th. Made this day 20 miles. During a severe gale from the N. N. W. the sand cut like a knife and it was altogether a most disagreeable day. This day saw a little timber on some hills to the south of the river about 5 miles distant also 2 bands of wild horses. Killed one bull so poor as to be uneatable.

28th. Killed buffaloe plenty today. Came in sight of the chimney about noon made 22 miles wind still high N. N. W. One of our outriders saw six Indians mounted today.

29th. Nooned at the Chimney lat. 41° 51'. After travelling this forenoon 11 miles afternoon 10 miles.

30th. Passed through between two high blufs through a pretty good pass and avoided going between one of them and the river where there are bad ravines. Made this day 22 miles to Horse Creek.

31st Made after crossing Horse Creek at starting about 20 miles.

June 1st. Made 15 miles to Laramies fork just before coming to which we made a cut off of about 3 miles over and about 5 miles by the river forded this fork with ease and made 8 miles up the Platte in afternoon. At the crossing we found 13 of Sublette's men camped for the purpose of building a fort he having gone ahead with his best animals and the residue of his goods he left about 14 loads.

2nd. Made along the river 5 miles then struck out into the hills about W. N. W. and made 12 miles to a little creek. In the afternoon made 13 miles to pretty large creek and camped for the night the whole course this day about W. N. W. Left at noon camp a bull and cow whose feet had worn out.

3rd. Made 15 miles and nooned on the river this course N.W. by N. and cut over the hills about ½ the way the river taking a bend quite to the N. and passing through bad rocks. Afternoon made 6 miles cutting two very bad blufs but still following the river and camped on it.

4th. Forded the river and made W. N. W. 17 miles along the river and camped on it. Sublette one day ahead.

5th. Made along the river 24 miles along the river.

6th. Made along the river 24 miles W by N.

7th. Made 12 miles along the river to the Red Butes so called and is the place at which the river turns S. W. and we leave to strike for Sweetwater. Sublette 2 days ahead weather chilly and windy. Poor grass for several days.

8th. This morning I had intended to have turned out the horses at 2 o'clock and guarded them but during the night the horses appeared uneasy and appeared to think there were Indians about which induced me to keep them up until sunrise when we started W. S. W. from the Red Butes and made 18 miles to the high ridge of land. Then one point more to the South and 12 miles more to a small creek with poor grass. Several of the horses nearly done up for want of grass and from fatigue. This day killed two grisly bears and many buffaloe. A little shower toward night.

9th. Made S. W. 10 miles and made Rock Independence on which W. L. Sublette had noted that he had arrived on the 6th but I think he could not have done so before the 7th. I noted my name then made S. W. along the creek 4 ½ miles to a place where the creek puts through cut rocks each side perpendicular and about 60 feet high. The trail goes through another place on a level and about 100 feet south of the river the rock intervening then made 6 miles W. S. W. between mountains but on a level and along the creek.

10th. General courses W. S. W. and along Sweetwater high granite hills on each side. Made 25 miles.

11th. W. 10 miles then N. W. 9 miles to camp on Sweetwater.

12th. S. W. forenoon a cut off of 10 miles to Sweetwater afternoon S. W. 9 miles along Sweetwater. Long, 110° 30'.

13th 3 miles along Sweetwater S. W. then took up a ravine to the W. N. W. about 1mile then W. by S. 9 miles to a creek of Sweetwater running into it about 8 miles off and S. E. Then W. by S. 7 miles to another creek of Sweetwater running about S. E. and emtying into it at about 10 miles Sweetwater appears to run in cut rocks.

15th, Made due west 5 miles and crossed a small creek of Sweetwater which comes from a point of granite rocks about 2 miles from which we passed then W. 7 miles to a spring of good cold water and good grass. Wind River mountains now bear N. N. W. and are covered with snow about 20 miles distant, latt. 42° 44'. Afternoon made W. 6 miles to Sweetwater Creek main body going about S. E. and coming out of cut rocks then W. by S. 16 miles over broken ground to one fork of Sandy running S. by E. Here horses were tired buffaloe plenty.

15th. W. N. W. 9 miles to Big Sandy where we found buffaloe plenty. My hunters not yet come in been out 4 days fearful they have been scalped.

16th. Made down the Sandy S. W. by W. 15 miles then 4 S. E. by E and camped on this stream. So far the grass is miserable and the horses are starving and also at last night's camp they eat something that has made many of them sick, the same thing happened two year since on the next creek west.

17th. S. S.W. 10 miles down Sandy which makes here a bend to the right. Afternoon S. 9 miles passing at three miles the mouth of little Sandy and camped without any grass.

18th. 12 miles in the forenoon S. S. W. making small cut off afternoon W. S. W. 7 miles camped in good grass.

19th. About S. by W. 8 miles and camped 1 mile above the mouth of Sandy on Green River or Seckkedee. On the night of the 17th I left camp to hunt Fitzpatric and slept on the prairie in morning struck Green River and went down to the forks and finding nothing went up again and found rendesvous about 12 miles up and much to my astonishment the goods which I had contracted to bring up to the Rocky Mountain fur Co. were refused by those honourable gentlemen. latt. 41° 30'.

20th. Made W. S. W. 8 miles then S. by E. 15 miles to Hams Fork running here S. E and a small stream.

21st. Same camp.

22nd. Same camp

27th. Moved up the river N.W. 10 miles grass here pretty good but little timber and none but willows for the last 6 miles.

To 3rd. July. Same camp then up Hams Fork 10 miles N.W. moved up the fork about W. by S. 12 miles. Too many Indians with us for comfort or safety they let their horses among ours so that it is impossible to guard any of them.

4th. Moved up the creek about 1 mile then leaving it made W. by N. over a divide and by a pass which occurs in the lowest part of a high range of hills 7 miles then W. 13 miles down a ravine which had a little water in it to its junction with another small run and the two are called Muddy. Here we celebrated the 4th I gave the men too much alcohol for peace took a pretty hearty spree myself. At the camp we found Mr. Cerry and Mr. Walker who were returning to St. Louis with the furs collected by Mr. Bonneville's company about 10 pack and men going down to whom there is due 10,000$.

5th. Made down Muddy 5 miles W. then N. W. cutting a divide into a small ravine which has a little water in it 8 miles then leaving the ravine cutting moderately high land to Bear River 4 miles. Then down Bear River N. by W. 4 miles to camp.

6th. Made down the river N. N. W. 5 miles to Smiths Fork which is a short stream from the N. E. by N. and nearly as large as Bear River then same course 3 miles more then N. W. 5 miles here comes in Kamas creek from the N. then W. N. W. 3 and crossed Bear River three more and recrossed then cut over some high hills. Same course 8 miles more and struck the river again then down the river same course 1 mile to camp nothing to eat. Due south of this camp about 5 miles is the little lake so called which is about 20 miles long.

7th. Made 3 miles N. N. W. and passed a little creek the same course 6 miles along the river, then 3 miles N. W. to camp. All day fine grass. During this day a multitude of fine springs coming into the river. Today killed one bull.

8th. Made N. W. 10 miles then 10 miles W. N. W. to a place where there is soda spring or I may say 50 of them. These springs throw out lime which deposits and forms little hillocks of a yellowish coloured stone. There is also here a warm spring which throws water with a jet which is like bilge water in taste. There is also here peet beds which sometimes take fire and leave behind a deep light ashes in which animals mire. Killed one bull today but so poor as to be hardly eatable. Having in the course of the day lost a horse will remain here to hunt him up.

9th. Same camp. Assended a mountain and from it could see that Bear River took a short turn round sheep rock about 2 miles below the spouting steam and goes south as far as I could see. There are in this place many hundreds of mounds of yellowish stone with a crater on top formed by the deposits of the impregnated waters of this place. Killed one buffaloe.

10th. Moved N. by W 3 miles cutting a range of hills then N. N. W. 17 miles to Blackfoot on which I found Bonneville again and plenty of buffaloe and killed 3 grisly bears. During the day passed many small funnel shaped holes in the lava having the appearance of small craters.

11th. Made W. 6 miles cutting a range of hills then following in a valley formed by these hills and another range. Made W. N.W. 10 miles to a little brook running N. by W. to camp. Buffaloe today. Saw one Blackfoot on foot in the hills who ran like a good fellow.

12th. Made W. 3 miles and came upon a small creek which was said to be Portneuf it may possibly be .the same water as that we camped on last night but running S. by E crossed this and a high range of hills and struck a stream which is said to be Ross Creek this runs about W. After 9 miles more camped. Saw but few buffaloe today.

13th. No buffaloe, saw elk on Snake River which we struck after 6 miles W. by N. In some small slew saw a great quantity of fine trout about 2 lbs. weight.

14th. Went down the river about 3 miles and found a location for a fort and succeeded and killed a buffaloe near the spot.

15th. Commenced building the fort and sent our 12 men to hunt to be gone 12 days and continued at work on the fort a few days and fell short of provisions and was obliged to knock off in order to obtain food sent out some men for buffaloe they returned in two days with plenty. The 12 returned the 28th day at night. On the 26th a Frenchman named Kanseau was killed horse racing and the 27th was buried near the fort. He belonged to Mr. McKay's camp and his comrades erected a decent tomb for him, service for him was performed by the Canadians in the Catholic form by Mr. Lee, in the Protestant form, and by the Indians in their form as he had Indian family, he at least was well buried.

30th Mr. McKay left us and Mr Lee and Capt. Stewart with him.

6th. Having done as much as was requisite for safety to the fort and drank a bale of liquor and named it Fort Hall in honour of the oldest partner of our concern, we left it and with it Mr. Evans in charge of 11 men and 14 horses and mules and three cows. We went down the river S. W. 4 miles and found a ford crossed and made N. W. 7 miles to the head of a spring and camped in all 29 strong. Fort Hall is in latt. 43° 14' long. 113° 35'.

7th. Started at day light and travelled 10 hours as fast as possible N. W. by W. 30 miles to the Bute, being the most southwardly one and from it the other two Butes bear N. N. E. the farther about 20 miles off the other midway the Three Tetons about 100 miles off and bearing N. E. The day was hot and we suffered some for water and found but a small supply on the N. side of the bute a miserable chance for our horses and not a good one for ourselves.

8th. Started it sunrise and made N. W. 10 miles to Godins River then crossed it and made in the same direction 12 up the river and camped in fine grass. Where we struck the river there is no grass nor until we camped above I am told it is fine. Found no appearance of buffaloe.

9th. Made due W. 16 miles striking for the N. side of it a pretty high hill and struck up the mountains close on the N. side of it then wound into the mountains in a S. W. course finding water several times and cutting a divide struck a small thread of water at 5 miles. This we followed 3 miles N.W. and struck a pretty large creek which we followed N. N. E. 1 mile and camped. Just at starting killed a bull and separated from Abbot and a small party of trappers accompanied by Antoine Godin whom I sent out for beaver.

10th. Made 7 miles down the creek N. N. E. to Godins River the same we left day before yesterday then N. W. 3 miles then west 14 miles. Today saw a large fire in the mountains on our left suppose them to be Diggers keeping for safety in the hills the Blackfeet trouble them even here. Saw one band of buffoloe cows today killed one calf. The party I parted from *viz* Antoine and Abbot are before us on this river.

11th. Made W. 9 miles then 18 S W the angle of the two courses occurs at what is called the Spring prairie which is about 10 miles over in the centre of which there are three tolerable butes. These butes when you approach from the east look like three but when from the west show but as two. This day killed an old bull very strong.

12th Moved 3 miles up the creek S.W. at which place the creek divides into about equal parts. The one going south I took by the advice of one who said he had passed before followed this up one mile and a branch going E. 3 farther another E. 4 miles farther looked so bad camped. Took a horse to explore the route. ½ mile above camp the stream branches the right at small distance heads in an amphitheater of inaccessible mountains followed the left 4 miles S. by E, and this also heads in an amphitheater. We drove 2 bulls before us which we killed they being unable to pass. I climbed up the clefts and in passing over the snow had liked to have been killed in the following manner.

Passing over some snow and on which the water was running and being afraid of caving in I missed my foothold in a slippery place and went gradually sliding down to a precipice but succeeded at last in averting my progress to destruction by catching the only stone which projected above the icy snow. I however reached the summit and looked into another defile running E. like the one I came up. Got to the bottom again and found one of our two mules gone and being in want of meat packed the other with part of one of the bulls and walked barefoot to camp during the night through an infernal rough, rocky, prickly, bruisy, swampy, woody hole.

13th. Moved down creek back to the commencement of the South Fork then took the other about S. W. by W. at two miles up a creek from the N. forming about half of the stream then three miles farther where the rest divides into two parts very small.

Passed the mountain in a south course between these last forks up a gentle fine trail and not more than 1 mile to the top then down by a very steep bad trail. South still along a branch of Malad 5 miles to tolerable grass and camped. This last part of the route about the worst road that I ever passed.

14th. After shoeing some horses that were lamed yesterday started and made 9 miles S. S. W. at 2 of which got a small creek from the N. E. at the end of the 9 miles got a fork of about equal size to the one I came down from the S. W. then made S. E. by S. 10 miles and camped. Got a creek from the N. E. at 2 miles of it and at 7 one from the S. W. Saw no game today the dusky grouse plenty for three days past. Horses much knocked up with sore feet.

15th. After crossing the stream passed up a ravine S. W. to its head then crossed some low grassy hills and at 12 miles crossed a small creek going S. E. this creek forks at this place then at two miles in all 14 miles S. W. Crossed another which we followed two miles S. S. E. then left it on our left and cut a pretty high hill 4 miles S. S. W. and came down to the plain of Snake River then 3 miles W. to a creek with a fine bottom but no water except what remains in little pools, but excellent grass. Here found two lodges of Snake Indians.

16th. Made 28 miles W. following the main trail which is good perfectly level and distinct except in one place where it crosses several small branches which in the spring I presume are miry which occasions the traveller to go in no particular place. During this days march I observed some low hills on the South side of us which gradually approach and at this camp are about 8 miles distant, between us and them a little river appears to run to the W. which I am in hopes is Reeds, other wise called Big Woody. Today the travelling was fine and many little streams of water cross the trail at this camp which is on a very small thread there commence small irregularities just enough to note the place.

17th. Made 20 miles due west over a country with easy hills good and distinct trail and often water in very little streams. Country mostly burnt out by the Indians who have passed here lately going up to buffaloe. Killed some dusky grouse and dug some *kamas* which assisted our living a little also found some choke cherries and saw one Indian at a distance on horse back who fled.

18th. Made over a hilly country 12 miles W. until we passed a high stony hill then bending N. W. made 10 miles more over a stony hilly but distinct trail with not much water. Saw a track of a bull made this morning although there is very little old signs in this section. Camped on a nearly dry creek running W. Today lost 2 horses.

19th. Left the little run on which we camped last night going here N. N. W. on our right and put out as near as I could judge W. 10 miles the first three over a divide of high steep hills then taking a little run followed it out of the worst hills. Along this run were many little Indian camps. We then left it and went W. N. W. 15 miles and struck Woody River in cut rocks at about 7 miles of this last course struck the run on which we camped last night at Woody. We saw plenty of salmon but had no means of catching any of them. This day found a colt in the Rush probably left by the Indians on which I mean to breakfast tomorrow morning being short of provant.

20th. Followed the river down W. by N. 22 miles. In the course of the day traded of some Indians enough salmon for a lunch and consumed the remaining provisions.

21st. No breakfast. Feel very much purified (?) in the flesh. 12 miles down the creek W. At noon found Indians of whom we traded enough salmon with a dead one we picked up in the brook and a few birds for a dinner afterwards. Traded 2 bales salmon of the Indians.

22nd. Made 5 miles W. then the trail cut a point of higher ground of about 2 miles and again struck the river and crossed it. Made on the other side 7 miles W. in all this day 15 miles W.

23rd. Made West 9 miles and found a small village of Snakes of whom we could only trade a very few salmon then 5 more in all 14 miles along the Big Wood W. and arrived at Snake River which we forded by wetting our packs a little. Here we found a few lodges of very impudent Pawnacks of whom we traded a half bale of salmon. Afterward 4 miles N. along the W. side of Snake River and camped near a few lodges of Indians.

24th. 6 miles N. then made a cut off N. N. W. 4 miles to R. Malheur where we found but three or four Indians and consequently got but little salmon and consequently may starve a little between this and Walla Walla. Afternoon 7 miles N. passing not far from the river. I had forgot to note that on Big Wood River the Indians attempted to steal some of our horses but the horse guards discovered them and they failed. Scorpions are here quite common two nights since I was just about laying down when on my blanket I saw something move I folded it in the blanket and on carrying it to the fire found it to be a very good sized scorpion. This day at noon parted from Richardson and 8 men to go up Malheur and other creeks to trap. There is something melancholy in parting with men with whom one has travelled so far in this uncertain country. Our party is now 17 boys Indians *literati* and all.

25th. This days march was in many different courses but I average them at 23 miles N. W. and camped just before where the trail finally leaves the Snake River and at the same camp where I overtook two years since my men who without orders were leaving the country while I was up Malheur trapping. Traded this day about 70 salmon which makes a tolerable supply of provisions for the cut to Walla Walla.

26th. Made about 20 miles in about a N.W. direction up Brule. Last night lost two horses which I think were stolen and today two more gave out. I now think of leaving two men behind to bring up some of the worst animals otherwise I fear I shall loose many of them.

27th. After leaving Sunsbury and Briggs to bring up the worn out horses I left and making a cut off to the right going up a ravine across another and down a third came again upon Brule, at the open prairie and camped for noon at the upper end of it on a little run and cashed 24 bars lead and 18 traps. General course N. W. 14 miles afternoon 9 miles N. W. W. following the little creek up and camped on a little prairie near the head of it of about 20 acres. Here there is two trails one N. W. the other N. the N. W. One I shall try.

28th. Here taking the left hand trail we followed it 12 miles N. W. when it disappeared. I then took a N. course and at 8 miles came on Powder River which we followed down about 5 miles and camped. This afternoon I shall go out to see where the trail crosses the river. This day killed an antelope and a fawn and saw fresh elk track.

29th. Turned up the creek again and after arriving at where we first struck the river made 6 miles W. by N. then into cut rocks then W. N. W. 4 miles more and nooned on a little water in a ravine. During the forenoon two men whom I had left behind with the poor animals brought up all but two. Also during the forenoon two men got lost and our hunter got lost yesterday all missing tonight. Afternoon made 8 miles N. W. and camped in cut rocks on the main river at a place apparently not frequented either by Indians or whites but there are salmon here but we have no means of catching any without waiting too long. I think by the looks there are beaver here but will ascertain in the morning in order that my trip here may not be entirely lost.

30th. Made 8 miles up the creek through cut rocks during which time killed one salmon and two otter so much provisions and nooned on the Walla Walla trail. West Fork the east being the one I descended on my first tour afternoon made N. N. W. on the trail. Here plain and good 15 miles at 5 of which crossed another fork of Powder River but dry at 5 more a little water and at camp a little and but a little. Country rolling and soil good. At our camp two lodges of Kiuses.

31st. Made 15 miles N. N. W. Good soil and not very hilly and nooned at the Grand Ronde where I found some Kiuse Indians, Capt Bonneville and two of Mckay's men and learned that Capt. Stewart and Mr. Lee passed two days before. Afternoon took the Walla Walla Trail N. N. W. 12 miles and camped at a very small prairie with a little stream going N. W. Killed 5 hens today. On allowance still.

1 Sept. After about 5 miles descended a very bad mountain and followed a dry creek then assended another bad mountain and nooned without water at 8 miles of very bad going. Afternoon making along a ridge of mountain 16 miles arrived at the Ottilla (?). The trail plain, the ground stony about N. W. course but indirect so far from the Three Butes. Every day has been thick smoke like fog enveloping the whole country. Last night we camped at 10 o'clock having found no water and the whole country burnt as black as my hat affording as poor a prospect for a poor sett of horses as need be.

2nd. Left camp behind and proceed across the Utalla River to the N. and up a mountain then took a slight ravine going N.W. and crossing several trails until the ravine leads to a dry willowed creek going N. E with a little water in puddles. Then N. W. up a ravine to the height of land which is a gentle slope then leaving the trail and going a few hundred yards to the left followed a dry ravine to the Walla Walla River. 22 miles in all N.W. then down the Walla Walla W. by N. 10 miles to Fort Walla Walla where I found Mr. Pambrum who did the honours of the fort in his usual handsome stile. Also found Capt. Stewart and Mess Lees who arrived two days since. Mr. Mckay for some reason remained in the mountains.

3rd. Remained at Walla Walla this day and made arrangements for going down at night Capt Thing and the residue of the party came up.

4th. In morning left Walla Walla in a boat hired by Capt. Stewart after proceeding 4 miles obliged to come to land to tighten the canoe.

5, 6, 7th. Down the river and landed to hire canoes at the Dalles for the party still behind.

8th. Waiting at the Dalles for party.

9th. Waiting at same place party arrived at night with news that they drowned one horse and the jackass in crossing the river, I valued him more than 10 horses as a breeder.

10th At noon having with difficulty hired three canoes started down the river with three Indians on board. Wind high and soon increased to a gale swamped one of the canoes which frighted the Indians back. Obliged to lay by with two of the canoes behind.

11th. Walked back and brought up the two canoes. Gale still furious and finding that my people were not good boatsmen enough to follow me left the two boats in charge of Capt. Thing and at noon put ahead made about 10 miles and swamped the canoe.

12th. Gale still violent and canoe so leaky as to require one man to bail the whole time. Kept on until noon and camped until night when it calmed and we put ahead and made to the Cascades the roar of which warned me to camp. Here overtook Capt. Stewart.

13th. Made our boat a little tighter with some pitch obtained of Capt. Stewart and made the portage of the Cascade carrying our things about 1 mile and letting our boat down with ropes. Raining hard made til 9 o'clock at night when it rained so hard that that with the leakage we could keep the boat free of water no longer and put ashore.

14th. At 2 o'clock in morning cleared up a little and we put on but it kept drizzling. At 9 o'clock. made the saw mill above the fort and got some breakfast not having eaten since noon the day before. At 12 o'clock arrived at Fort Vancouver where I found Doct. McLaughlin in charge who received us in his usual manner. He has here power and uses it as a man should to make those about him and those who come in contact with him comfortable and happy.

15th. Early in the morning having hired another canoe put ahead and in a rainy day at about 12 o'clock. met the brig *May Dacre* in full sail up the river. Boarded her and found all well she had put into Valparaiso having been struck by lightning and much damaged. Capt Lambert was well and brought me 20 Sandwich Islanders and 2 Coopers 2 Smiths and a Clerk.

16th. Kept on up the river in order to make Fort Vancouver and pay my respects to Doct. McLaughlin but the wind failed and we could not.

17th. Took the gig and went up to Tea Prairie to see about a location but found none.

18th. Came on board and put down the river for Oak point where we mean to examine for a location.

19th. Came too at Carnean's (?) house and concluded to remain at least for the winter.

20th. After setting the forges at work and commencing a coal kiln houses etc, started up the River Wallammut in a gig. The gig followed the Wallammut 1 mile then took a creek to the right and after 5 miles came to the farm of Mr. Thomas Mckay, where I was treated with great kindness by La Bonte his foreman and of him procured horses and proceeded by land until near night over hilly wooded country. Near night came out into large plains of good lands surrounded with good timber some oak and overtook Mess. Lees who had started the day before me and camped with them. They are in search of a location.

21st. Put out in the morning. Day's travel through good lands rolling sufficient and assorted timber and water. At 3 o'clock. came to and crossed the Wallamut at Duportes[1] house and from him got fresh horses and proceed up on the E. side of the river to Jervais 10 miles.

22nd. Not suiting myself as to a farm returned to Duportes and went to look at a prairie about 3 miles below his place and concluded to occupy it. It is about 15 miles long 7 wide surrounded with fine timber and a good mill stream on it. Laid out a farm. Afternoon took a canoe and descended as far as falls.

23rd. Made the portage of the falls and was taken violently sick of vomiting and purging probably caused by having eaten some Lamprey eels. Recovered toward night and arrived at Fort Vancouver and finished an arrangement in regard to trade.

24th. Went down the river to the vessel.

25th. Making preparation for sending out parties.

26th. Ditto and sent off Sunsbury to trade horses at the dalles. Sent Stout up the Wallammut with 2 men and implements to commence farm and started myself up to Vancouver on buisness.

28th. Up the Wallamut with Mr. Nuttall and Townsend and Mr Stout.

29th. Going up to the falls and went a small distance up the Clackamas River to look at a spot there found it would not do. Saw there a chalk formation.

30th. Returning down the rivers.

31st. At night reached the vessell at Carneans. From this time until the 13th Oct. making preparation for a campaign into the Snake country and arrived on the 13th at Vancouver and was received with great attention by all there.

14th. Made up the river 12 miles.

15th. Made up the river 11 miles.

16th. Made up the river 13 miles to the Cascades.

17, 18, 19th Delayed by strong winds and making portage on the last day at night sent a division off under charge of Capt. Thing

---

1. This name is given as "Dapattys" on the map.

20, 21, 22nd. Same camp with nothing to eat but what we catch out of the river with our lines not liking to broach our stores for the voyage.

23rd. At sundown our boats arrived from above and I immediately started up the river we pulled all night except stopping to cook at midnight.

24th. After taking breakfast and giving the Kanackas two hours sleep we put up the river with a head wind. Day raw and chill.

25th. Arrived at noon at the Dalles and found all the people well and but one horse traded.

26th. Started Capt. Thing with 12 Kanackas and 6 whites and all the best horses.

27th. Remained at same camp and traded 5 horses at about $5.00 of goods each.

28th. Started the boats back and Hubbard down by land with 13 horses for the farm.

29th. & 30th. Same camp traded 4 horses.

31st. Started up the River Kanackas on foot for want of horses and goods on miserably poor animals. To the 7th Nov. moving slowly up the river during which time and before traded 18 horses and 600 lbs dried salmon which I have reserved for provisions after we leave the river when I know we shall get none and having hired a canoe for Walla Walla dispatched her with this salmon, 2 loads of traps, one woman, one Indian and two whites. She sank once but we recovered all and suffered one day's delay only to dry the fish. We have lived chiefly on trash and dogs fearing to commence our stock of provisions expecting to get little or nothing all winter and I do not mean to starve except when I can't help it.

8th. Traded one horse. A few drops rain today and for more than two thirds of the days since the 1st of the month. Kept along the river traded 8 dogs today being a 2 days' rations.

9th. Moved along the river. Traded 1 dog but no horses.

10th. Left camp and went into Walla Walla found Mr. Pambrum well and good natured, and got the news that Capt. Thing's 12 Kanackas had deserted him and that he had gone in search of them on their trail.

11th. Went to Capt. Thing's camp and learned from Mr Baker that the Kanackas had taken about 2 bales of goods and 12 horses. Returned to Walla Walla on the way met the men who went with Capt. Thing they had not been successfull. Dispatched an interpreter Mr. Richardson and two other men down the river in a canoe to head the fellows.

12th. Moved camp up the river a small piece for grass having crossed yesterday. No success in trading horses today. The Indians appear to think their fortunes are to be made by an opposition but they will find their mistake. Today got word that the Kanackas had not touched the Columbia nor passed the Utalla River and that Richardson had got a party of Indians to accompany him and horses and had taken up pursuit on land.

13th. Richardson still out. At night dispatched 4 men after two Kanackas that have been seen by the Indians about 15 miles below Walla Walla on the main river.

14th. Robinson and Richardson's party returned with no success Robinson had seen the track of shod horses within 5 miles of Walla Walla.

15th. At 10 o'clock this morning dispatched Richardson and Robinson with two men to trace out the track seen by Robinson.

16th. An Indian brought in one shod horse which had been taken by the Kanackas he found it at the Utalla River and brought word that there saw two of the scamps had bought a canoe and gone down leaving no horse except fat which they (the Indians?) took and one alive which he brought in.

17th. Robinson and Richardson returned no news yet of the rest.

18th. Finding there is no immediate hope of getting the Kanackas I today dispatched Capt Thing to Fort Hall having 19 (?) men *viz* 4 Kanackas 10 white men and himself, a fur (?) man and three Nez Perces 19 in all. This is a picked up lot and I have great fears they will commit robbery and desertion to a greater extent than the Kanackas have done but I was obliged to trust to the chance it is late and the Blue Mounts, are now covered white with snow although the grass is green here within 30 miles of them.

19th. Went up the Walla Walla River about 7 miles and raised a deposit of goods which I had made in the ground there fearing that some of Capt. Thing's men who knew where it was might desert and raise it and attempt to go to the Spanish Country. I am now quite sick with a fever but must keep doing,

20th. Spent the day arranging packs for a move . Weather clear and cold with much hoar frost and mist.

21st. Deposited the spare goods on hand at Walla Walla Fort

22nd. Finished arranging for moving and have given up all the horses still missing *viz.* 2.

23rd. Moved down the Walla Walla River and camped on the Columbia about 6 miles below the Walla Walla taking leave on the way of Mr. Pambrun the gentleman in charge of the fort. Still not well.

24th. Moved about 15 miles down the Columbia and camped, without wood night quite cold, near some bad rapids just above the mouth of the Utalla where I have a cash of traps which I intend to raise.

25th. Moved about 15 miles down the river and camped. I had forgot to mention that on the 23rd in the morning when I was about loading the horses I found that Ira Long a sick and as we have supposed crazy Kanacka was missing I then thought that he would go at once to Walla Walla but do not hear of him. Yet I am at a stand to make up my mind whether he went out of camp and died suddenly or drowned in the river or ran off. What he should run off for no one can conceive as no duty had been required of him and he had tea and other luxurys given him on acct. of sickness that no one else had. It is a very strange affair to me. Today I hear that one of the two Kanackas who went down the river in a canoe as per former report has been killed for killing horses by the Indians. Other reports say a Kanacka has killed an Indian. I also hear that 6 of the runaways are on the heads of John Days River the whole of which store's I take to be lies invented to tell me in the hopes of a small present of tobacco. We live on dogs chiefly good luck traded 4 today.

26th. Made about 12 miles down the river and during the day traded a young fat dog.

27th. Moved about 14 miles down the river traded one poor little dog and 4 dried salmon. We hear such contradictory and impossible accounts from the Indians of the Kanackes that I do not know what to believe.

28th. Moved down the river 15 miles traded nothing all day. Providentially killed one goose which made supper and breakfast for 5 of us. Snowed a little this day and of course not much comfort for a little cold and wet spoils all the comfort of our camps.

29th. 16 miles down the river killed nothing traded 2 dogs and some little deer meat dried. Snowed all the first part of the day and uncomfortably cold rains. Tonight very uncomfortable some of us have no coats (?) men grumble.

30th. The rain of last night changed to snow and this morning the earth is white and the weather cold made 12 miles and crossed John Days River then 3 more along the main river and camped with nothing but grass to cook our supper.

31st. Made today 12 miles the last of yesterdays and some of today's march. Pretty bad travelling for the horses owing to cut rocks. Camped one mile up the river of falls called by the French "*Revieu des Shutes*". I do not know if from the numerous rapids of this river or its proximity to the great falls of the Columbia which are about 3 miles below its mouth. There is here a small village of Indians from whom I understand by signs that the two Kanackes who descended the river stole horses here or killed horses and in some wrangle with the chief concerning it one of the Kanackas shot him. I shall be sorry if this is true as in such case I shall be obliged to make a signal example of him both in order to quiet the Indians and prevent their rising upon the whites and as a terror to the other Kanackas.

Dec. 1st After trading 4 dogs and a few salmon and roots and ascertained that there was no ford above or near us and that the road lay on the river we moved camp down to the mouth and crossed at a rapid and tolerable deep ford then assended the hill by a ravine and descending again struck a good sized Beaver Creek at 6 miles due South. While on the divide could see far ahead of a dreary, snowy, exposed country without a stick of timber to relieve the eye except far in the distance a black looking mass like a cloud of pine timber.

2nd. Moved camp early and left the creek on which we camped by a ravine to the right running S. S. W. followed it to the height of land then down a ravine to the creek on which we camped last night 6 miles. Followed this creek 3 miles S. S. W then S. S. E. to the loft of the creek by a ravine 5 more and camped. We here find some little oak timber traded today about 30 lbs. dried deer meat.

3rd. Made 16 miles to the River des Shutes S. S. E. and camped near about 20 lodges of Indians. Had to buy what little wood we used a thing I mortally detest. Last night about 12 sett in to snow before morning turned to rain which lasted all day the coldest I ever knew and blew a gale in our teeth this has been a miserable uncomfortable day. The first part of it we assended gradually until we reached a high ridge then descended suddenly to the river. On the ridge considerable snow and the whole country covered with little round cones of earth denoting that the winds blow over this divide continually and strong. Grass is far as I could see pretty good.

4th. Moved camp S. S. W. 3 miles and camped on the fork of the river coming from timbered hills to the W. N. W. We hear that the two Kanackas have been followed by the Indians and killed in revenge for killing one of them and their horses.

5th. Same camp trying to trade horses get none yet.

6th. Same camp.

7th. Same camp.

8th. Same camp.

9th. Same camp. During all this time traded but one horse, but fared well enough for food as we obtained as many dogs as we could eat during the time. Gully my Indian having lost his horse went out to hunt him and as I believe with a determination to quit me he found his horse and sent it to camp by an Indian with word to send his things with some trifling excuse but I kept the horse and things. The Indian whom he sent said he would go and take the horse for which I gave him a flogging and he went off. During this time we percussioned 3 rifles our powder being so badly damaged as to render flint locks useless. In this vicinity there are elk and deer as we trade their meat and skins of the Indians in small quantities the grass here is good and here I cashed some goods our horses being too poor to carry them on.

10th Moved but without our guide whom I had engaged who was among the missing when we started and I suppose engaged only to get something but without intending to start. We took a S. S. W course and crossed the fork on which we had camped for some days past and after mounting the small mountains which range along this fork found an extensive plain beyond which white and high rose a range of mountains. Disheartening to look at but ahead is the word and the spirit seems to raise with the occasion.

This range runs E. and W. Made this day 11 miles to the foot of the range along which is a small stream (?). Here we *cached* some provisions for our return route and some loads of dry goods which our horses are too weak to carry.

11th. S. S. W. and mounted the mountains which we found much less formidable than they appeared to be the earth and trees are covered with a heavy hoar frost which at a distance made them look as if covered deep with snow of which there was but little. These mountains have scattering groups of pine timber and some oak and the little plains in them have brown (?) cedars similar to those of N. E. but still of a different sort. But yet the robins in considerable number feed on the berries which reminded me of old pleasures and home where I have often been out to shoot these birds from the laving (?) but these are too painful to be indulged and the present evil is enough without calling up old joys to enhance it. Made this day 15 miles and camped on snow water with good pine wood. Day cloudy wind N. E. and cold. Saw the first elk and deer sign for some time. They say we cannot cross the divide to Clamat but I will go as far as I can.

12th Engaged an Indian guide last night but he too it seems has backed out as I cannot find him this morning. Made one mile down the ravine in which we camped and came to a small creek running about E. then assended the hills and after 5 miles came to a larger creek then 3 miles more where the trail gave out. Then courses S. S. W. then struck S. by E. 3 miles and crossed a small creek this and the last running E then 3 miles more and camped on a dry ravine. All these last courses S. by E. Grass this far pretty good and country timbered and prettily levell today with small prairies. Saw much elk and deer signs but killed none.

13th Made 5 miles S. by E. over level timbered with small openings country and came to a creek with very bad cut rock banks at least 400 feet high. We had much difficulty in getting our horses down to the water and up the opposite bank but succeeded after laming several of our horses. This creek is rapid tolerably large and runs N. E. We then made 3 miles S. by E. and camped. The snow here covers the ground and the horses have to dig for their food. Saw today 12 deer and a great quantity of elk and deer sign and one bear track.

After camping went out to hunt but could kill nothing. Today the first clear day for four days the fog lifted a little and enabled us to see a range of snowy mountains on the west side of us and one very high bearing S. W. distant about 25 miles. Should we have any considerable fall of snow now we should loose all our horses they could not subsist with much more than there is now. All the dog meat which we have brought with us from the last Indians is done and we have now to look to our guns to supply us or eat our horses. We have about 4 bushells of rice and flour in camp for cases of extremity and a little dog grease. Small game there is none we have but 10 lbs of powder along and that damaged. Go ahead very cold for the 4 last days.

14th Made S. E. 4 miles to a very small creek running in an immense chasm into which we got and camped the grass being good and our horses having had nothing last night except what they dug up from beneath several inches of snow. Saw many deer today but killed none. Sent our hunters out after camping all but one returned empty and him I suppose has lost himself in the forests as I heard a gun late at night and returned several shots. Weather still quite foggy and very cold.

15th S. E. by E. 4 miles and down the ravine. The snow growing less and less visibly in this direction got out of the woods and saw the country bare of snow. Here found a lodge of Indians who have 32 horses traded one of them and have the promise of trading two more in the morning. The man missing last night came in this morning.

16th. Traded the two horses one of which cost 82½ cents of beads first cost. Made E. down the ravine 2 miles then struck a good trail crossing the ravine and going off S. S. W, which I followed over rocky high land 8 miles and came to a very large creek. I should think it must be at least one-half of the River des Shutes at least running in an immense chasm into which we descended and camped in good grass and plenty of dry wood which makes us very comfortable for the night is very cold. During the march over the high land saw a chain of mountains on our left and the other side of the river white with snow and partly wooded.

17th. Went up the creek W. S. W. 2 miles when it turned south and we forded it at a deep ford, horses suffered much from the coldness of the water. Then wound S. E. up the opposite bank of the river very high and precipitous 2 miles more. Here saw many deer killed none after attaining the height made 8 miles S. S. W. through timber and snow then S. S. E. 4 miles also through timber. Saw several places where deer had been killed by the wolves which are here numerous and very large. Camped at a little grass the first seen today where the horses can dig up a little food. The country ahead appears more open we have now a little rice to eat and no meat begin to look at the horses still cold.

18th. Made S. S. E. 12 miles to a small creek. During this days march a snowy range of high mountains in points lay along our right and front stretching so that our course today just doubles their eastwardly termination at a place where probably a fork of the river Des Shutes passes. This range runs N. E. and S. W. still farther on our left and apparently on the other side of the same river there is another range running N. by S. Today saw a very great amoun of sign and deer and have concluded to stop and hunt tomorrow and rest the horses. Tonight a little snow squall.

19th. Same camp. Went out hunting killed 2 deer and several wolves. This day came to us 5 Walla Walla Indians who are out hunting they camp with us tonight they say that the game comes down from the mountains in the winter on account of the snows which is the occasion of its being so plenty. At this time one man out of camp tonight probably lost shall wait tomorrow for him if he does not come in the meantime and take another hunt for meat which is now quite a luxury.

20th. Same camp. Killed one deer found the lost man.

21st. Made S. S. E. 15 miles toward the eastwardly termination of the range of mountains which has for some time been visible on our right. At this point we can see no mountains, but a little farther on the left they commence again apparently the same range which we have seen for some time ranging on the E. side of the river. Killed no game today but saw plenty.

22nd. S. E. by E. 10 miles and struck a small creek which though very rapid was so hard frozen over that we crossed it on the ice then N. E. 1½ miles and came to a very large creek which I take to be the main river. It is about as large as the other fork which we crossed on the 17th inst. Country a little more broken. Deer plenty but killed none. Today a little warmer than usual.

23rd. Started up the river E. S. E. and gradually in 4 miles travel rounded to a S. S. W. course and made 12 more the last 6 of which the snow increased in such a manner that tonight we find no grass for our horses and being afraid to advance with them another day's march I have determined to send them back. And with 3 men I propose to build canoes and assend as far as I can and ascertain if it is possible to get the horses through and if so to send back for them and if not to ascertain if there is beaver and if so trap it if not further advance in this quarter is useless. Tonight set in to snow hard but soon turned to rain.

24th. Snowed and rained all last night and still snowing with a gale of wind from S. S. W. Nearly all the horses gone astray about 12 having found all but one killed a poor horse for food and sent the party all but three back to find grass for the horses. Cut down two large pines and commenced two canoes. Gale all day with occasional snow and rain.

25th. Same camp gale S. S. W. Snow and rain all day a miserable Christmas worked what little we could on the canoes.

26th. Day fair and calm warm go ahead making canoes.

27th. Day fair calm and warm still at the canoes.

28th. day fair calm and warm still at the canoes and eating horse meat.

29th. Fair weather and mild.

30th. Fair weather and mild. Sick with indigestion.

31st. Fair weather and mild all so far south wind. Myself better and finished the canoes and horse meat at the same time *viz*; this evening at supper the men have called our two boats *Black Snake* and *Triton*.

1835 Jany 1st, Started in the morning in the canoes about 5 miles by the river about 2½ miles due south and came to a rapid. In attempting to assend filled with water and afterward in towing with the line she broke loose and went down stream we recovered her after a long run and assended again to the rapid and it being near night camped. Killed today one fine fat goose. Warm south wind rain. Snow deeper as we proceed and is now about 2 feet. Country rough and covered with pines. Set 4 traps for beaver today and am in hopes to have one for breakfast.

2nd. Went to my traps found nothing then made snow shoes and set out with one man to explore the river took a due south course and in 3 or 4 miles came unexpectedly to the river there running smooth. I was happy to see it as I was entirely tired of this mode of travelling my shoes were too small and I frequently sunk into the snow and it bothered me much to get out again. Sometimes I would tread on my shoes and fall down and on the whole I thought I could get along better without them. Returned to camp killed three ducks for four of us small allowance with our men. Took our boat up to the rapids and spent the residue of the day in getting our canoe past the rapid most of the time up to my middle in this cold water. Had to make a portage at last of about ¼ of a mile. The river here makes a detour to the E. and around S to west to the place where we take our things across.

3rd. Raised my traps and found one beaver caught the largest I ever saw I think he weighed 65 lbs. and killed one duck a very seasonable supply of food. The residue of the day finished making the portage and sett 8 traps. The other boat also got setting above. Snow today and rained hard last night nearly all night. Wind Strong N.W. the first wind beside S. since 10 days.

4th. Found but one beaver in our traps. Took a jaunt up the river at about 6 miles straight line S. the river forks into two apparently equal streams. Followed the left one about 2 miles S by E. and returned to camp tired enough having found only sign enough in this distance to set 3 traps. The river winds so that we have to paddle twice the real distance. Rained and snowed some during the day. Saw for the first time on this route swans they appear plenty here. Country still timbered but much more level.

5th. Caught 3 beaver. Rained and snowed hard all last night and part of today. Raised camp and camped about 2 miles below the forks mentioned yesterday. One of the beaver caught today would weigh I should think 70 lbs. and our fries look finely with sundry roasting sticks around full of meat the beaver are fat and we live finely again. Wind strong and south.

6th Rained all the forenoon and hail and snow all the afternoon. Caught no beaver saw very little sign. Heard a rapid or fall ahead. Killed 2 swans so fat that we could not eat all the grease a rare thing in this country to be troubled with fat. Seems good to live well after poor horse meat and short supply. Shall lay down the course tomorrow when I get it more accurately today being too thick to see and the river more winding than ever timber less plenty and very small and but little of the large kind of pine. Country as far as we can see very level with here and there a round conical mountain.

7th Started up the river to sett traps found sign for but one and returned to camp. At the same place as last night killed one swan which would weigh I should think 35 lbs. too fat to eat. One we eat yesterday yielded nearly 2 qts. of oil more than we could eat with it. These birds are delicious it is strange that one only does two of us two meals that is to say a day. They don't eat so in the states. Day pretty cold wind S. W. Strong. Little snow today and some sun. Out the bed of the river is a sort white stone or hard clay the same as found on the Clacamas. I think it is of the chalk formation.

8th Remained all day at same camp on account of a severe snow storm. It snowed all day and fell about one foot. Blew strong from the South which is almost constant wind here.

9th went down the river and raised some traps we had set there and returned to same camp. The river from the last place to which I brought it runs S. E. 1 mile at which point a fork coming from the eastward but it was frozen up so we could not assend it. Then south 5 miles to this camp.

10th Snowed and rained all last night hard and today so we are blessed with about 8 inches of slush makes everything very uncomfortable did not move camp.

11th. Last night grew cold and set in for a hard snow storm with a gale of wind from the W. S. W. which continued without intermission until sunset today so we did not move camp. The cracking of the falling trees and the howling of the blast was more grand than comfortable it makes two individuals feel their insignifance in the creation to be seated under a blankett with a fire in front and 3½ feet of snow about them and more coming and no telling when it will stop. Tonight tis calm and nearly full moon it seems to shine with as much indifference as the storms blow and whether for weal or woe, we two poor wretches seem to be little considered in the matter. The thoughts that have run through my brain while I have been lying here in the snow would fill a volume and of such matter as was never put into one, my infancy, my youth, and its friends and faults, my manhoods troubled stream, its vagaries, its aloes mixed with the gall of bitterness and its results *viz* under a blankett hundreds perhaps thousands of miles from a friend. The blast howling about, and smothered in snow, poor, in debt, doing nothing to get out of it, despised for a visionary, nearly naked, but there is one good thing plenty to eat health and heart.

12th. Started up stream and made S. 6 miles at which point there is a considerable creek coming in from W. S. W. water as warm as the main river and not frozen up. Then 3 miles S. S. E. and camped. Saw but little beaver sign today. River not very rapid but winding. Saw only two swans could not kill them. Caught one yearling beaver. Spit snow all day at night set in to snow hard. Moderately cold wind S. but moderate.

13th 6 miles W. by N. creek very winding and more rapid than usual and camped just below a severe rapid. Fine sun in the forenoon but cloudy and snow spits in the afternoon and this evening.

14th Snowed about 4 inches last night. Today pretty cold passed the rapid on the south side of the south channel there being a small island at this place just above the island there is a raft of drift timber which extends across the whole river this we made a portage of for about 6 rods. At the rapid I hauled the canoe wading in the water about waste deep and remaining in it about 3 hours and got quite numb but at last got through with it. We then assended the river 3 miles more in good water but very winding S. W. to make which I think we paddled 8 miles to another rapid not severe. Finding that it would take some time and being obliged to return to camp soon concluded not to pass this rapid and returned to the first rapid and set 6 traps. Day windy from S. W. and some snow and sunshine.

15th. Last night excessively cold the cracking of the trees kept me awake part of the night and night before I was kept up most of the night by a fever arising from indigestion. Today cold calm and clear. As the sun got high it was extremely pleasant and this is the only day I have seen that would pass for a pleasant one in a good climate this winter. Went to the traps found nothing. Decended the rapid after another cold job in the water and returned to our camp of the 13th inst. On the way down saw 5 swans the first since the 12th but killed nothing but 3 ducks. We are getting short of provisions again. At evening very cold again.

16th Started down the stream and made the portage of the falls about one hour after sunset. Last night the ther. must have been 10 below zero and the river scum over with drift ice which made us make haste for if we should get frozen up here it would be hard times. For food the water fowl and beaver would be done and other game there is absolutely none and to travel would be almost impossible there is four feet of snow. However we could try snow shoes. Killed 4 ducks and one swan today the latter would weigh at least 45 lbs. a very seasonable supply as all our food gave out this morning. Day calm sunny. Not very cold tonight strong south wind and rain.

17th Moved camp down stream about a mile and found our other boat with Mr. Richardson and Robinson. The latter during the severe cold had frozen his toes and fingers and the former was unwell with a numbness in his hips. They reported to me that the beaver on this creek had made them sick probably this was what was the matter with me there is plenty of wild parsnip here. They raised camp with us and we stopped the canoes where we built them and made a portage of ¼ of a mile this severe work in deep snow. We then decended about 3 miles and came to rapids part of which we let our boats over by the line in about ½ mile more came to worse rapids and made a portage of about 1/8 mile. Then immediately let the boats down further rapids about 100 rods to do which I had to remain in the water the whole time. It was after dark when I got through the other boat got nearly through and gave it up and I suppose have camped without fire or food. The river falls at each of these carrying places at least 50 feet. Rained most all day.

18th. Went up above the last rapid to see the other boat found them comfortably camped they made a portage of their things and I attempted to run their boat empty. Just as I took the Shute the bow struck a rock I did not see she swung round filled at once and commenced whirling over like a top I hung to her and passed without further damage than mashing both of my feet severely between the boat and a rock. Was in much pain all this day but not very lame. We run by the river about two miles and passed some bad rapids then made a portage of about a ¼ mile into a slew of the river which we followed about ¼ mile further. Then were forced to make a bad portage up a steep bank of lava about 100 feet this portage about ¼ mile. We then ran about two miles further and camped. Snow here not so deep as above and apparently diminishing fast. Men much tired and discouraged and wish to abandon the canoes which I do not mean to do until I am obliged to. *Cached* at the first portage today 22 traps. Good weather today.

19th. Started down stream and ran a continuous rapid for about 2 miles. We let our boats down about ¼ mile then crossed the river and let the boats down a few rods and finding the river was pretty much all rapids and falls concluded to abandon the boats. *Cached* all but our blankets, books, ammunition, axe and kettles and took it on foot with about 60 lbs each on our backs and 1 foot of hard snow into which we sank sometimes and sometimes not. It however diminished as we proceeded we made about 6 miles and saw plenty of deer and camped killed one which was just in time as a little piece of swan was all the meat left in camp.

I am very tired and hungry but the deer will cure all this. There is little snow at this place. Our camp I think cannot be far off on the other side of the river I can see a grassy plain of about 30 miles long and about 5 wide bare of snow. Snowed a little this morning day fine tonight freezing a little.

20th Started late sore footed but with a full belly and an addicion of about 20 lbs meat each we made about 6 miles and passed our camp of the 22nd and 23rd *ult*. About 1 mile further we crossed a small fork the one we before crossed on the ice then S. 2 miles and camped and tried hard for a deer but could not get one although we saw a great many. Day fine this evening cool. Grass not much covered with snow. See no sign of camp yet.

21st. Made 2 miles N. to the river and camped. Took a turn down the river about 5 miles to look for some sign of our camp found a little Indian sign of about the same age but nothing of our people. Afternoon went out to a high hill to the W. and made a large pile of brush and after dark set fire to it in order that if our people are near that they may see it and come to us. Sent a man over the river to look but he could not cross but he saw one of their camps. Shall go tomorrow and ascertain if it so. Killed nothing today so we shall have no breakfast in the morning. Day fine tolerable cool 1 inch of snow last night which went off today.

22nd. Snowed part of last night and rained the residue and the forenoon of today. Snow the rest and part of the night. In morning our hunter went out and wounded a deer which the wolves ran down but before he could find him they had eaten up all but enough for

2 meals. This morning breakfasted on two beaver tails which I had laid by and forgotten so we have not yet on this trip lost a meal as yet. Myself in the morning made a raft and endeavoured to cross the river but found I had selected a bad place and could not do it. Went above found a better place made another raft and succeeded. Found one of our camps so we now have some clew to camp and shall push for it after getting a small supply of meat beforehand. Wind strong southwardly. Camped this night in a cave of the rocks one mile S. of last nights camp.

23rd Moved down to camp of 22nd inst and went out to hunt. Killed nothing myself but Mr Richardson killed a fawn so we have 2 meals ahead besides two nights' supper. Mr R. is sick of a bad cold in his chest and some biles on his neck and cannot carry his pack. Rained steady all day.

24th Made 12 miles N. by W. and using what looked like a fine ford I tried to wade the river but at first failed. Went a little lower and succeeded and got back safe but benumbed with cold and after warming myself at a fire which the rest had built took my things across and built a roaring fire to warm the others as they came over. Here found some beaver cuttings saw but little deer or sign. Today cold wind W. cloudy. Snow nearly gone.

25th. Made 10 miles N. and seeing a little deer sign stopped and our hunter went out during the march we heard a gun on the west side of the river we fired guns and were answered. Toward night a little Snake Indian came to us and induced us to go to their camp which was among the cedars about 5 miles N. E. We found them without meat but we bought of them a lean dog of which we made supper and enough left for breakfast so tis rub and go. There were three lodges they had no guns but had killed much deer as proved by the number of skins they had last night and this forenoon. Snowed about 5 inches today rained and melted most of it. No water except snow and that dirty at this camp.

26th Under the guidance of a Snake Indian we struck N.W. to the river 7 miles and forded it at a rapid and waist deep ford then W. by N. 4 miles and came to 8 lodges of Snakes. Here our guide I suppose heard that our camp had moved and backed out of his job by running away. We then struck N. W. 8 miles and came to the small river on which we camped the 18th, 19th and 20th *ulto*. Here we saw one

Indian who ran from us who appeared to be a Snake. While we were debating which course to pursue we espied 4 Indians on the opposite side of the creek these we spoke and they informed us where our camp was and one of them took my pack to it. They had killed several deer but we thought to get to camp and did not take any. We made from the creek N. N. W. up a very steep high hill 5 miles and coming very dark we camped for the first time this trip without supper and me without blanketts and tired enough.

27th Got up and having; no breakfast to cook or eat started the earlier and moved N. N. W. 2 miles and the rest refused to go further preferring to wait until some chance Indian should come along hunting to take them the right way to camp. I having no pack started in quest of it and passing the N. N. W. course in 1½ mile found it on a little thread of water running N. and deep snow. During the time we had been gone they had killed 20 deer and had not starved, the Walla Walla Indians are here hunting. They go out on their horses and run them and as the deer get tired the Indians get good shots at them but the number wounded is much greater than that killed, on these the wolves feast at night and keep up a continual howl. After these last comes the ravens for their share. I found missing from yesterday 6 horses among which was my two fine riding horses and three others which have been stolen by the Snakes who are up to this kind of dealing today sent men to look for the 6 and they brought but one. Day fine for any country and warm tonight freezing cold.

28th Sent out two men again for the 5 missing horses and after finding the residue which not until noon started N. by W. and after 12 miles struck the old trail on which I came up about 6 miles from our camp of 16 and 17. Day very fine. Nothing to eat tonight but a little flour. Camped on a little stream made by the thawing of the snow.

29th Rose early and without any breakfast started down the valley on which we camped last night which joins a large fork of the Des Shutes in about 3 miles from this and leaving the old trail on which I came up to the left made N. N. E. 2 miles. Then leaving the valley to the left made 1½ miles N. E. then going down a very steep and high cut rock bank E. 1 mile crossed the large fork of the Des Shutes about 2 miles. Below my camp of the 16th and 17th *ulto*. this ford is deeper and more rapid than the one I made before, possibly the stream is higher on account of the thawing of the snow. We are camped with about 12 lodges of Walla Wallas they have at this moment a good supply of meat deer which they are drying, I presume they have not often so much on hand as they seem to value it highly on my arrival. I made the chief a good present to induce him to influence his people to trade but as yet have traded of root and meat but about 3 days supply. I intend waiting here three nights in order that they make another hunt and then perhaps I may get a sufficient supply to take me down. Tomorrow is Sunday and there will be neither trading nor hunting in this camp this is my birthday but I have forgotten how old I am.

30th This unless my reconing is wrong is Sunday. At day dawn the chief called the Indians to prayers which consist of a short recitation followed by a tune in which all join without words after which a note in accord to wind off this is repeated several times on Sunday and is a dayly practice. At daylight today the two men sent for the horses came in and brought 4. 2 of which were my riding horses. This day warm as June in N. E. and no snow in this valley.

31st The Indians commence their meal with religious ceremonys and then come and beg a smoke. The day is also closed with religious ceremonies. Traded about 2 days provisions of the Indians. Day fine as summer and the grass begins to start a little.

Feb. 1st Started from camp early and made 8 miles N. by E. over a trail which we followed the latter part of the 16 *ulto*. I then laid the course S. S. W. to make our camp of the 16 and 17 which was about 1 mile above our last night's camp. Traded today about 2 days' provisions. Looked at the rocks a little and as the country has been the same as far as I have been a description of the bluffs here will answer for the whole. There are some cut blufs of basalt in its original position but they are chiefly a very coarse sand stone of an ash colour in layers some of which are finer and some coarser it is soft and is composed of rubble stone of lava and primitive rocks. It sometimes contains organic remains bones, I have taken out of it in a fossil state a small piece of which I have preserved. Today cloudy and on the high land over which we came today it was quite chilly but in the valley of the small creek on which we are camped it is warm. Latter part of the day sunny.

2nd Moved camp N. by E. 8 miles over a plain and pretty good trail leaving entirely the route which I followed coming up. The Indians killed some deer. Grass appears better. Day cloudy or foggy until about noon when the sun came out like April in N. E.

3rd This day the Indians concluded not to move camp I therefore requested the chief to call on his people to come and trade meat. They traded about 6 days' provisions and I left them following the trail N. by E. 8 miles to a creek which we crossed in our march of the 12th *ulto*. The banks of this creek is of fine deep red clay and at this camp there is a hot spring too hot to bear the hand in long and smoking like a coal pit it tastes of sulphur and iron and deposits a whitish substance on the pebbles as it dries away. We hear for the first time this season the croaking of the frogs. Trail good, grass good. Day cloudy and chill. Ther. in spring 191°.

4th. Early in morning took my thermometer to ascertain the heat of the spring found it to be 134° and took a good bath by going a little distance down the stream to find a suitable temperature and this first time for a long while feel myself pretty clean. Rose camp and crossed the little stream on which we camped and leaving the Indian trail struck N. N. E. and in 6 miles came to the main river Des Shutes along which we found a small trail we made 4 miles N. and camped. During this distance the river could be run by a good boatman but it is almost a continued rapid. The rocks of this march appear to be all shades between green and red similar to the earth. It appears by being porous to be volcanic. The first course of the march very miry the last firm and pretty good. Grass improving. Day cloudy in morning sunny this afternoon. Saw much big horn and deer sign by the way.

5th Made along the river 1 mile N. then west 2 miles up a mountain then N. 1 mile and down a ravine then E. N. E. 2 miles to the main river again and down a ravine then 7 miles N. by E. along the main river and camped. Trail plain all the way but very hilly and stony. Grass good. Day at first cloudy and on the mountain much hoar frost in afternoon sunny. The upper part of the mountain was of mica slate very much twisted. This afternoon the rock was volcanic and in some places underlaid with green clay. Saw today small holders of a black-rock which from its fracture I took to be bituminous coal but its weight was about that of hornblende perhaps it might be obsidian but I think was heavier than any I have ever seen. River all this day's march might be run if there is no bad place where I cut the mountain saw big horn trails but not the game.

6th Made along the river 4 miles N. by W. during which space saw nothing that might not be passed by a good boatman. Then mounted the W. bank of the river and came to a large cedar plain 3 miles N. by

W. then N. by E. over the plain 6 miles more to tinkers camp. In crossing at this camp wet my cases with all my papers by a horse falling in the river while fording. Day cloudy with a little snow. Found this branch some higher than when I passed up here. We found and raised a small *cach* which I made on my way up and during the march sent two men to raise another which I made at the next camp above. From these Indians I hear that of my runaway Kanackas 10 took the trail over the Blue, one was drowned in crossing some ford, one froze in the upper country, that the residue rafted the Snake River, one more died somehow about the falls, that 7 are gone down to Vancouver. Tonight traded 8 dogs for their fat to kill the lice on my horses.

7th Early in the day the two men sent to raise the *cach* came in with its contents undamaged exchanged at this camp a poor little, lame, mare for a tolerable horse in pretty good order. Traded for a knife each 6 dogs today used the grease of these dogs to kill the lice on my horses that are nearly covered with them. Day cloudy but not cold in the valley. Mount Hood bears ½ point N. of N. W. Sick myself of a bowell complaint. *Cached* at this camp 11/3 bales corn and 7 setts shoes and nails.

8th N. N. W. 16 miles in the first place 2 miles to the top of an elevated range of woodless hills which skirt the west side of the creek on which we camped. Then down the slope of these hills 4 miles more. During this space much snow then struck into a little creek which we followed 6 miles then up the left bank of this creek to another and larger fork of the same 4 miles and camped in good grass. This creek comes from the S. W. and is now as large as the small creek on which I camped the first night after leaving the mouth of the River Des Shutes on my way up. There are several Indians with me who say that once there was much beaver on this creek but that the British Cos have trapped it out. Day cloudy a few drops of rain.

9th Moved camp early on a plain and good trail N. N. W. 10 miles to the Dalles. After following on this trail 3 miles we came to a small creek coming from the W. S. W. and joining the one on which we camped last night and at 5 miles more another which either joins the same very near the Columbia or goes into the Columbia. found Soaptilly (?) and a few more Chinooks at the river of whom I traded one horse and a canoe they report 7 Kanackas gone down and that one was drowned at the falls and one froze in the mountains leaving one unaccounted for rained a little today.

10th Started early in a very leaky canoe which kept us bailing all the time and made 8 miles N.W. 5 W. and 3. S.W. 1 west and on account of high wind camped about noon. A little rain as usual.

11th At about sunsett last night the wind lulled a little and we made a start but the wind continued high and about 2 o'clock we arrived at the Cascades a little above which we camped this morning. Went to the Cascades and there found Mr Ermatinger with a brigade of 3 boats taking up the outfits for the upper forts also Capt. Stewart Mr Ray and one more gentleman. Made the portage and in 12 hours made the saw mill.

12th In the morning made to Vancouver and found there a polite reception and to my great astonishment Mr Hall J. Kelley he came in Co. with Mr Young from Monte El Rey and it is said stole between them a bunch of horses. Kelley is not received at the fort on this account as a gentleman a house is given him and food sent him from the gov. table but he is not suffered to mess here. I also found 7 of my runaway Kanackas they appear to be very sick of their job so I have concluded not to be severe with them. I hear also that Fort Hall has traded 300 skins up to what time do not know or how true also that Tom Bule & Harry two more of the runaways are with some of McKay's men on Snake River they will probably fall in at Fort Hall.

13th Went down to the station at Carneaus (?) and found all well and doing pretty well. This is Sunday and I have lost 3 days somewhere. During the residue of this month sent Mr Richardson to the Dalles with supplies for the party which I left above trapping he had tempestuous weather and was gone 13 days. Myself took a trip up the Wallamut to look after the farm and my Taylor who had deserted me during the winter. After Richardson had gone I took a small canoe and proceeded up the Columbia and in my progress got filled with the violence of the wind and quantity of rain. I arrived at Vancouver in the morning 23rd Feb. and met a reception such as one loves to find in such a country as this.

24th Started down the Columbia to the mouth of the Wallamut up which about 4 miles to the head of Wappatoo Islands. Here finding the canoe too deep to proceed against the rapid current of this river now very high we put down the west slew and crossed over the first bank of the river into the waters back and went to the farm of Mr Thomas McKay and procured horses and went by land. This took us all of the 25 and 26 both of which days it rained hard. All the little streams made us swim our horses and some of the open .prairies were swimming and much of them wading. At night of the 26th arrived at Sandy camp just above which I had begun a farm.

27th Went to the farm and found the Taylor and Sloat the foreman gone down to see me they having heard of my return. During the day went up to Mr Lee's place in order to get Babtiste to school with him in which I succeeded.

28th Returned to Camp Sandy. Rain today.

29th Started for McKay's Farm during a hard rain and snow.

30th Arrived at McKay's Farm.

31st Back to station at Carneaus (?) place and here found my runaway Taylor.

March 1st From this time until the 8th employed him in getting out coopers stuff and timber for a house boat which I intend to build.

Apl 13th Sunday I suppose employed in getting out stuff for the house boat in cutting 8000 hoop poles and in building a canoe 60 feet long wide and deep enough to chamber barrells of which she will take 25. She is clean of knotts, shakes, and almost of sap and 27 feet cut off the same tree of the same kind of stuff. The whole tree was 242 feet long and this by no means the largest tree on Wappatoo Island this is of the Spruce kind today. I am on my way down to Fort William where the brig lay to regulate matters there. I have just parted from Mr McLaughlin Esq. on his way to view the Fallatten (Tualatin) plains I suppose with some idea of making him a farm there some day. I have now out of 21 people 7 sick and little work can be done after deducting from the remaining 14 a provision boat to trade food and enough to take care of the sick. Up to the first of this month it rained continually and about ¼ of the time since. I find the ploughs which I brought from the States of no use in the new lands here. No news as yet from brig or Capt Thing. So far with much exertion we provided ourselves with food but the whites in this country are exhausted of all kinds.

Copy of a Letter and a Statement of Facts Pertaining to a Claim Based upon Operations Involved in the Two Expeditions

Camb. Dec 13th 1847

Dear Sir,

The papers herewith enclosed are in continuation of the subject brought to your notice in my letter of the 5th of April last which was accompanied by copy of statements relating to claims of John McLoughlin Esq., formerly chief Factor in charge of the H. B. Co's western district comprising all the territories occupied by that Co west of the Rocky mountains. but who has since retired from their service, and resides at Oregon City. This statement or memorial was dated previous to the late treaty of boundary with Great Britain, and under the impression that his rights would be subjected to the capricious justice of the new settlers who had then formed a provisional government. I conceive that the said treaty fully secures his rights, or should they not be secured by the treaty, you will oblige me by securing them so far as in your power. I have placed the copy of his memorial as above stated in your hands for this purpose. At this time I shall confine myself to my own interests in Oregon. Having gone to Oregon in march 1832 for purposes recognized by the convention then existing between the U. S. & G. B. having formed establishments there of the same character and for the same purposes, as those formed previously by the N. W. & Hudson's Bay Cos. having maintained one of the same through tenant to the present time, and having after two expeditions, accompanied by much suffering and expenditure of five years time, and more than $20,000 in money, established the nucleus of the present American settlement in these regions, I ask the American government to place my interests in that country on as favourable a basis, as the treaty of boundary places those of British subjects whose possessions are of the same character.

The recommendation of the President would benefit only actual settlers, and would entirely exclude me. It seems to me a law might be passed consistent with justice, granting a pre-emption to all Americans who have ever resided in Oregon, and who occupied land there, and continued to hold the same either directly or by agents or tenants, to the absolute extent of the property so occupied, as it was at the period of the organization of the provisional government of Oregon. And to all Americans actual settlers, occupying lands after the organisation of said provisional government, and until the extension of the laws of the U. S. over the territory, a pre-emption to all the lands so occupied not exceeding one square mile.

I do not believe a law mainly such as proposed above would benefit a single American except myself. I do not know one other who has occupied more than a mile square, while there are several British subjects who have done so, and whose claims are all secured by the treaty whether large or small. And unless some such law is passed it appears to me that I am to be stripped of all my rights, and that the great sacrifices I have made will inure to the benefit of all concerned except myself. That you may better understand why I desire some protection from the government I herewith send a statement of facts No. 1, and a petition to Congress No 2. I remain very respectfully
    Your obedient Servant.
          Nathaniel J. Wyeth.

To Hon. J. G. Palfrey, M. C.

(Statement of facts No. 1)
On the 10th day of March 1832 I left Boston in a vessel with 20 men for Baltimore where I was joined by four more, and on the 27th left by railroad for Frederic Md from thence to Brownsville we marched on foot, and took passage from that place to Liberty Mo. on various steamboats, which place we left for the prairies on the 12th of May with 21 men, three having

deserted, and on the 27th of May three more deserted. On the 8th of July we reached Pierre's Hole at the head of Lewis River where was then a rendezvous of trappers and Indians. We remained at this place until the 17th at which time my party had been reduced by desertion and dismissal to 11 men, and then started for the Columbia arriving at Cape Disappointment on the 8th Nov. 1832, one man having died on the route. There I learned that a vessel on which I relied for supplies had been wrecked at the Society Islands. This intelligence discouraged the party so much that all but two requested a discharge.

Of the 8 who then left me 5 returned to the U. S. by sea, one died there in 1834 and two remained as settlers. In the Spring of 1833 I commenced my return to the states with the two remaining men. When I reached the mouth of the Yellowstone one left me to remain with some of the trappers until I should return. With the other I reached the States, and soon after fitted out a vessel for the Columbia, and on the 7th Feb. 1834 left Boston for St. Louis where I organised a party of 70 men for the overland trip arriving at the head waters of the Snake or Lewis River in July 1834, and on the 15th of that month commenced to build Fort Hall, and after placing it in a defensive condition left it on the 7th August following for the mouth of the Columbia. On the 15th of Sept. I reached Oak Point 75 miles from its mouth where I met my vessel just arrived after a voyage of 8 ½ months, having been struck by lightning at sea and so injured as to be obliged to go into Valoaraiso to repair. This vessel was fitted for the salmon fishing of that season. Her late arrival caused me to detain her until the following year.

During the winter of 1835 this vessel went to the Sandwich Islands with timber and card returned in the Spring with cattle, sheep, goats and hogs which were placed on Wappatoo Island where in the meantime I had built an establishment called Fort William on the southwesterly side of the island and about 8 miles from the H. B. Co's post of Vancouver. At this post we grazed all the animals obtained from the Islands California and from the Indians, planted wheat corn potatoes peas beans turnips, grafted and planted apples and other fruits, built dwelling house and shops for working iron and wood, and in fact made a permanent location which has never been abandoned.

Made this my personal residence during the winter and summer of 1835. In the autumn of that year I proceeded to Fort Hall with supplies, having sent some previous to that time. During the winter of 1836 I resided at my post of Fort Hall, and in the spring of that year returned to Fort William of Wappatoo Island whence I carried more supplies to Fort Hall arriving there the 18th June, and on the 25th left for the U. S. by way of Taos and the Arkansas River and arrived home early in the Autumn of 1836. The commercial distress of that time precluded the further prosecution of our enterprise, that so far had yielded little but misfortunes.

It remained only to close the active business which was done by paying every debt, and returning every man who desired, to the place whence he was taken, and disposing of the property' to the best advantage. All the property in the interior including Fort Hall was sold, it being necessary in order to retain that post, to keep up a garrison for its defence against the Indians, and to forward annual supplies to it, an operation at that time beyond our means. Fort William at Wappatoo Island requiring nothing of that kind was retained, and the gentleman then in charge Mr C. M. Walker was directed to lease it to some trusty person for 15 years unless sooner reclaimed. Nothing having been heard from Mr Walker for a long time I sent a request to John McLaughlin Esq. for the same purpose and also to have the island entered in my name at the land office established by the provisional government.

That the original enterprise contemplated a permanent occupation is clearly shown by the instructions to the master of the brig Capt Lambert When I arrived on the lower Columbia in the autumn of 1832 as herein before stated there were no Americans there nor anyone having an American feeling. So far as I know there had not been since Mr. Astor retired from the coast. Of the 11 men which I had then with me three remained until I again arrived in the autumn of 1834 and 19 of those who then accompanied me including the missionaries remained permanently in the country.

Nathaniel J. Wyeth

ALSO FROM LEONAUR
AVAILABLE IN SOFTCOVER OR HARDCOVER WITH DUST JACKET

AN APACHE CAMPAIGN IN THE SIERRA MADRE by John G. Bourke—An Account of the Expedition in Pursuit of the Chiricahua Apaches in Arizona, 1883.

BILLY DIXON & ADOBE WALLS by Billy Dixon and Edward Campbell Little—Scout, Plainsman & Buffalo Hunter, *Life and Adventures of "Billy" Dixon* by Billy Dixon and *The Battle of Adobe Walls* by Edward Campbell Little (*Pearson's Magazine*).

WITH THE CALIFORNIA COLUMN by George H. Petis—Against Confederates and Hostile Indians During the American Civil War on the South Western Frontier, *The California Column, Frontier Service During the Rebellion* and *Kit Carson's Fight With the Comanche and Kiowa Indians*.

THRILLING DAYS IN ARMY LIFE by George Alexander Forsyth—Experiences of the Beecher's Island Battle 1868, the Apache Campaign of 1882, and the American Civil War.

INDIAN FIGHTS AND FIGHTERS by Cyrus Townsend Brady—Indian Fights and Fighters of the American Western Frontier of the 19th Century.

THE NEZ PERCÉ CAMPAIGN, 1877 by G. O. Shields & Edmond Stephen Meany—Two Accounts of Chief Joseph and the Defeat of the Nez Percé, *The Battle of Big Hole* by G. O. Shields and *Chief Joseph, the Nez Percé* by Edmond Stephen Meany.

CAPTAIN JEFF OF THE TEXAS RANGERS by W. J. Maltby—Fighting Comanche & Kiowa Indians on the South Western Frontier 1863-1874.

SHERIDAN'S TROOPERS ON THE BORDERS by De Benneville Randolph Keim—The Winter Campaign of the U. S. Army Against the Indian Tribes of the Southern Plains, 1868-9.

WILD LIFE IN THE FAR WEST by James Hobbs—The Adventures of a Hunter, Trapper, Guide, Prospector and Soldier.

THE OLD SANTA FE TRAIL by Henry Inman—The Story of a Great Highway.

LIFE IN THE FAR WEST by George F. Ruxton—The Experiences of a British Officer in America and Mexico During the 1840's.

ADVENTURES IN MEXICO AND THE ROCKY MOUNTAINS by George F. Ruxton—Experiences of Mexico and the South West During the 1840's.

AVAILABLE ONLINE AT **www.leonaur.com**
AND FROM ALL GOOD BOOK STORES

www.ingramcontent.com/pod-product-compliance
Lightning Source LLC
Chambersburg PA
CBHW031618160426
43196CB00006B/183